A TASTE OF WRITING THE SOUTHWEST

Edward Abbey Interview

"Just by virtue of being alive—living things—we deserve to be respected . . . beginning with our pet dogs and cats and horses. Humans find it easy to love them. And we should try to love the wild animals, the mountain lions, and rattlesnakes. . . . I think a tree, a shrub deserves respect as a living thing. You can go beyond that—to the rocks, to the air, because it's all part of a whole."

Tony Hillerman Interview

"I come from the poor-boy end of Oklahoma, raised on a small farm. I went to an Indian school my first eight grades. We were not allowed in the playgrounds, but the experience taught me what it was like to be a minority problem."

Waiting to Exhale by Terry McMillan

"I have tried being honest, telling them as diplomatically as I possibly could that they just weren't right for me, that they shouldn't take it personally because there was somebody out there for everybody. Which is how I became 'the bitch.' I wanted to tell all of them to come back and see me after they grew up or got some serious counseling."

Barbara Kingsolver Interview

"I'm not going to braid my hair, put on beads, and rename myself 'Soaring Barbara' and say, 'This is the way to believe,' but there's something I admire about the Pueblo Indian world view, which incorporates an awareness of our place in the food chain and our habitat and a real solid awareness that if we foul our nest, we're in big trouble."

DAVID KING DUNAWAY wrote and produced the radio documentary series on which this book is based, "Writing the Southwest." He is a professor of English at the University of New Mexico and the author of *How Can I Keep from Singing: Pete Seeger*, *Huxley in Hollywood*, and *Oral History*. Sara L. Spurgeon is writing her dissertation on southwestern literature at the University of Arizona.

WRITING THE
SOUTHWEST

David King Dunaway
and Sara L. Spurgeon

A PLUME BOOK

PLUME
Published by the Penguin Group
Penguin Books USA Inc., 375 Hudson Street,
New York, New York 10014, U.S.A.
Penguin Books Ltd, 27 Wrights Lane,
London W8 5TZ, England
Penguin Books Australia Ltd, Ringwood,
Victoria, Australia
Penguin Books Canada Ltd, 10 Alcorn Avenue,
Toronto, Ontario, Canada M4V 3B2
Penguin Books (N.Z.) Ltd, 182–190 Wairau Road,
Auckland 10, New Zealand

Penguin Books Ltd, Registered Offices:
Harmondsworth, Middlesex, England

First published by Plume, an imprint of Dutton Signet,
a division of Penguin Books USA Inc.

First Printing, October, 1995
10 9 8 7 6 5 4 3 2 1

Copyright © David King Dunaway, 1995
All rights reserved

Novena Narratives copyright © Denise Chavez, 1995
"Night Horses" and "Every Word, Everything" copyright © Simon Ortiz, 1995

The Colorado Endowment for the Humanities assisted with the research for this volume.

Acknowledgments for permission to reprint appear on pages 267–268.

Ⓟ   REGISTERED TRADEMARK—MARCA REGISTRADA

LIBRARY OF CONGRESS CATALOGING-IN-PUBLICATION DATA
Writing the Southwest / [edited by] David King Dunaway
and Sara L. Spurgeon.
p.   cm.
Includes bibliographical references.
ISBN 0-452-27394-3
1. American literature—Southwestern States. 2. Authors,
American—Southwestern States—Biography. 3. Authors, American—
Southwestern States—Interviews. 4. Southwestern States—Literary
collections. 5. Southwestern States—Intellectual life.
6. Southwest, New—Literary collections. I. Dunaway, David King.
II. Spurgeon, Sara L.
PS566.W75   1995
     810.8'0979—dc20   95-13241
                                                                        CIP

Printed in the United States of America
Set in Cheltenham Book
Designed by Leonard Telesca

PUBLISHER'S NOTE
Some of the extracts in this book are works of fiction. Names, characters, places, and
incidents either are the products of the authors' imaginations or are used fictitiously, and
any resemblance to actual persons, living or dead, events, or locales is entirely
coincidental.

ACKNOWLEDGMENTS

▲ ✧ ▼ ✧ ▼ ✧ ▲

A book based primarily on oral sources owes its greatest debt to its narrators: in this case, the writers who spoke at length with us and who lent us their works. A number of other writers also discussed participating in this project, including Leslie Silko, Bernice Zamora, N. Scott Momaday, and Jimmy Baca; though other commitments prevented their involvement, we thank them and hope to include them in our future work—perhaps even in a second volume.

The authors acknowledge with thanks the funds for the research of this volume from the Colorado Endowment for the Humanities and, particularly, Maggie Coval and Jim Pierce.

A number of scholars assisted us in our selection of authors and works, including Vera John-Steiner, Larry Evers, Joseph Flora, Paula Gunn Allen, Rudolfo Anaya, Valerie Smith, and Teresa Marquez. Ruth Dickstein of the University of Arizona Library and Jana Giles and Sara Ranney of the University of New Mexico assisted in our research. Thanks go, too, to Danielle Perez at Plume and to Loretta Barrett, who placed this title with Plume.

Friends and family have kept our spirits up through long interludes on the road and in the library: Alexander Dunaway; Nina Wallerstein; David Ewing; Russell Goodman; Chellis Glendenning; Greg Roberts; Marcy Steinberg; Colleen, Paul, and Trent Spurgeon; Diane Fernandez; Mae Ihla; Peter Cordero; and Sancho and Tonto.

This volume is dedicated to Stan Steiner, who provided the initial inspiration for this literary gathering; wherever he is today, we hope he is riding easy with those Golden Spurs presented to him by the Western Writers of America.

CONTENTS

▲ ❖ ▼ ❖ ▼ ❖ ▲

FOREWORD — *Poorly written*
THE SPIRIT OF THE PLACE

▲ ❖ ▼ ❖ ▼ ❖ ▲

The works of the writers collected between the covers of this book reflect diverse styles and content. The Southwest has always been a richly textured land when it comes to ethnic backgrounds, and yet few anthologies of the past have reflected this reality. This book, and the radio series on which it is based, is innovative in giving voice to the various communities of the region.

The writers included here infuse their stories with their own distinctive backgrounds. We write in English, yet our personal and cultural language is reflected in our stories. Here you will find the spirit of Navajo and Acoma chants, the homespun Spanish of the Nuevo Mexicano villages, the beat of Afro-American real talk, and the older, established Anglo writers and the newcomers. Collectively they reflect the reality of *el norte*, the north side of this frontier region.

I once wrote that the true literature of this country would not be known until all the communities that comprise the nation are acknowledged. I feel the same way about the literature of this region. We, the writers, represent various and distinct communities. We are a border people, half in love with Mexico and half suspicious, half in love with the United States and half wondering if we belong. We live in a great space, separated by great mountains, harsh deserts, and the Rio Grande. This book and the radio program that was the genesis of this collection help span those distances.

What do we mean by writing the Southwest? Are we describing surface or soul when we say a Southwest sensibility

Posits a special attachment to the people and the land.

is reflected in our literature? For me, writing the Southwest means that the writers in this book have a special attachment to the people and the land of the region. I'd like to offer some ideas on that attachment.

Reflecting one's sense of place in one's stories has at times been construed as regionalism. Critics often take it upon themselves to decide for us what constitutes universal literature, and they have decided that allowing the sense of place to be an essential part of the story lessens it. I take the opposite view. By sense of place I mean the "spirit of the place," and I know that sensitive writers respond to that spirit as they write their stories. So for me the spirit of the place is an integral part of the story.

Takes issue with view that regionalism is not "universal."

Writers from all regions have allowed the spirit of the place to permeate their works. When I sit down to read a southern writer, I understand I will encounter a set of historical, cultural, and language traditions that I *know* are the materials of the southern writer. Thus, the literature of each region reflects a tradition. That tradition is the spirit, the mythopoetic, of the place and its people. Each new generation of writers struggles to create a new way of telling the story of the people and the place, a new voice that will capture the time. But these new voices still continue to reflect the writer's deep sense of tradition.

Writers do have "a room of their own," meaning that the writer's place is the center of the universe for the writer. We in the Southwest know that every area is inhabited by the spirits of the place, so the story cannot be separated from the *spiritus loci*. The language, style, concerns, and perspectives are uniquely the writer's; and each story will add to the body of work from the region, but each work will also be guided by the spirit of the place, the soul of the community and the land.

A story from the prairie states should present the reader with the essence of the place and people. The writer fails us when the story *isn't* suffused with the spirit of the place. To read a story from New Mexico and one from Iowa and feel that either story could have taken place in either locale defeats the story. Even the most abstract and existentialist story has an essence, because writing must reflect the soul of the place. Even the story most separated from its *spiritus loci* reflects the

Q. What is the "soul" or "spirit" of a place? Brainstorm the "soul" and "spirit" of Michigan, and then try to categorize/classify responses.

essence of the place. The spirit of the place guides us, and we cannot help but honor it in our stories.

The spirit of the place precedes us because the earth did not come to us, we came to the earth. The conciousness of the universe is infused in the earth, and we have come to learn from it. I think this is true for all regions of the earth.

Cities also have a sense of place, a spirit of the turf. I feel the spirit of people and place when I read the black, white, Jewish, and Nuyorican writers from New York. The traditions of the writer, the collective memory of the place, help spark the writer's creativity. Writers infuse their stories with their language, tradition, food, music, tempo, and individual styles; they are driven by the spirit as they add to the communal history. Stories establish a tradition even as they rework the *yes* materials of the past to create a new, contemporary voice. Stories are links in historical continuity.

Literary history grows in increments, and each region of this country plays a role in defining the literary inheritance. The specific history and persistance of spirit in each community dictates that there can be no one national epic. There are critics who hold up *Moby-Dick* as the American novel which best describes us, and yet from where I sit, *Moby-Dick* is a regional novel. Its spirit is of New England, the ocean, and whaling as a way of life. It presents a worldview quite foreign to me, and quite foreign to the regions west of the Hudson River. This does not lessen its importance; the human struggle and conflict within the novel touch me. The novel captures not only the turmoil of its characters, it reveals the spirits of the place. Those same spirits lend their power to the overall essence of the work.

The argument that a regional novel cannot address universal human emotions is a specious argument. *Moby-Dick* may be a regional novel, but its portrayal of the human condition is universal. Writing from a sense of place does not limit the exploration of universal human emotions that will resonate with readers. In fact, this is the challenge to the writer, to write from a sense of place and explore the human condition so deeply and profoundly that the work can touch the heart of any reader.

Sense of place does not merely mean that a writer uses the

Place = more than landscape

landscape of the place as background. It means that the spirit of the place affects and influences the characters by shaping their consciousness. We are all the products of our place and community, and while we may expand our horizons in any given lifetime and actually write about many places, we still reflect in our stories the *spiritus loci* which shaped our imagination. It is that shaping of the creative imagination that is the power of the place.

The mythos of a group is shaped by the place it occupies. The longer a particular group lives in a place, the more deeply attached the group is to that place. Elsewhere I have written the very gods of the place rise from the features of the landscape. The deities of our place inhabit the earth, and our imagination resonates to their creative powers. The sensibility of the living force of the earth is engrained in our psyche.

We see the process at work in Greek mythology. The ancient Greek gods rose from the mountains, oceans, storms, springs, and rivers; the god or goddess became the spirit of the place. As humans we are heir to the deities that rise from and walk in our region; those gods are the muses which influence the writer's creativity. The writer responds to the spirit of the place, and thus links the past to the present.

Historical continuity is a reality which anchors us. The human psyche needs this anchoring in the face of evolution. We change and grow and must adopt new archetypes to our original storehouse of symbols. That storehouse of images is necessary for coping with and interpreting the constant changes of evolution. Those primal images are our connection to human history, hieroglyphs of the spirit which help us transcend our daily life and feel connected to a purpose in the universe. The *spiritus loci*, therefore, is an evolutionary gift. The spirits of the place help us interpret the way; the spirits not only feed our creativity, they help us see our connection to the totality of life, and thus help keep us in harmony.

Our stories reflect on this mystery, and so there is a spiritual intent in the creating of story, no matter how gross the subject matter. We are more than the scattered parts our stories portray; the intent of the story is to create meaning, to reflect a center. Writing is our communication with that spirit, a prayer asking that our community be spared the violence and evil that gravitate toward the sacred.

Throughout our time on earth nature's forces have been harsh and chaotic. Violent storms, earthquakes, ghosts in the bush, the fear of night, and wild fires have plagued us. Our personal nature reflects the violence and evil abroad, and yet the spirits of the place remind us there are original archetypes of order and harmony. Spiritual evolution takes place in each new generation, and we reflect that in the stories we tell. Writing reflects that evolution, so we become what we compose. By writing stories we give order to our lives; we give order to the place we call home.

In today's often violent and cruel world, we need to probe the depths of our personal and communal souls, find some internal sense of harmony, and make it part of the vital energy of our stories. This is a responsibility handed down to us by the old storytellers who knew and communicated with the spirits of their place.

For me, a touchstone of good writing is that which transports me into the life of the characters. To be moved into the realm of the characters of the story means to feel the place, the food, music, language, and history of the character's surrounding. Taken a step further, the power of literature is to transport the reader into the very core of the mythic and poetic world of the story.

Is the spirit of the place available to every writer, I am asked. If writers are the dream catchers, the story catchers of the place, and if writers are the sensitive shamans of the community, then they should be able to feel the pulse of the place and communicate it in story. Thus, writers who are newcomers to the Southwest can convey the sense of place as they are moved by the spirit. This collection includes some of those newcomers whose antennas respond to the region and its people and who are able to express the soul of the region.

Still, the gods of the place do not reveal themselves overnight. Evolution in a place marks the soul and psyche of a group, that is, the spirit of the place leaves its imprint over generations. The myths of a community that have to do with the "coming into being" are the first stories of the group, and thus the earliest stories and traditions of the Southwest region belong to the Native American communities, those who first settled the region. Here covenants with the gods were formed; here ancestral voices still speak to us from across the span of time; here the landscape is still inhabited by spirits.

Myths, those stories that tell of our coming into being and learning to deal with our humanness, are powerful forces that shape the communal psyche. The myths of this region are the bedrock of belief, identity, tradition, and the other cultural nuances of the first communal groups of the Southwest. The mythic stories feed not only our creativity, they also tell us that if we are to survive on this land we must listen to the stories of the place.

One theme explored in southwestern literature is the conflict we have created with the fragile earth of the region. The Southwest is an arid region; desert and formidable high mountains dominate. There is little arable land. As new groups enter the region, the amount of land each group can occupy becomes smaller. Cultural sharing and adopting used to occur; now we see more displacement taking place. Widespread development is shrinking the land base and the water available. This reality is an emergent theme in our literature.

The first Native American groups to inhabit the land were communal groups. Language and spiritual sensitivity kept them together, and kept them evolving stories from the first myths. The newer migrations into the Southwest brought not only different languages and religions, but a rugged individualism which stood in opposition to that communal spirit. A second important theme in our literature segues into the first. Can the mythic individual of the Old West learn to survive in the communal circle, or will his needs destroy the spirit of the place that drew him there in the first place?

The newer arrivals to the Southwest must learn that to survive, the community must share land and water. The land, climate, and the indigenous people have taught the newcomers this simple lesson. We sense the reverence in the farming ways, in communal survival, and in the stories.

We are beginning to realize that the earth is a fragile planet. We call her mother earth. We say we are riding spaceship earth and we have to take care of the ship. We call the earth Gaia, a living organism, and develop theories of the interrelationship of all things. But abstract statements like this don't move people to mend their ways. They don't mobilize people to act. Very few of us are actually working to save the Amazon rain forest, or the whales, or the ozone layer, or the Northwest forests. We go right on destroying regions for their resources. Our obsession with development is destroying the earth.

As the bumper sticker suggests, perhaps we need to think globally and act locally. The psyche is tuned to its intimate sense of place. From the intimate and regional we can make universal statements. The desert we destroy here today will create droughts in Africa; the water we use from the aquifer will spell disaster in the Amazon.

One service the writers who are writing the Southwest are performing is alerting the people to the destruction of their place, their homes. The new information age is carrying our stories around the earth, and we also read stories from distant places. The communication creates a bond. The creative power of our spirits moves from our region to envelop the earth.

The literature of the Southwest forms part of the literary history of the United States. That it has not been included in the canon of literary history does not lessen its importance. Generation upon generation of natives from this region told stories around the campfires, while hunting, at play, while building shelters, having babies, and otherwise carrying on the work of family and community. Generation upon generation passed down the stories of origin, the gods, the proper ceremonies and ritual, the relationship of the people to the spirit world. This is what the most profound meaning of sense of place describes: our relationship to the spirit of the earth.

Yet, we do not really know our Native American inheritance. There are writers who are recording and building on the indigenous oral tradition and making it known. From their works we learn that we have not only destroyed each other, we have destroyed stories. The stories which carried the history and soul of the people were destroyed. Until we acknowledge the genocide of people and their stories, we cannot make peace with ourselves. This is what the new writings of the Southwest are doing. Making peace with our neighbors, making peace with the gods.

We must acknowledge the history and traditions that came before us. We must celebrate all of those stories of the ancestors, even as we celebrate each new poem or story told today.

There is a vigorous sense of experimentation in style and language going on in the region. We are a multicultural, multilingual region. Here native languages mix with the high-tech languages of science. The language of the people of the villages, *los vecinos*, mixes with New Age lingo. The old dances for rain and harvest, prayer to the *santos* and the *kachinas* mix with the boom of the latest musical fashion. If we learn to listen to each other, maybe the country will learn to listen to its various communities.

Change is constant, and yet beneath the flux the old values resonate. Writers listen to the people and the place for inspiration. That listening is the catching of dreams, the catching of stories. The voices are the spirits, the ancestors, the hum of the earth itself. The writer who is in tune with those voices is truly blessed. The spirit has come to move the story. Writing is a participation and sharing in the place and the people. The writers in this book have listened. Now we invite you to listen as they share their stories of joy and tragedy, stories inspired by love and the spirit of the place.

Rudolfo Anaya
Alburquerque, Nuevo Mexico

PREFACE

▲ ❖ ▼ ❖ ▼ ❖ ▲

Americans in general have at best a vague idea of the American Southwest—culturally, politically, or geographically. Some no doubt see it as something like the wonderful 1990's film *Tombstone*, or the popular movies of the 40s and 50s. The Southwest/West is a land of buttes, mesas, redskins, gunslinger desperadoes, and Frito bandidos, where the language is not necessarily American, and tourists call the state tourism bureaus to inquire about the rate of exchange, the frequency of Indian raids, and the availability of accommodations with plumbing.

Other Americans equate "Southwest" with Native American silver and turquoise jewelry; trendy colonial Spanish-American furniture, architecture, artwork, and cuisine; a style of dress that is based on Diné (Navajo) fashions of the early twentieth century; Pueblo pottery; Navajo rugs; and green chili in everything from vodka to focaccia. These Americans, often among the more intellectual and privileged, believe that *Southwest* and *Santa Fe* are synonyms; they perceive the "Southwest/Santa Fe" as a major loitering place for spiritual trekkers, featuring restorative mineral baths, adobe houses floored in saltillo tile, bent junipers, and cliff dwellings in exotic locales where UFOs, Native gods, and spirits still sing and weep among the magnificent ruins of Chaco, Mesa Verde, Bandelier, and Canyon de Chelly, and can be evoked, enjoyed, and videotaped. When I mentioned to an English friend that I had returned to New Mexico after more than a decade as a

Californian, he said, "Oh, really! You've moved to the New Age center of the world!"

Others come here because it can be perceived as an excellent place for reformation while remaining both exotic and quaint: It's as close to a third world country as one can get while retaining the conveniences, personal and political safety, and the comfortable efficiencies the United States provides its inhabitants. As such, it offers many of the preferred ingredients for the Eastern liberal and radical establishment's favorite pastime: revolution without danger to anyone other than the Natives, whether Indian or Spanish-American.

As a daughter of the Southwest, born and raised in the central mountains of New Mexico by parents who were themselves native New Mexicans, and as a contemporary mixed-blood descendant of the Keres Pueblo peoples who have lived in this region literally since time immemorial, these pop-American versions of *mi país* (my country) are very far indeed from the ordinary and astonishing realities of the place. And to this tri-cultural daughter of the tri-cultural and ancient Southwest, it is necessary that the Southwest be viewed as an aesthetic location, the psycho-cultural place that shapes and gives meaning to the daily habits, possessions, perceptions, values, and personal and community styles of its people that are reflected and refined in its literature.

The material created by Anglo writers of the Southwest arises out of contexts framed as much by Eastern American thought as by Pueblo, Navajo, and Hispanic/Spanish language style, theme, and philosophical preoccupation.

The three strains of thought that characterize southwestern literature, as well as its contemporary social and political movements, blend into a differentiated yet harmonious whole because the land itself is the overarching presence in all the major works by Southwestern writers.

There are three cultural bases that define southwestern cultural identity: the Pueblo, the Mexican Hispano, and the American. The latter influence is as present in the thought and style of African, Lebanese, Syrian, Greek, Chinese, Japanese, and Jewish America as in the Anglo-American segments of the American community; and the commonality of American culture is nowhere more visible than in the Southwest where its presence is still largely marginal, unassimilated at any but superficial levels into the deeper identity of the Southwest.

I am pleased to introduce this study of southwestern writing compiled by Professor David Dunaway from his interviews and background research for his radio series, "Writing the Southwest." David comes to Albuquerque by way of Berkeley and Huxley's Los Angeles, and his route lends a perspective to his presentation and understanding of Southwest literature that is unique. It is drawn as much from his understanding of contemporary western and coastal American literature and culture as from a more formalist approach to Southwest literature. This broader perspective enables Dunaway (and his co-author, Sara Spurgeon) to present the literary produce of this high plateau/mountainous, arid land within its true tri-cultural framework.

Working with David on "Writing the Southwest" and preparing to write this preface have given me the opportunity to reflect on my sense of the Southwest, its cultural characteristics, terrain, spiritual, and aesthetic qualities. I have spent many diverting hours thinking about how I go about identifying a place or quality as "southwestern," comparing my sense of my country to the more official identification Dunaway and many Anglo experts broadly define as the Southwest.

In their introduction, Dunaway and Spurgeon comment that "By 'Southwest' we refer primarily to Arizona, Colorado, and New Mexico, states which share the Colorado plateau, the upper Rio Grande valley, and the arid land surrounding them. This region is bounded," they continue, still citing the historian Lawrence Powell, by " 'the land east of the Rio Colorado, south of the Mesa Verde, west of the Pecos, and north of the border.' "

I am not particularly comfortable with an historian's definition of this cultural and historical construct, the Southwest, preferring a Native, nativo, or generations-long Anglo inhabitant to articulate this space. I am equally at a loss to discern why a map is used to draw the parameters when there are more telling pieces of information that define it beyond the mesas, mountains, rivers, and geopolitical borders. Indeed, many might place southern California in the Southwest, geo-

argues that geopolitical boundaries of Southwest are inadequate.

graphically and culturally, while others are of the opinion that Oklahoma, at least its western portion, must be included within the general cultural-political borders of the American Southwest. Zane Grey might have included Utah and more of southern Colorado than Powell includes, while others would exclude most of Texas, Oklahoma, Arizona, and southern California.

Cultural geographies, far more than geological or political ones, give rise to cultural artifacts such as literature, and it seems wisest for readers of this collection to think on the cultural dimensions of our "tri-cultural" spiritual-psychic location rather than on the geopolitical ones.

For true Southwesterners, the land is central to their multiplicit identity, but it is one of several dimensions of that identity. Given that, the Southwest encompasses southern Utah, which is presently populated by a large Diné community, an even larger presence of Yei (holy people to the Diné), and Katsina (Pueblo supernatural beings), goddesses and gods who inhabit some unknown dimension that corresponds to that area. That presence defines the entirety of the region known accurately as the Southwest, and includes eastern and central Arizona, northwestern to northeastern Mexico, all of western, central, and northern New Mexico, and the portions of Colorado that lie adjacent to the Rio Grande.

These borders, drawn in largely geospiritual terms, can be intuited by exploring the southwestern landscape. One can readily perceive its particular identity through its characteristic sounds, smells, colors, textures, tastes, and ambiance both subtle and overt. A major indicator is the kind of social and spiritual structure the local Native people enjoy, a subject best assessed by careful study of petroglyphs and petrograms, samples of the local corn and chili based foods, the noticeable influence of Spanish-colonial ambiance, and a particular "cowboy" or Anglo rancher outlook and the accompanying scattering of "anglo" artifacts of various kinds and degrees of permanence.

As I see it, the Southwest is that space shaped by the deep understandings possessed and expressed by the ancient Pueblos, Mogollons, and Maya and their descendants, the Hohokam,

Southwest : ① narrative with aesthetic of land-animal-human interchange.
② Spanish/Indian synthesis characterized by presence of the living dead.
③ Characters of the American mythic West — the knight quest.

Preface / xxi

Pueblo, Pima, Yaqui, Diné, and Mexicans of Aztec-European descent. It is this bedrock of a particular kind of Native American civilization and embodied in its central narrative that best distinguishes southwestern literature from that of any other region in the Western Hemisphere. That central narrative is characterized by a particular aesthetic that is rooted in the ongoing relationship, or conversation, among the human, the plant and animal, the land, and the supernaturals, each perceived as members of the same geospiritual community.

Upon this ever nourishing cultural terra firma rests a second layer, Southwestern cultural-spiritual narrative. The Spanish-colonial presence in the narrative tradition of the Southwest is as tightly interconnected to the Native ground as the grass, junipers, sage, mesquite, cottonwoods, and arroyos are to the basic terrain. It is because of this tight connection of the Maya/Aztec Spanish narrative tradition to the modern American's sense of place that locations from Monterey to central Mexico can be seen as fundamentally Southwestern. Certainly their narrative tradition bears many of the characteristics of Pueblo/Maya thought, although there are a number of dimensions of that narrative that remain distinct from that of the core Southwest.

This heritage—that of the Spanish colonial built upon and tightly bonded to the Pueblo/Maya cultures that both precede and presently inform it—gives its particular quality to the work of Hispanic Southwestern writers. Of late, that quality has been defined as "magico-realism" by the literati, but that is, of course, the translation of a complex psycho-cultural phenomenon rendered for intellectual consumption of the intelligentsia, much as Ceasar Vallejo's bicultural Portuguese Colonial-Mapuche' articulations of Peruvian worldview were designated "surreal" at an earlier period. This literature is characterized primarily by the active and compelling presence of the dead—as living—and the legendary quality of most Hispanic literature of the Southwest.

A number of characteristics of this writing mark the work of South American writers such as Borges, García Márquez, and Allende. Yet sufficient differences exist in the way they render a Spanish/Portuguese–Native American worldview that one may see them as distinct. It is not the marked presence of

Spanish or Portuguese language, Catholicism, violent revolution, and magico-realism or surrealism that characterizes certain writers as southwestern of Hispanic ambiance and descent, but a complex of other characteristics within which the powerfully Spanish/Portuguese colonial experience is rendered into contemporary literature.

One writer who belongs in the southwestern cadre because her work shares all of these distinguishing characteristics is Laura Esquivel (*Like Water for Chocolate*). If some enterprising literary genius from my father's hometown, Seboyeta, New Mexico, had written a novel, it could read and mean almost exactly the same as *Like Water for Chocolate*.

The third dimension of the psycho-spiritual ambiance, the distinguishing aesthetic ambiance of the Southwest, is the Anglo pioneer, cowboy, prospector, U.S. Army, forts, ranges, mesquite and cattle, "blue shadows" on the Santa Fe Trail, tumbling tumbleweed, rangy, tough cowboy ponies and gentle cowboy humor, gunslinging outlaws, sheriffs and marshals, careful, seamed Anglo ranchers, livestock growers, traders, railroad magnates, priests, preachers, bureaucrats, and shopkeepers.

These are the characters who people the modern American myth of the West, a modern narrative whose roots lie deep in the Celtic wanderer cum knight-and-lord who anciently peopled and wandered from Anatolia, moving onto the Iberian peninsula and along the trans-Alpine range into Western Europe. Those people migrated over the millennia into the British Isles and finally came to rest in the American Southwest/Mexico. A Santa Fe writer who most clearly represents this tradition is Roger Zelazny, whose Avalon series is as southwestern/Celtic-contemporary as any work produced by an "anglo" writer in the contemporary period.

The more settled members of the newest emigré community include insurance and real estate sales people, restaurateurs, and hotel magnates—Conrad Hilton was raised in tiny San Antonio, just outside of Socorro, New Mexico—high-tech managers and technicians, computer hackers, pilots of F-15 jets, radiant glow-in-the-dark children of the nuclear age, nuclear astrophysicists, mountaineers, and strong women of every class: bankers, ranchers, pilots, adventurers, politicians—and

most recently New Agers, yuppies and feminists moved from
the recently overcrowded and expensive west coast.

Here in the ancient cradle of American civilization, these
most recent comers hope to replicate their version of paradise
on Hispanic/Pueblo/Anglo southwestern grounds in new laws,
new ordinances, "green" environmental structures, gun, alcohol, and tobacco control, and the pretty overlay of gentrifica-
tion that conceals brutal power management, and prettifies the
truly monstrous.

"Ay, poor New Mexico," sighed once Governor Armijo, "so
far from heaven, so close to Texas." Today our recently de-
feated Governor, Bruce King, one of Armijo's Anglo-rancher
political descendants, might similarly sigh, "Ah, poor New Mexico, so close to remodeling, so far from its *corazón*."

When these various strands combine, they result in writing
that is Southwestern in aesthetic quality, theme, structure,
point of view, and deep meaning. A truly Southwestern work
almost inevitably combines the ancient, the medieval, and the
contemporary in ways that yield maximal meaning comprehen-
sible within several contexts.

One of the prime characteristics of *mi país*, the Southwest,
is its power to ever change and remain essentially the same.
Magically, it has for millennia retained its singular aesthetic
identity while incorporating great deviations from its central narrative core. To this the narratives themselves testify,
as does the differing quality of the wind—*el viento, nitch'i,
ai'tah'yah*—singing their (for the polytheistic pueblos hear a
number of distinct "winds") various songs in the full-leafed
cottonwoods, aspens, and juniper of July, when the lightning
flashes and dazzles, the sky clouds thick and deep, the blue-
black flies crowd round the blue wooden doors, the Shiwanna
(rain people, supernaturals) return, and the hard rain pounds
the earth, writing its nature deep into the canyons, the arroyos, the acequias, the lakes, and rios.

Mi país is forever itself, though cultures and peoples, like
wind and rain, have over and over come to change it, from the
ancient ones of millennia past, through the Athabascans in the
ninth century, through the Spanish colonials who began their
incursions in the sixteenth century and continue today, and
through successive waves of Anglo emigration that have in-

undated us since the mid-nineteenth century. The process by which the Southwest is changed and ever remains the same began in time immemorial; one can only suppose that it will end there as well.

It may be that the theme song Dunaway has chosen for his radio series, one of my favorites since early childhood, "Don't Fence Me In," is the true song of the Southwest wind, and that it, as much as any corrido, chantway, or Pueblo dance, tells us who and where we are.

Paula Gunn Allen

INTRODUCTION

▲ ✧ ▼ ✧ ▼ ✧ ▲

For many, the literature of the American Southwest is frozen in amber, a scene out of Robert Sherwood's *The Petrified Forest*, where a Villon-spouting wanderer meets a desperado in a remote roadhouse. Yet the literary history of the Southwest is a dynamic, ever-changing fusion of the peoples who settled there and created its oral literature over the last millennium. In this volume, we set forth a representative selection of the region's modern literary riches.

There are countless ways to define this region. By "Southwest" we refer primarily to Arizona, Colorado, Utah, and New Mexico. In literary historian Lawrence Powell's terms, it includes "states which share the Colorado plateau, the upper Rio Grande valley, and the arid land surrounding them . . . the land east of the Rio Colorado, south of the Mesa Verde, west of the Pecos, and north of the border."[1]

Like the folklore of its people, the literary history of the Southwest is carved from its unique geography, which allowed ethnically diverse communities to coexist.[2] The tall ranges and deep valleys of southern Colorado and northern New Mexico separated Indian from Hispanic and Hispanic from Anglo settlements. The Southwest's great rivers (the Colorado and Rio Grande and their tributaries) have always determined the settlement of the region, its commerce, and its demography: in New Mexico alone, 80 percent of the state's population lives within thirty miles of the Rio Grande.

Riding over the smooth asphalt of the interstates today, one can easily forget that territories such as Arizona and New Mexico have been states for less than ninety years. This juxtaposition of ancient and modern, the fact that traditional cultures have maintained much of their histories and customs into a technological age, has given the American Southwest a literature unlike any other.

Literary History

The ancient literary culture of the Southwest blossomed with the Pueblo Indians, the nineteen tribes who trace their ancestry to the Mogollon and Anasazi settlements of the Colorado and Rio Grande valleys, from A.D. 600 to A.D. 1400. Today this tradition lives on in the writing of poet Simon Ortiz, of the Acoma Pueblo, whose luminous and textured works capture the startling beauty of the Southwest's high desert and mesas.

Alongside these Pueblo settlements came the Hopi, and later, the Navajo. (Included in this volume is the reservation-raised Shiprock poet Luci Tapahonso, whose poetics spring from the lyric Beauty Way of her Diné heritage and evoke the musical quality of her tribe's oral traditions.)

The Southwest's literary history before 1500 belongs exclusively to its earliest peoples. Their poetic forms were derived from traditional chants and songs; to this day, some traditional Indian poetic texts can only be performed as part of a ritual religious observance. Native American imagery depicts a world alive: sky, earth, mountains, animals, streams, and rocks have an inner nature as vital as that of humans. In these visions of oneness, it's possible to overlook the cultural differences separating the formerly nomadic tribes of the Southwest, such as the Apache and Navajo, and the more agrarian, such as the Hopi and Pueblo. For, despite differences among tribes, most share a parallel worldview of nature.

Traditional Native American poetry differs from the Euro-American variety by its impersonality. Poetry and song are only secondarily a vehicle for creative expression of individual experience, at least until well into the second half of the twentieth century. Individual authors stand out within the cultural expression of their families, clans, villages, and tribes. These traditions pass along a people's history, religious beliefs, mythic stories, morality tales, and aesthetic ideals. The beginnings of twentieth-century native writings in the Southwest are found in the biographies and autobiographies of the 1930s and 1940s: Acoma James Paytiamo's *Flaming Rainbow's People* (1932) and Don Talayesva's *Sun Chief: The Autobiography of a Hopi* (1942) are two examples. In fiction, Cherokee novelist John Oskison was publishing novels in the 1920s and 1930s. D'Arcy McNickle, the preeminent Indian novelist of the 1930s and 1940s, sometimes took up southwestern themes, as in *The Surrounded* (1936). And Cherokee humorist Will Rogers published numerous collections of his columns in the 1930s and 1940s. The Choctaw writer Todd Downing wrote mysteries set in Northern Mexico and the Southwest, such as *The Mexican Earth* (1940) and *The Lazy Lawrence Murders* (1941).

It is not until the Red Power movement of the 1960s, however, that we find the literary flowering which helped launch the Native American writers in this volume. N. Scott Momaday's novels began a literary resurgence: *The House Made of Dawn* (1968) and *Way to Rainy Mountain* (1969) set a new standard for writing about Native Americans.

An important point of confluence was the campus of the University of New Mexico in the early 1970s, when Simon Ortiz, Geary Hobson, and Leslie Silko were on the faculty and Luci Tapahonso, Joy Harjo, and Paula Gunn Allen were students.

Today's most famous native writers began their careers in an educational system which offered few models of native writing; thus modern Euro-American influences, from Keats and Shelley to Audre Lord, are heavily felt among contemporary Native poets such as Joy Harjo, Luci Tapahonso, and Simon Ortiz, who combine two or more disparate traditions into a vital new form, a unique mix of languages and cultures, old and new, that is the reality of Native American life today.

Many literary historians have noted the romanticization of Native Americans in the literature of this (and previous) periods; fewer have commented that this tradition is not exclusively North American, for it may owe as much to Chateaubriand, Rousseau, and Ernest Thompson Seton as it does to Fenimore Cooper. And tragedy has always been a part of this romance. Native Americans taught settlers survival, how to forage and cure themselves with plants from the forest;

and they were made sick, with foreign diseases. They accepted those seeking a haven for religious freedom; and to a significant extent lost their freedom to worship at traditional sites. They gave newcomers space for their imaginations and their communities; and they were confined.

Intermarriage further complicated a cultural mix which includes not only Indian and Anglo cultures, but also those of Spain and Mexico. In 1542, the Spanish explorer Hernando de Soto died in Oklahoma after coming westward with his men from Mississippi. Coronado first explored the upper Rio Grande valley and traveled across the plains of what would be New Mexico and Arizona in the 1540s. In 1595, Juan de Oñate began colonizing New Mexico for Spain.

Spanish settlers of the sixteenth and seventeenth centuries intermarried with the Indians of the region. From Spain they brought the lore of the explorer as well as more expressive forms of culture—songs and music; tall tales, called *cuentos*; and folk dramas whose forms persist in Hispanic culture today.

Chicana playwright Denise Chavez, for example, brings the voices of the borderlands to vibrant life in her dramas and stories. She is the cultural and literary descendant of earlier Hispanic poets and writers who created what was initially in the United States a literature of resistance. Chicana playwright Josefina Niggli wrote in the 1930s about the Mexican Revolution; the plight of illegal immigrants in the United States; and the volatile and changing role of Hispanic women caught between patriarchal Mexican (Spanish Catholic/Aztec machismo warrior roots) and Anglo cultures, and the economic demands of life north of the border, which required many of them to work outside the home.

Earlier Spanish conquistadors brought folk dramas and religious plays from Spain which survived and melded with the rituals of Mexican and American Indians. Along with new and older forms of dramas were the *corridos*, folk ballads telling of the exploits of Hispanic heroes who defied the strong arm of American expansionism, especially after the Treaty of Guadalupe Hidalgo in 1848 left many Mexican nationals on the north side of the new border between Mexico and the United States. The cultural conflicts and sometimes blatant racism they experienced in their new country caused the *corridos* to flourish throughout the Southwest, and some of them have survived up to the present day.

While many *corridos* were composed anonymously, some of the more famous, like "The Mexico-Texan" (1934) and "With a Pistol in His Hand" (1958), were published by scholars such as Americo Paredes, inspiring group solidarity and activism; and the protagonists of the songs became folk heroes in Hispanic communities. Many *corridos* still popular in Chicano communities such as "El Corrido de Gregorio Cortez" and "El General Cortina" can be traced back as far as 1859.[3]

Springing directly from this oral literature of protest were early modern Chicano works such as *Pocho* (1959) by Jose Antonio Villarreal, chronicling the lives of Hispanics in rural California whose parents came from Mexico, but who grow up speaking English, and later Tomás Rivera's acclaimed . . . *y no se lo tragó la tierra* [*and the earth did not devour him*] (1971), tracing the tragic realities of migrant farm workers in California and Texas. Today, Arizonan Alberto Rios writes of the border towns of the Southwest and of their struggles to survive, economically and culturally, the continuing arrival of English-speaking peoples.

Drawing from *corridos* and traditional dramas, as well as the folk belief in *curanderas* (witches/healers) common in rural New Mexico, Rudolfo Anaya, hailed by the *New York Times* as the most widely read Latin writer in the United States, weaves tales of witches and magic. In many ways, Anaya represents yet another branch of modern Chicano literature. Unlike the communities in the works of Villarreal, Rivera, and Rios, on the borderlands of California, Texas, and Arizona, many Hispanic villages in New Mexico are still quite isolated geographically, both from Anglo settlements and from new or continuing immigrations from Mexico. Many of their inhabitants, like Anaya, can trace their ancestry directly to Spain, thus leaving them a folk history related, but by no means identical, to that of the Mexican-American traditions of other parts of the Southwest.

The Anglo (non-Hispanic Euro-American) settlements of the region date principally to the early nineteenth century, when, following the Santa Fe Trail and more southerly routes, Euro-

American settlers poured into the region in search of gold, open spaces to homestead, and refuge from the urbanization of the East.

For the Anglo-American settler in the nineteenth century, literary culture consisted of the diaries, journals, and correspondence kept by the settlers and, in some few cases, mailed to the East for publication. Works which had an enduring effect were often those of individuals with formal education east of the Mississippi. In 1834, Albert Pike published *Prose, Sketches, and Poems, Written in the Western Country*. This and other literature derived from the oral traditions of the region, whether cowboy stories told on cattle drives or *cuentos* such as those of Joaquin Miller.

The continuing Anglo immigration—particularly after the 1848 Treaty of Guadalupe Hidalgo ceding much of northern Mexico to the United States—has taken place over the last 175 years. This multigenerational influx has continued the Southwest's dynamic mixture of cultures, languages, and literary traditions. Much of the new Anglo literature sprang from the experiences of easterners in the Southwest. Perhaps the most famous literary denizen of the Anglo Southwest was Charles Lummis, whose 1892 chronicle of his cross-country journey by foot from Cincinnati to Los Angeles, *A Tramp across the Continent*, fired the country's romantic visions of Hispanic and Indian settlements of the American Southwest. Lummis later published numerous articles, essays, books (including *Land of Poco Tiempo* (1902)), and magazines trumpeting the delights of the desert.

He also acted as mentor to another of the Southwest's long tradition of nature writers cum historians, Mary Hunter Austin. Austin's *Land of Little Rain* (1903) and *Land of Journeys' Ending* (1908) brought new life to the folktales of Hispanics, Anglos, and Native Americans from the region. Her work, along with John C. Van Dyke's *The Desert* (1901), established an early blueprint of Anglo relationships with the land (later explored in the works of modern western writers, such as controversial naturalist and philosopher Edward Abbey, who arrived in the 1940s).

In this volume, Anglo writing is also explored in the works of Frank Waters, whose family arrived in Colorado in 1870. In his footsteps followed the best-selling mystery writer Tony Hillerman, who moved to New Mexico in the fifties; John Nichols, author of *The Milagro Beanfield War*, *The Sterile Cuckoo*, and *The Wizard of Loneliness*, who migrated to Taos, New Mexico, in 1972; and by even later immigrants such as Kentucky native Barbara Kingsolver, whose wondrous novels have gained much critical acclaim. African-American novelist Terry McMillan, whose books top the *New York Times* best-seller list, is representative of the growing African-American presence in southwestern cities such as Phoenix, Albuquerque, Denver, and El Paso.

The balance of the population and the culture of the Southwest has shifted throughout the last ten centuries with each in-migration. After the Civil War, those writers associated with the "local color" movement in American fiction turned their attention from the South to the Southwest, resulting in a series of southwestern romances: a typical title is *The Old Stone Corral* (1888) by John D. Carteret, made up of tales of lost treasure and adventures on the Santa Fe Trail. Works such as Helen Hunt Jackson's best-selling romance *Ramona* (1884) glorified the Spanish Mission culture and beleaguered Indian communities, and it was hailed along with *Uncle Tom's Cabin* as one of the great moral novels of the century. These were balanced by the more realistic works of Adolph Bandelier, whose *The Delight Makers* (1890) portrayed the southwestern Indians whose prehistory this well-known archaeologist had preserved.

Alongside these works were those of the best-known popularizer of the Southwest, and one whose images have dominated America's imagination, Zane Grey; his classic early novels *Riders of the Purple Sage* (1912), its sequel, *The Rainbow Trail* (1915), and *Light of the Western Stars* (1914) spawned many imitators, as J. Frank Dobie writes: "From the days of the first innocent sensations in Beadle's Dime Novel series, on through Zane Grey's mass productions . . . the Southwest, along with all the rest of the West, has been represented in a fictional output quantitatively stupendous."[4]

In the twenties, the mythologized works of D. H. Lawrence (including essays and novels on New Mexico and Mexico, and stories, such as "The Woman Who Rode Away") described southwestern culture on a mythopoetic, symbolic level. Soon, another generation of southwestern writers emerged, including Willa Cather, whose critically acclaimed *Death Comes for the Archbishop* (1927) set a high standard for literature about the region.

Then came the first generation of Anglo writers born and raised in the Southwest, who took their region as their text. Frank Waters's Colorado mining trilogy, *Pikes Peak* (1932–37), was one of the earliest realistic treatments of an Anglo settlement by a native southwesterner, and his novel *The Man Who Killed the Deer* (1941), set in Taos Pueblo in northern New Mexico, made him one of the first Anglo authors to write seriously about Native American efforts at self-determination.

Beginning with Mary Hunter Austin's 1909 classic *Lost Borders*, literary adaptations of traditional Southwest folktales were published. Hispanic tellers of *cuentos*, such as Jaime de Angulo, wrote down their oral traditions. Frank Applegate's *Indian Stories from the Pueblos* (1929) and Frank Dobie's *Coronado's Children* (1930), along with Helen Hunt Jackson's *Ramona*, were actually national best-sellers. Such works fired the imagination of Sunday-supplement readers in the Midwest and East; their interest was eventually merchandized into the black hat–white hat icons of B movies of Hollywood in the 1930s, 1940s, and 1950s.

Postwar southwestern literature was dominated initially by Frank Waters, followed by essayists who interpreted the Anglo Southwest's traditions and myths to distant readers: one of these was Joseph Wood Krutch, whose *The Voice of the Desert* (1955) set the context for authors such as Edward Abbey and John Nichols. Paul Horgan, A. B. Guthrie, Willa Cather, and Pulitzer Prize–winning novelist Oliver La Farge whetted the appetite of a national audience for Southwest mystique. Works of more modern novelists, such as William Eastlake and N. Scott Momaday, are the immediate predecessors of Tony Hillerman, Barbara Kingsolver, and Linda Hogan; naturalists Henry David Thoreau, John Muir, John C. Van Dyke, and Aldo Leopold wrote in an American Romantic tradition which preceded Edward Abbey and John Nichols.

We speak of "Anglo" writers, but today this term's definition is under debate. Paula Gunn Allen uses the term "American" to refer to all non-Native, non-Hispanic inhabitants of this region. (This would include Asians, African-Americans, and other communities, many of whom have lived in this region for more than a century. Allen is herself half Lebanese.) Others use such terms more restrictively; yet all such rubrics are constructs, including "Southwest"—"Southwest of what?," one might ask. Instead of her "tri-culturalism," we might look towards a coming-together, *la confluencia*, of the peoples of the Southwest.

Oral Literature and the American Southwest

Just as there are many ways to delimit the Southwest's boundaries, scholars offer various definitions of oral literature; ours is drawn from two giants of the field: Ruth Finnegan and Jan Vansina. "The special nature of oral tradition," writes Vansina, "derives from the fact that it is an unwritten source couched in a form suitable for oral transmission, whose preservation depends on the powers of memory of successive generations of human beings."[5] Because of its physical and linguistic isolation, the Southwest's memories have lived on for centuries.

Most classic writings about oral literature in the Southwest draw on its Native American and Spanish-language manifestations across literary genres. Thus, one view of the region's Spanish folklore sees only survivalism of a culture originating in Spain—much as the great British folk song collector, Cecil Sharpe, viewed Appalachian folk songs in 1915. Yet Hispanic writers such as Rudolfo Anaya and Denise Chavez claim literary influences from Mexico and Native America as well as Europe. Most feel that rather than the preservation of a single form, southwestern Hispanic literature today is instead the fusion of often divergent worldviews.

Today's oral literature of the Southwest remains vital, a fusion of multiple sources: pop jingles and advertisements, traditional *corridos* and modern *rancheras*, country and western and blues, radio and television broadcasts.

As Paula Gunn Allen (Laguna Pueblo) writes in *Spider Woman's Granddaughters*, "Among native people, stories have been told from time immemorial into the present, [some] orally told stories and those that are told-on-the-page. To a native ear and eye, the told-on-the-page stories are sensible because they belong to a literary tradition the writer lives and thinks in."[6]

The overall method used in this volume is oral literary history—documenting the literary culture of a historical period or region via taped recordings. This is the application of oral history research to topics with a literary focus. The oral biography is one result of such literary study.

Biography sits at the meeting point between literature and history. The oral biography is a nonfictional life narrative researched primarily through interviews. Each author relates a narrative of his or her family, region, schooling, the sound- and landscapes of youth, and his or her oral traditions.

The oral biography format used here has an authenticity based on a three-sided collaboration among the biographer-interviewer, the author's oral tradition, and the author's life and community. Thus each author is approached personally as well as professionally. Personal narratives have always formed a major part of oral tradition in the Southwest. Few Hispanic women had formal education in the nineteenth and early twentieth centuries; and those who did lacked the support and the leisure time to write. Their lives were told rather than written—or not documented at all.

Radio and Literature: "Writing the Southwest"

Despite its title, this volume is as concerned with listening to the Southwest as composing it. This book had its origin in a radio series, "Writing the Southwest," which has shaped its text considerably.[7]

The use of radio to find new audiences for literature is not new—but its application to the literary history of the American Southwest is novel, and perhaps particularly appropriate.

As Rudolfo Anaya told the authors of this volume, it is not the exact texts of folklore, with their traditional tale types, that serve as a basis for his writing: "More importantly, I've used the *technique* of the *cuento*. I am an oral storyteller, but now I do it on the printed page. I think if we were very wise we would use that same tradition in videocassettes and in movies and in radio."

In *The Voice in the Margin: Native American Literature and the Canon*, Arnold Krupat contextualizes the work of contemporary Native authors, including Leslie Silko, Simon Ortiz, and others: literature Indian writers create must be understood as a continuing product of their timeless oral tradition. He suggests that there is no way to translate and present Indian oral performance in any completely satisfactory way.[8]

That is, on a page. Yet radio as an oral (spoken)/aural (heard) medium offers the public an effective way of appreciating Native American, Hispanic, and Anglo oral traditions in their own right, as oral literature. Southwestern literature is based on its oral literary traditions—even those texts that circulate exclusively in printed form.

"Writing the Southwest" offers this oral-based literature in what a folklorist might call an induced context (performed on radio); the tradition shifts from oral to aural. The aim of the series is to present literary adaptations of oral tradition to wide public audiences. The programs' greatest contribution may be in developing the growing audience for literature off the page. These documentaries, with special effects and music, offer an alternative to the books-on-tape format.

The pilot program, on Stan Steiner, winner of the Golden Spurs from the Western Writers of America, was produced in 1986 by an English professor trained in radio. This led to eventual funding from three state humanities councils (New Mexico, Colorado, and Arizona) and, in 1992, from the National Endowment for the Humanities (NEH).

Radio broadcasting and the Southwest's oral literature seem at first glance made for each other. When broadcast, literature provides an ear into our culture, one custom-built for radio and rich with the color and pacing of real speech.[9] Interviews with authors and critics may possess gem quality, but seem opaque; considerable cutting and polishing is done before the jewels show their luster. Broadcasting authors' oral interpretations of their work offers the authenticity of their own speech patterns and other nuances.

At the heart of this volume's aesthetic lies what might be called a radiographic imagination: the way we understand the world from what we hear. Of course, understanding what we hear is complicated by the fact that for most of us hearing rarely occurs in isolation from what we sense in other formats—particularly what we see. We speak of watching television or film, but in fact we hear this entertainment as thoroughly as we see it. Strip the sound from our favorite programs and the images which flash across the screen seem pallid. Compared to television, radio is not the absence of images but the enhanced and exclusive use of sound. Radio's aurality, its quality of being heard, allows the world to be mentally pictured by sound; thus it is less explicit than its sister visual forms. The mind populates literature from the pool of friends and acquaintances surrounding us.

For "Writing the Southwest," this has meant that via radio, the oral traditions of the American Southwest are presented on their own terms. Our imagination first dials in a soundscape of the natural and human-built environment, and then notes the interviews, narration, music, and effects which are auditorily superimposed on the soundscape by the producer. In responding to these elements, we think with our ears. This response may differ in kind from the way we read literature with our eyes.

In printed form, the story or poem is fixed. In oral performance, the work is subtly nuanced by the expectations of the audience sitting before the oral author. He or she notes the mood in the room and may embellish or foreshorten a text to match the occasion. Some of this is lost in radio, for there too the text is predetermined. Yet by its intangibility radio creates its own mood and texture for the literary moment, a different experience of a poem.

This play between orality and aurality is embedded in the chapters which follow. We read a life configured by being told, as opposed to being written; we hear the words of the author not only in their works but in their descriptions of the circumstances which underlie the text.

Characteristic Themes of Contemporary Southwestern Literature

Boiling southwestern literature down to a series of central themes risks reductionism and overgeneralization. Ironically so, for one of the principal themes of this volume is the over-shadowing effects of the persistent body of southwestern icons and stereotypes, often created by people who had never actually seen the Southwest.

A Sense of Place

"A writer without a sense of place is not likely to get very close to his material," once commented John Milton, editor of the *South Dakota Review*. If there is one topic to which the writers in this book return—Indian, Hispanic, African-American, and Anglo—it is the importance of being rooted and of the landscape. The Southwest is a region sparsely settled; three hundred miles of sky, desert, and mountains separate Denver from Albuquerque, and Albuquerque from Phoenix or El Paso. In regions peopled with institutions, edifices, and roads, where one urban area sprawls into another, it is hard to convey the spaciousness of the southwestern ecoscape.

We can mention that there are today regions where gas stations are seventy-five to one hundred miles apart; that there is no single "desert," but rather a half dozen recognized bio-botanical regions of arid and semi-arid land ranging in elevation from sea level to eight thousand feet; that because of its high elevations, southwesterners can drive in a few hours from foot-deep snow cover in dense pine forests to treeless, sun-baked desert plains.

Such contrasts illustrate the diversity of a region which shares only a few central characteristics: the presence of sun and the absence of water; large areas of unspoiled (or at least undeveloped) wilderness; the effects of altitude; and the pe-culiarly intense quality of the region's light, due in part to the absence of industrialization, urban sprawl, pollutants, and humidity in the atmosphere.

*"What's unique about the Colorado plateau, about this
area where the land is finally risen up out the heavy wet air
of the gulf, and your altitude is high, and you have cold
nights, and you can see a thousand miles, and it's dry, and
obviously nobody can make a living—this is not hospitable
country—it somehow puts you in an environment which
forces you into perspective; a very small human in a very
large landscape."*

—Tony Hillerman[10]

Culture/Peoples in Transition

Perhaps because of its geographical isolation from the rest
of the United States, the Southwest's industrialization and cultural homogenization have proceeded slowly; but they have
arrived. With this trend comes cultural hybridization, of which
a few snapshots may suffice: a band of teenage Navajos, playing in a school gym for their classmates dressed in tux and
basic black, singing tunes of Hank Williams & His Drifting Cowboys; Anglo immigrants from the 1960s who settled in com-
munes in the San Luis Valley of Colorado and New Mexico, who
stayed to the present day, wear their hair in ponytails, and
have as outbuildings tepees or hogans; a Hispanic executive of
Southwestern Bell, who on the weekends shifts from suit to
jeans and digs a six-foot hole in his backyard so that a whole
pig can be buried there atop live coals for a *matanza*, or pit
barbecue, who walks the Stages of the Cross on his knees
for Easter, yet spends Sunday mornings at the All-U-Can-Eat
brunch buffet at the local Howard Johnson.

Many factors combine to create this hybridization: radio,
TV, and film, which create homogenized images of one
(wealthy) culture shared by all peoples; the dramatic and ever-
increasing rate of ecological change, which has profoundly affected the ability of Native Americans and Hispanics to live in
their traditional relation to nature; and the economic change
involved in moving from a barter economy to a cash one. The
change can be as basic as the food generations after generations have eaten: Hispanic "chicos," or dried, ripe corn gives
way to canned hominy and then to Taco Bell, while salsa re-
places ketchup as America's best-selling condiment and many

Anglo families' favorite home recipes are for burritos or enchiladas. In Arizona and New Mexico today, Anglo girls are beginning to celebrate their fifteenth birthdays with *quinceñeras*—parties in the Hispanic tradition. Throughout the Southwest every Christmas *farolitos* (small paper bags, weighted with sand and lit by a candle) line sidewalks and rooftops in Hispanic and Anglo neighborhoods alike. We find cappuccino bars in rural Hispanic settings, and green chiles in bottles of Russian vodka.

One reason for this rapidly increasing cross-pollination of cultures is the growing urbanization of the region, forcing formerly isolated communities into close proximity. The increasing population of the Southwest's cities has also strained the natural resources in areas where urbanites have gone for recreation, particularly the mountains, lakes, and waters of the Southwest.

These ecological and economic changes inevitably produce shifts in culture. The Southwest's languages are fused: whether you call Spanish-inflected English caló, *pocho*, or Spanglish, English and Spanish have integrated in the Southwest in a way they have nowhere else in the United States. The characters in the works of playwright Denise Chavez and poet Alberto Rios code-switch between English and Spanish in the same sentence (or, in the novels of Hillerman, between Navajo and English). Such "code switchers" inevitably struggle with issues of identity, common to children whose parents speak one language and whose teachers and classmates speak another.

As Paula Gunn Allen comments in her preface, the words we use to describe the wind or physical features of the Southwest matter; naming is an act of love. So, too, do the various words used to describe communities of Spanish-speaking people carry subtle (and shifting) connotations.

"Latino" may be the most encompassing term, including such diverse groups as Cubans, Puerto Ricans, Europeans, Central and South Americans; the term appears most often on the East Coast or abroad. "Mexican-American" refers "specifically to those of Mexican ancestry who either came from Mexico to live in the United States or who are descended from Mexican parents or grandparents," according to one scholar.[11] (Of course "Mexican" is itself a mix of indigenous and European ancestry.) "Hispanic" describes those of Spanish descent and is particularly current in New Mexico and Colorado. "Chicano/a" is generally used by (and to refer to) those born after World War II; it connotes a sense of pride in a cultural identity which is both Indian (Native Mexican and Native American) and Hispanic.

Each of these terms allows for variations by class, education, and generation: a single family might include parents who identify themselves as Mexican-American, children who call themselves Chicano, and grandchildren who are "Hispanic."

In English we have no satisfactory term to translate *mestizaje*, the condition of being born between and within cultures. "Race-mixing" is a term for miscegenation, a crime in some states for most of this century. "Half-breed" is similarly derogatory, suggesting that a person is half as authentic. Yet being a *mestizo* is more accurately being a "two-breed," dual identities making a whole greater than its parts. Perhaps only when the United States has a majority of people of color as its citizens will it accept that we are all *mestizaje* in some sense and find a more healing expression, which allows choices other than assimilation or the denial of difference.

Today, cultural archetypes, such as La Llorona—the witchmother who keens by a river to seduce wanderers and lost children—are diffusing into Anglo, Hispanic, and even Indian variants, according to Rudolfo Anaya, who has written a volume on this recurrent motif.

Southwestern music has undergone a similar fusion: once western music was completely distinct from the accordion-based *norteño* or *conjunto* music, which was also distinct from Native American music. Today on KDTB-FM, a Navajo station in New Mexico, one is just as likely to hear Native American bands playing rock and roll on electric guitars, or Freddy Fender (a Hispanic) singing a country-and-western tune, as to hear Navajo chants. The same songs heard in the backstreet cantinas along the Mexican border are performed by country stars in the rock stadiums of Arizona and New Mexico. Even the instrumentation of southwestern music has changed and blended; the accordion, itself a contribution of the Czech, Polish, and German communities of south Texas, has become the dominant melodic instrument of much of northern Mexico and the border region.

A final illustration of these transitions is the dichotomy between urban and rural Indian communities: Navajos in maroon Ford pickups drive from their traditional hogans to the nearest mall to purchase Tony Lama boots and Levi's; traditional *curanderos* (healers) carry their dried herbs and roots in plastic sandwich bags; and many Navajos live only part of the year on the reservations, spending the majority of their days in the urban centers of Gallup, Albuquerque, and Phoenix. Luci Tapahonso writes of Navajo cowboys on the rodeo circuit; Tony Hillerman creates Navajo detectives; and many of *Writing the Southwest*'s native authors grapple with realities of a mixed-blood heritage and the struggle to live with a foot in both white and tribal worlds.

Communities distinguished by different languages, cultural values, and economic systems coexist, sometimes peacefully and sometimes with uneasiness or outright hostility, but they have always cross-fertilized to produce contemporary southwestern literature.

Myths and Stereotypes of the Southwest

Not only are the cultures and communities in the Southwest in transition or in stages of destruction and/or rebirth; the stereotypical images of western life and the roles assigned to the people who live in this region are also rapidly changing. Yet in America's popular culture, many southwestern stereotypes persist.

A fierce debate has traveled through the literary and historical scholarship on the modern Southwest and its settlement. Whose West was it, anyway? An empty, barren land, which Anglo settlers discovered and "civilized"? Or a region teeming with animal life and settled thousands of years earlier by Native Americans, and whose earliest Hispanic immigrants predated the Anglo arrivals by 250 years? Controversial scholars, such as University of Colorado history professor Patricia Limerick, challenge the status quo: "There's really a kind of an insult to Indian people in the notion of a White person who stands at the Mississippi River and looks into the horizon and says, 'It's open. It's free. It's mine.' "[12] Frederick Turner's famous "frontier thesis" has also been challenged, and some of the romantic legendry surrounding the settlement of the West has been discredited. Similarly, a reaction has set in to the New West historicism of Howard Lamar, Annette Kolodny, and Limerick; the revisionists are being revised.

Yet such debates are central to understanding the Southwest today. Electronic representation of stereotypes in films such as *Tombstone*, *Young Guns*, and *Geronimo*; in old radio series; and in television dramas from "Gunsmoke" and "The Rifleman" to "The Young Riders" and "Dr. Quinn: Medicine Woman" have created a climate where the inhabitants of the Southwest live in the shadow of the nation's expectations.

New Yorker writer Jane Kramer gives an example of this in *The Last Cowboy* (1978): "Henry Blanton [cowboy on the Texas Panhandle] deep in his bedroll, shoring up courage against the river's dead, called on John Wayne, Gary Cooper, and Glenn Ford. . . . On the day he brought his grandfather's chuck wagon home, [Henry and a friend] shared a momentary truce, mourning the West that was supposed to be."[13] Robert Berkhofer writes that to comprehend today's Indian, we must experience "the ideas and imagery used by Whites to understand [them]."[14]

Of course many of the Southwest's stereotypes are not benign, are even racial supremacist—the "lazy" Mexican, the "stolid" Indian, as expressionless as a totem pole. Some are not only racist, they are historical and culture anachronisms —southwestern Indians, for example, never carved totem poles; and yet the visitor's center at Navajo Tribal Park in Monument Valley is decorated not only with the totem poles of the native peoples of the Pacific Northwest, but with the feathered headdresses of the Plains tribes. This sort of massive cultural earthquake is a common theme among Native American writers such as Joy Harjo and Linda Hogan, who discuss their tribes' visions of "Indianness" and the struggle over who, in the future, will possess the power of defining what that is.

In this volume we trace how contemporary southwestern writers grapple with such historical stereotypes and their echoes in the confounding present. The authors reflect on intermarriage and social exchange among different ethnic groups; the growth of the African-American community in the previously tripartite Southwest, and how this and other population shifts are affecting the uneasy balance among the three dominant groups. The Anglo community, dominant in all other regions of the United States, will by the turn of the century become a statistical minority in both New Mexico and Arizona. Many of the writers in this volume feel the enormous changes convulsing the Southwest today are the birthing pangs of what American society as a whole will become in the twenty-first century. This painful and exhilarating process is viewed both with sorrow for a past that is gone forever, and with fierce hope for a future that these authors are attempting to mold today.

> *"A lot of us who grew up in the West, we've given up. To us it may seem that our world is completely changed and it's never going to be as it was when I was a child, never. . . . Things will not be like they were, of course not. They can't possibly, because they never were that way, never in the first place. To me the West is not dead. It doesn't have to be dead. Even though it's not there anymore, it is. The valley where I grew up was full of horses. In my head the horses are still there. . . . I feel like a very old man, but I still hear the horses."*

> —STAN STEINER, *interview with a Montana rancher*[15]

Finding Audiences for Southwestern Literature

American publishing has changed dramatically since the first book of psalms was published in Boston in the seventeenth century. The industry has always been one dominated by a few cities: Boston, New York, and more recently Los Angeles. Thus, the experience of being a writer in the distant Southwest, working on regional themes and seeking distribution on a national or regional level, has always been a problematic one. This isolation from the centers of power has had profound effects on publishing southwestern literature.

First, writers in the relatively unpopulated Southwest generally cannot make a living writing for an audience of their peers and neighbors; as Stan Steiner, author and editor of thirty books, told us:

> *"Since the publishing industry isn't here, and we have no ready access to the market, most people here don't write for New Mexico, they write for the audiences back East.*
>
> *"If the* New York Times *wants to run a page on the wonders of Santa Fe [Steiner was the author of one such article], and you write a piece on what Santa Fe is really like, then the* New York Times *won't print it—they want to believe in the myth of New Mexico. So the writers give in, writing falsely to themselves, falsely to their subject, falsely to their market to please the publishing industry back East."*[16]

When southwestern writers do pierce the thicket of stereotypes fencing the Southwest, they are frequently told their work is not of national interest; they are too "regional" in their concerns; their characters, often non-Anglos, are too exotic or don't fit the proper stereotypes; and their settings, whether urban or rural, are seen as being too distant and removed from the experiences of what the publishing industry considers its general book-buying public.

Because southwestern literature has its roots in oral tradition and not the Eurocentric literary fashions of New York or Boston, the southwestern writer faces the additional burden of finding an audience for a literary tradition often based in chants, songs, or oral folktales.

Despite a recent rise of interest in regionalism in publishing and literature—which has made writing from New England and the South so prominent—literature which takes a nonfantastic view of the Hispanic, Anglo, and Native American populations of the Southwest is still widely dismissed. The Southwest is said to be "poor book country": too many people speak and read Spanish or other tongues; the life experiences of the region are seen as marginal to mainstream popular culture. Even when writers have built a major national reputation for themselves—such as Rudolfo Anaya, whose *Bless Me, Ultima* has sold 360,000 copies despite being published (until recently) by a small press—their work is sometimes handled dismissively by publishers who do not believe that anyone in Maine or Wisconsin will be interested in their stories. A writer working in a conventional genre (Tony Hillerman with his Navajo mysteries) found a national audience only after his first five books appeared.

This situation may be changing today, because of the publicity and mainstream acceptance of writers such as Barbara Kingsolver, Terry McMillan, and Rudolfo Anaya, whom *Newsweek* recently called "Poet of the Barrio" (though Anaya doesn't publish poetry) and because of a *Time* article, "Don't Fence Them In," on contemporary southwestern writers. With the movement of writers such as Denise Chavez from small Chicano-Chicana presses to prestigious national publishing houses like Farrar, Straus, and Giroux, southwestern writers may no longer indulge in the pain (as well as the luxury) of literary exile.

This periodic groundswell of interest in the Southwest— from Santa Fe style architecture to the rash of films set in the region (*Thelma and Louise* and *Raising Arizona*)—poses a challenge to the writers in this volume: how to write their own stories, and not the ones editors, publishers, and critics expect in advance from this region. For those groups traditionally silenced by a dominant Anglo culture, this can be particularly difficult. As Michael Dorris wrote in the *New York Times*, "[American culture has] laid out a single range for Indians to inhabit: savage-savage to noble-savage. Indians [and other minorities] embody the concept of 'the other'—a foreign, exotic, even cartoonish panorama against which 'modern' (that is, white) men can measure and test themselves."[17]

As ever, the descendants of the old settlers of the Southwest must work and live alongside those more recently arrived. From this *mezcla* emerges a culture as rapidly changing as the clouds of a stormy summer afternoon. What is permanent is the land and its shadowy contours.

What you have before you is not a definitive collection so much as a selection of major writers from a region, helping us make sense of what it means to live and write in their territory today. We define this region not in the abstract, but by listening closely to how a few of its authors see and hear it. We are concerned less with determining who is or isn't a southwestern writer than we are with the act of inscribing culture in a time and place.

You can read this book straight through, as a sampler of the contemporary literary riches of a region, or keep it by you as a literary companion as you read. This volume is an attempt to find a broad audience for the diverse voices from across the cultural and racial spectrum of the Southwest. It is dedicated to the unconventional reader, in and outside the region, who will help these writers tear down the literary barbed wire and open up the range of human possibility, exposed under the flaring sun of the American Southwest.

NOTES

1. Lawrence Clark Powell, *Heart of the Southwest* (Los Angeles: Dawson's Book Shop, 1955), p. xi. For an extended discussion of this topic see James Byrkit, *Journal of the Southwest*, vol. 34, no. 3, Autumn 1992, pp. 257–387.

2. William DuBuys, *Enchantment and Exploitation* (Albuquerque: University of New Mexico Press, 1985), passim.

3. Americo Paredes, *A Texas-Mexican Cancionero* (Champaign, Ill.: University of Illinois Press, 1976). See also J. D. Robb, *Hispanic Folk Music of New Mexico and the Southwest* (Norman, Okla.: University of Oklahoma Press, 1980).

4. J. Frank Dobie, *Guide to Life and Literature of the Southwest* (Dallas: SMU Press, 1952), p. 175.

5. Jan Vansina, *Oral Tradition: A Study in Historical Methodology* (Chicago: Aldine, 1965); Ruth Finnegan, "A Note on Oral Tradition and Historical Evidence," as excerpted in Dunaway and Baum, *Oral History: An Interdisciplinary Anthology* (Nashville: American Association for State and Local History, 1984, 1995), pp. 94, 103. These definitions are derived mainly from fieldwork in Africa.

6. Paula Gunn Allen, *Spiderwoman's Granddaughters* (New York: Fawcett, 1989), p. 6.

7. "Writing the Southwest," a thirteen-part radio documentary series on contemporary literature, was produced by David K. Dunaway at the University of New Mexico from 1986–94, with assistance from the state humanities councils of New Mexico, Arizona, and Colorado

and from the National Endowment for the Humanities. Its original broadcast was in October 1995.

8. Arnold Krupat, *The Voice in the Margin: Native American Literature and the Canon* (Berkeley: University of California Press, 1989), p. xx.

9. Some of the aesthetic principles of radio are discussed in David Dunaway, "Radio and the Public Use of History," in Dunaway and Baum, *Oral History*.

10. Interview for "Writing the Southwest" with David K. Dunaway, December 11, 1986.

11. Tey Diana Rebolledo, "Hispanic Women Writers of the Southwest," in *Old Southwest/New Southwest*, Judy Lensink Temple, ed. (Tucson, Ariz.: Tucson Public Library, 1987), p. 60.

12. Patricia Limerick, quoted in the *Albuquerque Journal*, Nov. 11, 1990.

13. Jane Kramer, *The Last Cowboy* (New York: Harper & Row, 1978), p. 2.

14. Robert Berkhofer, *The White Man's Indian* (New York: Knopf, 1979), p. xvi.

15. Stan Steiner, *The Ranchers* (New York: Knopf, 1980), pp. 200–201.

16. Interview for "Writing the Southwest" with David K. Dunaway, December 16, 1986.

17. Michael Dorris, *New York Times*, April 21, 1992.

EDWARD ABBEY

▲ ✧ ▼ ✧ ▼ ✧ ▲

Ed Abbey is perhaps the best-known modern southwestern
writer. Author of over twenty novels and essays, his name
has become synonymous with the deserts of the Southwest
and with radical environmentalism. Called "the Thoreau of the
American West," he is at once representative and atypical of
the writers covered here. Abbey's work veers from passionate
paeans to the earth to strident demands for its protection. The
deserts and mountains of the Southwest, which are at the core
of Abbey's writing, are living elements in the works of nearly
all the authors assembled here.

Abbey, however, was born in the East—his is an Anglo perspective on the land, and most of his fictional characters are
white males. His work does not shy from the uneasy coexis-
tence and forced intimacy in the Southwest of Anglos, Indians,
and Hispanics. The modern westward journey of the easterner,
echoed by Barbara Kingsolver, John Nichols, and Stan Steiner,
and harkening back to Zane Grey and Mary Austin, begins here
with Edward Abbey.

> *Ed Abbey invented the Southwest we live in. . . . His
> words were driven by a moral energy, a biting tongue, and
> thank God, by an abundant sense of humor. Want to keep
> Arizona beautiful and healthy? Let's make half of it a wilder-
> ness. Want to bring the Colorado River back to life? Let's
> blow up Glen Canyon Dam. There are damn near twenty
> books. Read them and see.*
>
> *Here's what I think: when I'm dead and dust, people will*

still be reading Edward Abbey, because the stuff he wrote is still alive.

—CHARLES BOWDEN[1]

Edward Abbey has been called by the *New York Times Book Review* "a living American artifact, part maverick, part pastoral extremist, part semi-hermit, part latter-day Jeremiah Johnson."[2] His works have inspired a generation of environmental writers, people such as John Nichols, Barry Lopez, and Annie Dillard, and have won him scores of enemies and fanatically loyal readers.

In both his life and his work, Edward Abbey was a walking, talking paradox. He was a revolutionist who admitted to being so "tender-hearted"* he hesitated to swat flies. He celebrated life but rejoiced in death. (On the occasion of his funeral, he left written instructions that all mourners were to sing, dance, listen to bagpipe music, and be fed corn on the cob.) Even his death was something of a mystery. Abbey died on March 14, 1989, from a circulatory disorder. He was buried secretly by friends in "one of the four American deserts"; no one would say which. Today reports of Abbey sightings add to the lore of the Southwest.

He was born January 29, 1927, in the Allegheny Mountain town of Home, Pennsylvania, the eldest of five children. His father, for whom he had a deep respect and who greatly influenced Abbey's life and politics, was as paradoxical as his son. Paul Revere Abbey, although not highly educated, was extremely well read, a fan of Eugene Debs's school of socialism, and a consistent quoter of Walt Whitman. In other ways, he was a typical Allegheny mountain man; a woodsman and crack shot who scrambled to support his family through the Great Depression by competing in shooting matches with the Pennsylvania National Guard while selling subscriptions to the *Pennsylvania Farmer.*

In his own words Ed Abbey was a hillbilly, an easterner by birth who spent most of his life waging a violent, passionate

---

* Unless otherwise noted, all direct quotations in this chapter are from the interview with Jack Loeffler on Jan. 1, 1983. In subsequent chapters, unattributed quotations are from interviews with the authors.

love affair with the American West. It all began in the boxcar of a freight train when he was seventeen years old. Abbey had left Home, Pennsylvania, to see the world, receiving from his father a twenty-dollar bill and a warning not to be a sucker. He crossed the continental United States, riding freights and hitchhiking.

His first view of the Southwest, Abbey later wrote, "struck a fundamental chord in my imagination that has sounded ever since." This, despite an incident at the freight's first stop at Flagstaff, Arizona, where he was promptly arrested for vagrancy. After a night in the town drunk tank, he was left at the city limits and warned never to return—a prophetic opening to Abbey's sojourn in the West, and a harbinger of his troubled relationship with authority of any kind.

He returned to Pennsylvania, via New Mexico, and joined the army, spending two years in Italy as a clerk-typist, from 1945 to 1947. Just months after his discharge his anarchistic tendencies began to surface. He became a student at the Pennsylvania State Teachers College, where he first came to the attention of the Federal Bureau of Investigation by posting a notice on a public bulletin board announcing a draft protest— boldly signing it "Edward Abbey." The document was turned over to J. Edgar Hoover, becoming the first of the memos, letters, and reports that would eventually create a dossier two inches thick.

He left Pennsylvania soon afterward and moved to Albuquerque, which he had walked across during his return home from his western journey, to attend the University of New Mexico. There he received a joint B.A. in philosophy and literature and began to write seriously. Abbey edited the student literary publication, *Thunderbird*, which before his editorship had as its motto, "Pleasant Reading for Every Member of the Family." This he soon changed, ending up blackballed for publishing the following quotation, sarcastically attributed to Louisa May Alcott, on the front cover of its March 1951 edition: "Man will never be free until the last king is strangled with the entrails of the last priest."

In his final year as an undergraduate, Abbey began his first novel, *Jonathan Troy*, a coming-of-age story about a young man from a Pennsylvania mining town who dreams of life in a gauzy, mythologized western frontier—a West Abbey sought both to recapture and to replace with his own mixture of myth and legendry.

Upon graduation, Abbey was awarded a Fulbright Fellowship to study the works of Robert Burns at the University of Edinburgh. By this time, however, he had grown disenchanted with the rigid structure of academic research; he spent the year finishing *Jonathan Troy* (published in 1954 to muted critical enthusiasm) and, as he put it, "gadding about Europe." His first wife, Jean, who had accompanied him to Scotland, became so disgusted with his wanderings that she flew back to the United States and mailed him divorce papers.

When his money ran out he returned to Albuquerque, married his second wife, artist Rita Deanin, and worked temporary jobs—as a social worker, factory worker, and seasonal laborer for the Forest Service. Despite his low opinion of university life, he had always excelled there; accepted for graduate study at Yale, he lasted all of two weeks in New Haven before heading back to the Southwest and reenrolling at the University of New Mexico for an M.A. in philosophy, completing a master's thesis entitled "Anarchism and the Morality of Political Violence."

In 1956, the year he finished his graduate degree, he also published his second novel, *The Brave Cowboy* (adapted for the big screen as *Lonely Are the Brave* in 1962). This book chronicles the tragic story of a cowboy who risks his life to free his best friend, who is imprisoned for refusing to register for the draft. This work was followed by *Fire on the Mountain* (1962), about an old rancher who refuses to give up his land to the government for a nuclear testing ground. Both books reflect a recurring theme: the heroic but doomed individual standing up against bureaucracy and government.

The summer of 1956 marked another watershed event in Abbey's life. He took a job as seasonal ranger at Arches National Monument near Moab, Utah. Although he despised the Forest Service in general—accusing it of selling out America's few remaining wilderness areas to ranching and lumber interests—Abbey periodically worked as a ranger and fire spotter. (It was the kind of job, he claimed, that allowed for solitude and the time to write in the most inspiring settings possible.)

During the next few years he wrote three novels, which he later called "absolutely terrible" books; all of them were rejected by publishers. He was frustrated, and on the brink of giving up writing altogether, when a friend suggested he assemble a book of nonfiction from the journals he had kept while working as a forest ranger. This collection, eventually published as *Desert Solitaire* (1968), collapsed three stints with the Forest Service in Utah into a fictional year in the life of a ranger.

The success of this volume finally allowed Abbey to live off his writing, and it remains the book upon which his reputation rests. "Abbey writes with a deep undercurrent of bitterness," wrote the *New York Times Book Review*. "But, as is not infrequently the case, the bitter man may be the one who cares enough to be bitter and he often is the one who says things that need to be said. In *Desert Solitaire* those things are set down in lean, racing prose, in a close-knit style of power and beauty."[3]

Reviews like this established Abbey's freelance career as an essayist for popular magazines. By the early 1970s, he was commissioned to provide the text for several coffee-table nature books, including *Cactus Country*, published by Time-Life Books in 1973. Though writing for mainstream publications, Abbey remained an anarchist and a fierce defender of the wilderness. His years with the Forest Service in Sunset Crater, Organ Pipe Cactus National Monument, Death Valley, the Grand Canyon, and Glacier National Park—some of the most spectacular natural wilderness areas in the United States—had left him horrified by the rate at which they were being destroyed to serve the interests of lumber and mining companies, ranchers, developers, and tourists who insisted on paved roads rather than hiking trails leading directly to every scenic vista. Abbey termed this infernal alliance "industrial tourism." In *Desert Solitaire* he had written, "Wilderness is not a luxury but a necessity of human spirit, as vital to our lives as water and good bread. A civilization which destroys what little remains of the wild, the spare, the original, is cutting itself off from its origins and betraying the principle of civilization itself."[4]

His love for the few remaining wild places reached a spiritual plane, and his writing reflected this quasi-religious reverence in prose poems to the earth, often possessing the mood and cadences of psalms. "Writing," Abbey insisted, "is a form of piety or worship."

Yet there was nothing ethereal in his love for the wilderness. His most famous novel, *The Monkey Wrench Gang* (1975), is a how-to book for would-be anarchists and nature lovers, detailing methods for disabling everything from bulldozers and giant earth-moving machinery to billboards, which Abbey considered "visual pollution."

He openly advocated any action, short of endangering human life, to protect wilderness areas from development. While some term this terrorism, Abbey insisted it was sabotage: "The distinction is quite clear and simple. Sabotage is an act of force or violence against material objects, machinery, in which life is not endangered. Terrorism, on the other hand, is violence against living things. I'd say that a bulldozer tearing up a hillside, ripping out trees for a logging operation or a strip mine is committing terrorism—violence against life. I feel that when all other means fail, we are morally justified—not merely justified, but morally *obligated*—to defend that which we love by whatever means are available."

Unsurprisingly, one of Abbey's favorite quotes was Walt Whitman's famous "Resist much. Obey little." Another was Thoreau's "Now. Or Never." The connection to Thoreau, as well as to Emerson and other nineteenth-century American Romantics, has been acknowledged by Abbey and by his critics.[5] He admired in equal parts Thoreau's nature writing, his civil disobedience, his activism in the antislavery movement, and his protests against the Mexican-American War. In 1982, Abbey published one of his best-known collections of essays on these themes, *Down the River with Henry David Thoreau and Friends*.

To his friends, Abbey often denigrated his impact on the environmental movement, saying he had hidden behind a typewriter while others (like those in the radical environmental organization Earth First!, inspired by *The Monkey Wrench Gang*) stood on the front lines. Despite the brash, outspoken, confrontational persona he created in his writing, in person Abbey is described by his friends as painfully shy, courteous, and willing to go out of his way for a friend or fellow writer.

To his detractors, Abbey was a dangerous fanatic, encouraging an adolescent (if not solipsistic) rejection of law and order in favor of self-indulgent, homemade justice. He placed nature's needs before those of humans; and many believe his anarchist visions would have made a chaos out of the West, as it inevitably filled with immigrants. Abbey was the original NIMBY (Not In My Backyard), a New Age frontiersman who sought to roll up the woods after him, as Gary Snyder once joked. As critics have pointed out, he had his faults: he was mired in political rhetoric and misogyny; his female characters, though lovingly described, never seem to have the best lines. He abused alcohol. He was more effective at championing the rights of nonhuman species than he was at supporting his own family, particularly his first two wives and children.

Ironically, the man with such a passionate love of life was stricken with disease while relatively young, fifty-six. As early as 1983 he knew that he was dying, and in his final years he wrote with renewed vigor, publishing three collections of essays and two novels before his death in 1989.

After news of his death, testimonials arrived from those who knew him. New Mexico writer John Nichols, author of *The Milagro Beanfield War*, wrote that Abbey had "ten times the number of enemies required to be considered an honorable man."[6] Barry Lopez commented on Abbey's "caustic accusations and droll humor, his Western skepticism. . . . Abbey's self-effacing honesty, the ease with which he can admire someone else's work without feeling he diminishes his own— these are qualities wonderful to find in any human."[7]

Abbey's close friend and biographer, Jack Loeffler, speaking of Abbey's last days, said, "He took as many adventures as he could in that final decade. I could hear from him this sense of needing to be a good father and a good husband in light of the fact that he knew he was dying by degrees. . . . He had absolutely no fear of death. He was completely exonerated from that, somehow."[8]

Perhaps Abbey had intimations of his mortality even before the medical establishment confirmed it. Images of death abound in his writing. His 1971 novel, *Black Sun*, traces his hero's search for lost love, culminating at the bottom of the Grand Canyon with vultures circling overhead. Critics have read this as an allegorical journey to the underworld, watched over by the birds most closely associated with the death of the physical body.

In *Desert Solitaire*, Abbey confronts death several times. On a solitary hiking trip near the Havasupai Indian Reservation, he attempted to descend a canyon wall via a series of deep potholes filled with rain water, each spilling down to the next lower hole. Halfway down the canyon wall, however, he discovered the pothole he had just slid into did not empty out to another, lower hole. The previous grip was twenty feet above his head, the floor of the canyon a hundred feet below. The only way out was up the sheer, wet wall of featureless stone. For perhaps the first time in his life, and over a period of several hours, Abbey truly believed he would die there, alone. Although he managed to pull himself up the rock wall to safety, the experience left a profound impact, reflected in the dark images of *Black Sun*, *The Brave Cowboy*, and other works.

Later in *Desert Solitaire*, Abbey gives this advice to the unlucky traveler lost in the desert, with his characteristically odd and startling mixture of mysticism, sarcasm, and black humor:

> When you reach this point [of dehydration] you are doomed. Far better to have stayed home with the TV and a case of beer. If that happy thought arrives too late, crawl into the shade and contemplate the lonely sky. See those big black scrawny wings far above, waiting? Comfort yourself with the reflection that within a few hours, if all goes as planned, your human flesh will be working its way through the gizzard of a buzzard, your essence transfigured into the fierce greedy eyes and unimaginable consciousness of a turkey vulture. Whereupon you, too, will soar on motionless wings high over the ruck and rack of human suffering. For most of us a promotion in grade, for some the realization of an ideal.

▲ ❖ ▼ ❖ ▼ ❖ ▲

The interview in this volume, which Jack Loeffler conducted with Ed Abbey, actually began on a camping trip to the Superstition Mountains of southern Arizona in the final days of 1982.

Abbey and his lifelong friend (and eventual biographer) were blocked from taking a six-week journey by revelations of Abbey's declining health. Then on New Year's Day 1983, the pair broke camp and drove out to Abbey's writing cabin, near the base of the Tucson Mountains, with Loeffler's tape recorder and some notes. Both were dressed in camping garb: Abbey wore a T-shirt with the legend Live Free or Die, the motto of New Hampshire. He had on a pair of blue jeans, canvas-topped GI combat boots, a bandanna around his neck, and a corncob pipe in his mouth. The small cabin included an old manual typewriter, a map of the Sonoran Desert, an old Wobbly poster, some landscape paintings, and a 1911 edition of the Encyclopaedia Britannica.

The study door was open to the Sonoran Desert to the south, and a wind played gently in the background.

Excerpts from this interview were published in a book by Loeffler, Headed Upstream: Interviews with Iconoclasts. *Writes Loeffler: "We were both saddened by the knowledge that the number of campfires we would share in the future was limited by Ed's mortality. This interview was part of a single conversation that lasted over 20 years. The mood was influenced by that strange heightening of awareness that comes with having been battered by the natural elements of a totally successful camping trip. We had already been the best of friends for many years and knew each other as well as two robust heterosexuals can possibly get to know one another."*

The reader is left with an exchange between two anarchist compañeros *which captures Abbey's clipped eastern accent and his boundless enthusiasm for the ecoscape of the American Southwest.*

EDWARD ABBEY:

I get a lot of hate mail—which I'm very proud of. Actually, I've done most of my defending of the West with a typewriter, which is an easy and cowardly way to go about it. I most respect those who are activists, at least in this area of human life. The people who carry on the fight, who do the difficult work of organizing public resistance, who do the lobbying and the litigating, the buttonholing of Congressmen, or in some cases, run for public office, who draw petitions and circulate them, who do the tedious office work and paperwork that have to be done to save what's left of America. I respect those people very much. I respect them much more than people who merely sit behind a desk and write about it.

I think human beings have made a nightmare out of their collective history. Seems to me that the last 5,000 years have been pretty awful—cruelty, slavery, torture, religious fanaticism, ideological fanaticism, the old serfdom of agriculture and the new serfdom of industrialism. I think humankind probably made a big mistake when we gave up the hunting and gathering way of life for agriculture. Somebody said that the plow may have done more damage to human life on the planet than the sword. I'd be inclined to agree.

I look forward to a time when the industrial system collapses and we all go back to chasing wild cattle and buffalo on horseback.

Human beings have as much right to be here as any other animal, but we have abused that right by allowing our numbers to grow so great and our appetites to become so gross that we are plundering the earth and destroying most other forms of life, threatening our own survival by greed and stupidity and this insane mania for quantitative growth, for perpetual expansion, the desire for domination over nature and our fellow human beings.

I've been a Joe Sixpack for much of my life—had to work various jobs, most of them rather tedious, simply to get by, make a living. No, I certainly don't blame working people. They're more victimized by this process than the rest of us. Most of them have their lives and their health threatened more directly and more constantly simply by the work they do, than we lucky ones who escaped that trap.

Just by virtue of being alive, we deserve to be respected as individuals. Furthermore, that respect for the value of each human being should be extended to each living thing on the planet, to our fellow creatures, beginning with our pet dogs and cats and horses. Humans find it easy to love them. We can and must learn to love the wild animals, the mountain lions and the rattlesnakes and the coyotes, the buffalo and the elephants, as we do our pets.

Beginning here in America—we should set the example. We have set the example for pillaging the planet and we should set the example for preserving life, including human life. We [should] simplify our needs and demands, so that we're not preying to excess on other forms of life—plant life and animal life—by developing new attitudes, a natural reverence for all forms of life.

We've got to teach our children sympathy for life and all living things. That begins as an individual, personal responsibility—develop the love for life in ourselves, try to pass it on to our children, try to spread it beyond the family as far as we can by whatever means are available. Teachers, writers, artists, scientists, performers, politicians have the primary obligation. A good politician is one with the ability to lead people toward this attitude. It's hard to think of any such.

Once we discover we have the ability to push things around, or to push other people around, most humans do not have the self-control to refrain from using such power. Science and technology give us absolute power over the rest of life, including human life. And power not only corrupts, it attracts the worst elements of the human herd. Power attracts the worst men, and corrupts the best.

Nothing's sorrier than an old man who has nothing to say, nothing to tell us, no wisdom to offer. A young man should be an adventurer. A middle-aged man should be a producer of useful goods for his fellow humans, a good husband to a wife, and father of children. And an old man should again be an adventurer, not physically as in youth, but an adventurer in ideas. And if you can live a full human life, that should be the life abundant for anyone.

*　*　*

I look forward to the day when somebody with a terminal disease (such as life) is going to strap on a load of TNT around his waist and go down in the bowels of Glen Canyon Dam, and blow that ugly thing to smithereens.

I think one should live honorably and die honorably. One's death should mean something. One should try to have a good death, just as one tries to have a good life. And if it's necessary to die fighting, then that's what we should do. If we're lucky, we can die peacefully. But few of us will ever live in such a world. There will always be something worth fighting for and something worth fighting against.

EXCERPTS

One Life at a Time, Please

. . . [T]here's something wrong at the heart of our most popular American myth—the cowboy and his cow. . . . Western cattlemen are nothing more than welfare parasites. They've been getting a free ride on the public lands for over a century, and I think it's time we phased it out. . . .

Overgrazing is much too weak a term. Most of the public lands in the West, and especially in the Southwest, are what you might call "cowburnt." Almost anywhere and everywhere you go in the American West you find hordes of these ugly, clumsy, stupid, bawling, stinking, fly-covered, shit-smeared, disease-spreading brutes. They are a pest and a plague. They pollute our springs and streams and rivers. . . . They graze off the native bluestem and grama and bunch grasses, leaving behind jungles of prickly pear. They trample down the native forbs and shrubs and cacti. . . .

But I do have some solutions to overgrazing. . . . I'd begin by reducing the number of cattle on public lands. . . . I also suggest that we open a hunting season on range cattle. I realize that beef cattle will not make sporting prey at first. Like all domesticated animals (including most humans), beef cattle are slow, stupid, and awkward. But the breed will improve if hunted regularly. And as the number of cattle is reduced, other and far more useful, beautiful, and interesting animals will return to the rangelands and will increase. . . .

If there's anyone still present whom I've failed to insult, I apologize.

Fire on the Mountain

"Here Lies John Vogelin: Born Forty Years Too Late, Died Forty Years Too Soon."

"Why forty years too soon?"

"I figure in forty years civilization will collapse and everything will be back to normal. I wish I could live to see it." . . .

Well—the summer rolled on, hot and dry and beautiful, so beautiful it broke your heart to see it knowing you couldn't see it forever: that brilliant light vibrating over the desert, the purple mountains drifting on the horizon, the pink tassels of the tamarisk, the wild lonely sky, the black buzzards soaring above the whirlwinds, the thunderheads that piled up almost every afternoon trailing a curtain of rain that seldom reached the earth, the stillness of noonday. . . .

". . . [M]aybe the Government is really in the right here, [the old rancher is asked]. If they need your land for the sake of national security, shouldn't you give it up? Which is more important, your private property or the national safety . . . ?"

"This is my home. I was born here. My father worked and fought all his life for this place. He died here. My mother died here. My wife almost died here. Now I want to die here, when I'm ready to die. I will not live here part-time as some sort of charity ward of the Government while they think up new ways to wedge me off completely. No, by God, I can't do that."

The Journey Home

If you're thinking of a visit [to the Southwest], my natural reaction is like a rattlesnake's—to warn you off. What I want to say goes something like this . . . you should beware of rattlesnakes; we have half a dozen species, all offensive and dangerous, plus centipedes, millipedes, tarantulas, black widows, brown recluses, Gila monsters, the deadly poisonous coral snakes, and giant hairy desert scorpions. Plus an immense variety and near-infinite number of ants, midges, gnats, bloodsucking flies, and blood-guzzling mosquitoes. . . .

It has been said, and truly, that everything in the desert either stings, stabs, stinks, or sticks. You will find the flora here as venomous, hooked, barbed, thorny, prickly, needled, saw-toothed, hairy, stickered, mean, bitter, sharp, wiry, and fierce as the animals.

Desert Solitaire

. . . [T]here is still much to see and marvel at, the world very much alive in the bright light and wind . . . the strangeness and wonder of existence are emphasized here, in the desert, by the comparative sparsity of the flora and fauna: life not crowded upon life as in other places but scattered abroad in spareness and simplicity, with a generous gift of space for each herb and bush and tree, each stem of grass, so that the living organism stands out bold and brave and vivid against the lifeless sand and barren rock. The extreme clarity of the desert light is equaled by the extreme individuation of desert life-forms. Love flowers best in openness and freedom.

Down the River with Henry David Thoreau and Friends

We glide down the golden waters of Labyrinth Canyon. The water here is smooth as oil, and the current slow. The sandstone walls rise fifteen hundred feet above us, radiant with sunlight, manganese and iron oxides, stained with old tapestries of organic residues left on the rock faces by occasional waterfalls. On shore, wheeling away from us, the stands of willow glow in autumn copper; beyond the willow

Edward Abbey / 15

are the green-gold cottonwoods. Two ravens fly along the rim, talking about us. Henry would like it here. . . .

"I never found the companion that was so companionable as solitude," writes Henry. "To be in company, even with the best, is soon wearisome and dissipating."

NOTES

1. Charles Bowden, *Tucson Weekly*, April 5, 1989.
2. Ted Morgan, *New York Times Book Review*, July 31, 1977, p. 10.
3. Edwin Way Teale, *New York Times Book Review*, January 29, 1968, p. 7.
4. *Desert Solitaire: A Season in the Wilderness* (New York: McGraw-Hill, 1968), p. 192.
5. See John Murray's article, "The Hill Beyond the City: Elements of the Jeremiad in Ed Abbey's 'Down the River with Henry David Thoreau and Friends,'" in *Western American Literature*, February, 1988; and James Aton's "Sons and Daughters of Thoreau: The Spiritual Quest in Three Contemporary Nature Writers," Dissertation, Ohio University, August 1981, p. 154.
6. *Tucson Weekly*, April 5, 1989.
7. Ibid.
8. Interview with David K. Dunaway, March 18, 1993.

RUDOLFO ANAYA

▲ ❖ ▼ ❖ ▼ ❖ ▲

Like Edward Abbey, Rudolfo Anaya lives and breathes the landscape of the Southwest. It is a powerful force, full of magic and myth, integral to his writings. Anaya, however, is a Native, a Hispanic fascinated by cultural crossings unique to the Southwest, a combination of old Spain and New Spain, of Mexico with Mesoamerica and the anglicizing forces of the twentieth century.

The result is a southwestern magical realism similar to that of Latin American writers such as Gabriel García Márquez and Isabel Allende, yet indigenous to the American Southwest. He draws on the many southwestern traditions of oral history and storytelling: the tall tales of Anglo cowboys, the *cuentos* of the Mexican-American communities, and the traditional stories of American and Mexican Indians.

> *"I have in my work a very oral approach that tries to seduce the reader into my place in the story as I'm telling it. I've used the technique of the* cuento *[the folktale]. I am an oral storyteller, but now I do it on the printed page. I think if we were very wise, we would use that same tradition in movies and in radio."*
>
> —RUDOLFO ANAYA

Rudolfo Anaya is widely acknowledged as the founder of modern Chicano literature. According to the *New York Times Book Review* he is the most widely read author in Hispanic communities,[1] and sales of his classic *Bless Me, Ultima* (1972) have surpassed 360,000, despite the fact that none of his books has been published originally by a New York publishing house. A *Newsweek* article featuring Anaya notes that his works "have become standard texts in Chicano-literature classes"[2] around the world. He has labored ceaselessly to promote publication of books by Hispanic authors in this country, even endowing a literary prize, the Premio Aztlan, out of his royalties. With the publication of *Alburquerque* (1992), *Newsweek* proclaimed him a front-runner in "what is better called not the new multicultural writing, but the new American writing."

Anaya himself epitomizes the "new American" on many levels, although he could more rightly be called an "old" American. His family lived originally in the ancient La Merced y Atrisco Land Grant, established in the late 1600s by the king of Spain, in what is now Albuquerque's South Valley. (Anaya still owns three shares of the grant, passed on to him by his father.) He traces his ancestry back to two brothers, Eugenio and Andres Anaya, Basque farmers who settled the fertile Rio Grande valley in the seventeenth century, before the founding and growth of the city of Albuquerque.

Although individuals can own shares of a land grant, the original purpose of these traditional holdings was to provide common land for a community, where all members could graze livestock, gather firewood, and draw water. According to Anaya, the original grant holders promised the land "would be held in perpetuity. It would be held forever into the future so that their children and their children's children would always have a home. A place of belonging."[3]

This deep respect for family and community, and a feeling of belonging to the land rather than vice versa, is a hallmark of Anaya's work, as is the difficult task of uniting pluralities— Spanish and English, country and city, Old World and New. The cultural crossroads of the Southwest, where the world of old Spain melded with that of Mesoamerica to become the *mezcla* (mixture) known as Mexico, then grew and spread and mixed again with the cultures of Anglos in the United States and with Native American tribes, forms the mythological basis of Anaya's writing and his family heritage.

His father's family eventually migrated eastward to the vast rolling plains, or llanos, of eastern New Mexico near the West Texas border. They were herders of cattle, the dashing, semi-nomadic *vaqueros* who were the precursors of later-arriving Anglo cowboys.

In the tiny village of Puerto de Luna on the Pecos River, *vaquero* Martin Anaya met and married Rafaelita Mares, the daughter of a farmer. She convinced her roving husband to move their family west to the village of La Pastura, just outside of Santa Rosa on the edge of the llano. Rudolfo Anaya was born there on October 30, 1937, saved by a *curandera*, a traditional midwife-healer, who successfully delivered him despite the umbilical cord wrapped around his neck.

The conflicting backgrounds of his parents, the wild *vaquero* and the steady tiller of the soil, along with the mysterious old wisewoman who delivered him, fired Anaya's imagination. In his autobiography, he wrote, "For me, it began there, with the blood of a farmer's daughter and a vaquero, commingling in the womb, to create a child who will come strangling on his own umbilical cord, pulled into the world by the strong hands of an old woman who understood life." These memories became the genesis of his acclaimed first novel, *Bless Me, Ultima*, a Chicano bildungsroman (coming-of-age story) in which a boy wrestles with the opposing forces of his family (a *vaquero* father and farmer mother); between traditional Catholicism and the even more ancient Indian mysticism of the *curandera-bruja*, Ultima.

But the forces pulling Anaya in different directions would not stop there. While he was still a baby, his parents laid him on a sheepskin in the middle of the floor and placed around him the varying symbols of the divergent lives each hoped he would choose. His father put a saddle in front of him; his mother—denied an education beyond first grade because she was female in a small ranching community—laid down a paper and a pencil. He crawled toward the paper.[4]

While Anaya was a boy, his family moved from the village of La Pastura to the small, nearby farming community of Santa Rosa. Anaya's father, still yearning for the wild freedom of the llano, built their house on the edge of town, atop a hill which sloped on one side toward the river, the church, and the school; the other faced the empty plains of his beloved llano.

His mother scratched out a meager garden in the rocky soil and his father worked at whatever jobs he found: as a cowhand, on a road crew, and as a laborer. The war years were hard; gas and tire rationing isolated rural families, especially on the llano, where pickups full of visitors arrived like prairie schooners, winding through the blossom-laden stalks of yucca and sotol, trailing clouds of dust.

Like most of the local children, Anaya and his brothers and sisters went barefoot in summer, and in winter wore burlap and newspapers wrapped around their shoes in place of galoshes. Despite its rural poverty, Anaya remembers his house as continually sheltering friends, relatives, and travelers. Hospitality was repaid with stories—*cuentos* or folktales. The great oral tradition of Mexican-Americans gave Anaya his first taste of the power of words, legends, and myths: "I would listen to those stories and I would be enthralled, enchanted. Not only the Hispanic Southwest, but the Indian Southwest has centuries of this tradition embedded in it—it's almost as if the oral tradition is alive in the landscape itself."

At the little school in Santa Rosa, Anaya first learned English, spurred by his mother's belief in the redeeming value of education. In 1952, when Anaya was fifteen, the family moved to Albuquerque, following the nationwide migration from rural areas to cities, in search of a better life. They lived in the barrio of Barelas in Albuquerque's South Valley; it was a tough neighborhood, but one in which Anaya, like the hero of *Alburquerque*, felt at home. Anaya was surrounded by family and neighbors who encouraged him to venture out into the bustle of city life during the postwar boom: "Downtown Albuquerque, Central Avenue, was alive with things that I didn't know from my small-town childhood—movies, cars, vitality, energy, workers. We used to come up from Barelas along First Street, which was full of wild cantinas, the bus station, the train station, a lot of activity. Even though Albuquerque in the early 1950s was still a cowtown, for me it was a big city."

The urban Chicano world was the setting of his next novel, second in a trilogy of Chicano New Mexico, *Heart of Aztlan* (1976), which looked unflinchingly at the scourges of barrio life—drugs, crime, racism—and their destructive effect on a rural Hispanic family recently come to the city.

As a teenager, Anaya survived a brush with death that in-spired the final portion of that trilogy, *La Tortuga* (1979). While playing with friends in an irrigation ditch, Anaya dove in head-first, struck the bottom, and shattered two vertebrae in his neck. Paralyzed from the spinal injury, he nearly drowned in the ditch before a friend pulled him out. He spent the rest of the summer in an Albuquerque hospital in a body cast, won-dering if he would walk again.

Despite predictions of his doctors, he did recover: fre-quently hiking, mountain climbing, and hunting in the rugged high country of northern New Mexico.

His time in the hospital brought meditations on sickness, healing, and diseases not only of the body, but of the mind and the emotions. He graduated from Albuquerque High School in 1956, the same year Abbey finished his graduate degree across town, and enrolled in Browning Business School in Albuquer-que. He found it unfulfilling and after three years transferred to the University of New Mexico. Anaya majored in English, graduating in 1963. He soon began teaching high school in Al-buquerque's South Valley, the very area his ancestors had farmed and ranched in the seventeenth century.

In college he dreamed of becoming a poet. In the long af-ternoons after teaching and in the silent hours of dawn, he later found himself drawn to the narrative power of fiction, remembering the haunting stories he'd heard as a child. In 1966, he married Patricia Lawless, the first person who be-lieved he could really become a writer, he remembers affec-tionately. She would become his first-line editor, critic, and supporter.

Anaya became deeply involved in the Chicano Power move-ment (chronicled in Stan Steiner's classic, *La Raza*), in part a reaction to racism in the academy: "We were Mexican stu-dents, unprepared by high school to compete as scholars. We were tolerated rather than accepted. The thought was still prevalent in the world of academia that we were better suited as janitors than scholars. Even in university classes, I was still corrected for allowing my Spanish accent to show."

Being Chicano and taken seriously as a writer was not easy. Anaya returned to the University of New Mexico to work on his M.A. in literature, which he received in 1968. Like Jack London's autobiographical hero in *Martin Eden*, Anaya wrote more manuscripts that he burned than those that ever saw the inside of a publisher's office. With Patricia's constant support, he worked for seven years on *Bless Me, Ultima* (1972). When finished, he mailed it off to all the major publishing houses in New York, each of which promptly rejected it. Despite receiving enough rejections to wallpaper a small room, he persisted, and it was accepted by a small Chicano press in Berkeley, California. It received the Quinto Sol Award as the best Hispanic novel written in 1971. The *American Book Review* noted, "Part of *Bless Me, Ultima*'s attraction is its feeling of authenticity, of trueness: it *sounds* right. . . . The fictional world of Las Pasturas, New Mexico is convincingly alive, changing, complex."[5]

In the late 1960s Anaya began exploring the Indian roots of his mother's Mexican ancestry, particularly the Aztec legacy that enriches the traditional mythology of Mexicans and Mexican-Americans. Along with his wife he frequently visited Mexico and studied the Taos Pueblo in northern New Mexico. In his readings, he discovered that many believe both the modern Pueblo Indians and the Aztecs to be descendants of the vanished Anasazi of the American Southwest. An Aztec myth holds that their ancestors came from a mystical homeland in the north, which they called Aztlan. Aztlan became a powerful symbol in the Chicano civil rights movement, representing the long history which many Chicano activists felt was denied and ignored by an Anglo-dominated U.S. educational system.

In 1974, Anaya was asked to join the English faculty at the University of New Mexico. There he completed the trilogy which included *Bless Me, Ultima*, *Heart of Aztlan*, and *La Tortuga*, which received the Before Columbus Book Award and helped win Anaya a fellowship from the National Chicano Council of Higher Education the same year.

Anaya worked to establish the creative writing program at the University of New Mexico. He published stories and tried his hand at drama. *The Season of La Llorona* was produced in 1979, and *Who Killed Don José?* in 1987. He returned to the traditional *cuentos* of his youth for *Cuentos: Tales from the Hispanic Southwest* (1980), an English rendering of Hispanic folktales. That same year he received both a writing fellowship from the National Endowment for the Arts and the New Mexico

Governor's Award for Excellence and Achievement in Literature; and he was one of twenty-three authors invited by President Carter to read at the White House. Always in demand as a speaker, he has lectured at universities across the United States as well as in Mexico, France, Israel, Brazil, and Canada. In 1982, he published another collection of his short fiction, *The Silence of the Llano*, and was awarded a three-year fellowship from the W. K. Kellogg Foundation.

On this fellowship he wrote his travelogue of China, *A Chicano in China* (1986). He notes in the introduction that he was journeying in search of the mythological and symbolic beginnings of the indigenous peoples of North America whose most ancient ancestors crossed the land bridge of the Bering Strait from Asia during the last ice age. The work spirals back in odd ways to his own beginnings as a writer and the image of the magical golden carp of *Bless Me, Ultima*.

Anaya spent the following decade writing, teaching, editing, and generally promoting the works of other Hispanic authors. He suggests that the creative explosion occurring in the West today is analogous to the southern literary renaissance of the 1930s; he also believes it is more difficult for western writers, particularly Hispanics, to receive serious attention from national publishers. Western and southwestern authors have been geographically more isolated from the eastern publishing centers than southern writers were. They have different stereotypes: "We have the myth of the West to contend with. That myth is rural, of ranches and small towns and the open landscape, with the hero against the gang of outlaws, and we're in love with that myth, we're part of it, and in a way we perpetuate it. Most of the writers in the West now live in urban areas and cities, and yet many of us still refuse to tackle the city as subject for the story."

Anaya has done just that in *Alburquerque* (1992). *Newsweek* called it his best work since *Bless Me, Ultima*: "It's a juicy tale about family, politics and a city where different cultures—Chicano, Anglo, and Native American—jostle for power."[6] It is also a far larger and more sweeping tale than his previous books. The hero, Abran, is of mixed races, with a gringo mother and an unknown Hispanic father, making him "a child of the line that separated white and brown." While searching for his father, the character becomes caught up in a political struggle involving real estate development in downtown Albuquerque and the hotly contested rights to the waters of the Rio Grande.

In 1993, Anaya retired from teaching to devote more time to writing and lecturing. He signed a six-book contract with Warner Books in 1994, including two new murder mysteries, *Zia Summer* (1995) and *Rio Grande Fall* (1996). He continues to explore literary forms—publishing an epic poem, children's stories, and more plays, as well as numerous editorials and essays. Anaya says, "I range toward finding the spiritual underpinnings of our community, our region, and our people. What interests me, in terms of perspective, is to search out, in my mestizo [mixed] world and mestizo background, those particular values of the culture that have to do with spiritual orientation, with value for human relationships, with healing those who are sick, with creating community, and creating a synthesis, not only out of the past, but out of the present."

▲ ❖ ▼ ❖ ▼ ❖ ▲

Rudolfo Anaya, when interviewed in his early sixties, looked more like a coffeehouse intellectual from South America than the son of a ranch hand. His wavy silvery-streaked hair, swept back over bushy, dark eyebrows, accentuated a rounded, flat face, reminiscent of his Basque forebears. His face is divided: laughing eyes with a hard-edged glint of irony counter a prim mouth which suggests inner restraint. When he laughs, one can't quite tell where the eyes leave off and the laugh begins.

Dressed in jeans and a flannel shirt for the interview, he might have been an older volunteer at the campus radio station, KUNM-FM, rather than the University of New Mexico's distinguished professor. His manner was relaxed as he discussed his life and work with a friend and colleague, on the home court of the campus where he had earned his three degrees and taught for twenty years.

In describing his boyhood on the sweeping plains of eastern New Mexico, he developed the intensity of those who travel often in their mind. The studio filled with his low, rich voice telling stories of padding barefoot through the summer thunderstorms and of climbing down into canyons to pick herbs. Later, he drew himself

up; suddenly the listener hears the cadences of the practiced lec-
turer, his pace quickening as he discussed the common barriers
keeping Western and Hispanic writers from a national audience.

In the last few years, Anaya has shifted his literary universe
from rural elegies to the hard-pressed street life of the barrios. As
he reads from his novel Alburquerque, *he trills the extra r, giving*
it the sound of the Spanish duke after whom the city was named.
His voice tightens as he reads his saga of greed for land and water
rights, and one remembers that he is, in his literary way, defend-
ing the land of his great-great-grandparents.

RUDOLFO ANAYA:

The llano is not exactly flat. It's not the plains country of
the Panhandle or of Kansas. It's more rolling hills, arroyos,
juniper and piñon trees. It has that spectacular beauty that
any stage has. I view the llano as a stage that is empty. It
seemed to me as a child I would look out across the llano and
I would see nothing, and then people would enter. Somebody
would come driving down the dirt road in a pickup truck to
visit my father, and my father would come from the house, and
soon there was a dramatic happening on that vast and empty
land.

The same thing happened when you went to the dance
halls. You would drive out in the llano all night to go to a
dance, and you would swear there was nobody there. But the
people would arrive and the dance hall would fill up, and there
would be wild polkas and waltzes, drinking and music, so for
a moment that stage draws to its center the dramatic impact
of people and the relationships they bring.

The sound of the llano is silence. It's a silence created by
a buzz, and the buzz to me is the sound of the earth. If you
stand very still, as I did when I was a child, I could actually
feel the earth turning. Then I had to think, What is this sound,
and what is it telling me? And then of course, if you listen very
closely, the sound becomes the sound of grasshoppers, of ci-
cadas, the wind rustling across the grass, the tinkling of a bell
on a goat, lizards darting here and there, and suddenly you

realize that that silence, that sound, is the sound of life itself.

I remember men talking with my father about how they used to be, how they used to work on the range, how they trained horses, who had such-and-such a horse, and what happened one night when they were on their way to a dance and they met a *bruja*, a witch, in the form of a fireball. They were personal experiences, a lot of them. They weren't just out of that body of folklore that we see in books. It's the personal experience that creates the living oral tradition.

My family was always puzzled by the fact that I began to write when I was an undergraduate at the University of New Mexico. They were interested, but they didn't quite know what to make of a budding writer in a family that had never produced writers, and didn't have too many books around the house. But they were very supportive of me continuing that strange thing I did in my little studio room, typing away at these stories.

In my academic training, the Romantics seem to be the ones that influence me the most. Later on, reading Native American writers helped me get in closer touch with the spirit of the place. But when all is said and done, how one responds and how one is affected by what we call the natural world is a very personal odyssey.

A long time ago I did an essay called "The Locoweed Perspective," and I say the writers of the Southwest, we are like horses that have gone out on the llano and eaten locoweed, and that madness is what is unique to us. It's obvious to me from my Hispanic background that that madness ties me into the magical realism of Latin America, and I understand that perfectly. But I see that also in the Anglo writers [of the Southwest] and in the Native American writers.

Southwestern writers possess a particular landscape that is not only geographic, but internal. Geographically, it extends from West Texas to the fault line in California, from southern Colorado across into northern New Mexico. The mix of cultures that has occurred in this region has been very unique. Also, the religious and spiritual processes of the Native Americans make this region very unique, and people who respond are part of the process. For me that is what we call the southwestern writer.

I think the kind of Catholicism that we had in New Mexico when I was growing up was a very medieval type; it had many exact rules. I grew up in the world of the church and what we call *los santos*, the saints. Is there a polarity or duality at work here? I'm just returned from Spain where I had the pleasure of sitting one afternoon and having a beer with a very important man of Mesoamerican thought and culture, Miguel León Portilla. I asked him, "Are *los santos* the kachinas?" And he did not hesitate, he looked at me and beamed and said, "Yes."

The person that I admire the most of the southwestern writers is Frank Waters. I think he is the one that created that sense of synthesis. He could talk about the Native American, he could talk about the Chicano, he could talk about the Anglo-American, their different ways of life, how they looked at the common land they have to share, and he got very deep into the collective memory of each group.

It seems to me that the Southwest and Mexico have been really important regions where many people have come to contribute their literature and their philosophies. I think we have to expand our knowledge, to acknowledge and learn more of the contributions of each group so that eventually we come up with a definition of the new mestizo, which for me is the New World man. This is the person that can synthesize divergent worldviews.

Right now we [Chicanos] live in a period of transition, almost a period of crisis, because so many of us are in the city, and I'm not sure that we have yet found the way to bring all of those ceremonies and all of that culture with us into the city. We're being drowned by popular culture. You know, you have a low-rider, with hydraulic lifts in the car popping and bouncing and jazzing up and down Central Avenue [in Albuquerque] with La Virgen de Guadalupe as a decal—one of the most powerful symbols the unites that Spanish world with the Mesoamerican world—and it's on a beautiful, customized low-rider going up and down [Route 66]. I think if we can keep enough of that knowledge of the symbols and of the history intact, then we're alright, we'll survive. But the day that, say, Ollie North becomes the decal on the low-rider, we've lost it.

* * *

I am an eclectic reader, and like Whitman, I take the world within me and chew it up and grind it and use it. I don't have any particular writer or school of writing that I've followed. In fact, we have created our own school, as Chicano writers writing about a Hispanic community in English, with everything that means and everything it has to do with language and myth.

I don't have to return to Europe or Spain for roots or for cultural identity. I have it right here in the New World. Once I defined that for myself and knew it within myself, it gave me a great deal of satisfaction. I am very much a New Mexican.

EXCERPTS

Bless Me, Ultima

Ultima came to stay with us the summer I was almost seven. When she came the beauty of the llano unfolded before my eyes, and the gurgling waters of the river sang to the hum of the turning earth. The magical time of childhood stood still, and the pulse of the living earth pressed its mystery into my living blood. She took my hand, and the silent, magic powers she possessed made beauty from the raw, sun-baked llano, the green river valley, and the blue bowl which was the white sun's home. . . .

There is a time in the last few days of summer when the ripeness of autumn fills the air, and time is quiet and mellow. I lived that time fully, strangely aware of a new world opening up and taking shape for me. In the mornings, before it was too hot, Ultima and I walked in the hills of the llano, gathering the wild herbs and roots for her medicines. We roamed the entire countryside and up and down the river. . . .

For Ultima, even the plants had a spirit, and before I dug she made me speak to the plant and tell it why we pulled it from its home in the earth. "You that grow well here in the arroyo by the dampness of the river, we lift you to make good medicine," Ultima intoned softly and I found myself repeating after her. . . .

Ultima's soft hands would carefully lift the plant and examine it. She would take a pinch and taste its quality. . . . She told me that the dry contents of her bag contained a pinch of every plant she had ever gathered since she began her training as a curandera many years ago.

Alburquerque

Abran and Joe drove south on Atrisco toward Central, then across the old Tingley Beach road. Tingley Beach was a large pond which ran parallel to the deep acequia on the east side of the Rio Grande. . . .

"If they build the big aquatic park the city is planning, la raza gets pushed out," Joe said. "My grandfather used to tell me the city was going to grow. 'Just don't let them get the pueblo land,' he said. If you give up the land, you die. The developers have built clear up to the Sandia Mountains. Now they're buying up the downtown barrios."

"What's left?" Abran asked.

"The river land. 'Water is blood,' my grandpa said, and now they need the blood to keep building."

"The conservancy won't let them," Abran said.

"Don't believe it, bro. See in the paper where Dominic is running for mayor? He cooked up a big water scheme. Gonna take the river right downtown. When men with money want to do something like that, the laws bend for them."

Who Killed Don José?

MARIA: You seem to have something on your mind.
DON JOSE: Didn't I tell you? Ramón's delivering my computer tonight.
TONY: A computer?
MARIA: He's going to put the whole ranch on a computer program—even the sheep.
TONY: I don't believe it.
MARIA: When most people are planning to retire, he's starting a new project. I tell him to sell the ranch and move

to Santa Fe, or Albuquerque, but no, the ranch is too important.

DON JOSE: Retire? Leave the rancho? My friends? My workers? No, impossible!

MARIA: You can't be responsible for them all your life.

DON JOSE: ¿Por qué no? Our family has been on this land for many generations. Your grandfather taught me to love the land and take care of the workers. He was a real patrón.

MARIA: But times have changed.

DON JOSE: So we change with them. Use computers.

TONY: Let me get this straight. The computer's going to take care of your sheep?

DON JOSE: Every single borreguito. I'm moving into the future.

TONY: Just be careful you don't move too fast, Don José.

A Chicano in China

Something about the vast courtyards between the buildings [in the Forbidden City] reminds me of Teotihuacán in Mexico. The walls, the smell, the sprigs of grass and weeds on the grounds. The dragon is everywhere, the flaming Quetzalcoatl of Mexico. I am on the right track. The face of the fierce dragon looks out at me from walls, from gargoyles, from decorative pieces, almost exactly as the serpent head in the pyramids of Mexico. This is my first clue. This is the door I seek. In the faces of the people it is written: the migrations of the people from Asia across the Bering Strait, down into the Americas, thousands of years ago. Those Asiatic people came bringing their dragon dreams. In the face of our guide, Mrs. Wang, I see a woman from Laguna Pueblo. I take a picture of a bronze turtle, a heron; both mean long life. The dragon means supreme power, the wisdom of emperors. Quetzalcoatl means supreme power. He was the god who brought wisdom and learning to the Toltecs of ancient Mexico. Quetzalcoatl, the savior prophet and god of the Americas. In what dream in Asia, millions of years ago, did he have his beginning?

N O T E S

1. Earl Shorris, "In Search of the Latino Writer," *New York Times Book Review*, July 15, 1990, p. 1.

2. Susan Miller, "Poet of the Barrio: Struggling for Power in the Southwest," *Newsweek*, September 21, 1992, p. 82.

3. Rudolfo Anaya, "Atrisco Heirs Ask for Continued Connection with Petroglyphs," *Albuquerque Journal*, July 28, 1990, Essay/Op Ed.

4. *Contemporary Authors Autobiography Series*, vol. 4 (Detroit, Mich.: Gale Research, 1986), pp. 15–28.

5. Ron Arias, *American Book Review*, vol. 1, no. 6, March–April 1979, p. 8.

6. Susan Miller, "Poet of the Barrio."

DENISE CHAVEZ

▲ ❖ ▼ ❖ ▼ ❖ ▲

Denise Chavez offers us the voice of a new generation of Hispanic women: educated, articulate, bursting with energy and drive. A native of the Mexican borderlands, she brings to her writing a keen eye for social pretenses and the frailties of the human heart.

Like Rudolfo Anaya, she is New Mexican; but where his New Mexico is the open range of the West Texas border and the bustle of Albuquerque, Chavez is rooted in the low desert of the southern border. The beauty and heat of this landscape informs her work and her characters. She too draws on the traditions of storytelling and folk dramas in the Hispanic Southwest; like Rudolfo Anaya, she revels in a distinctly American magical realism.

> *"Anybody that has eaten chile in New Mexico knows why we love our chile and why we love our land so much, because our writing is spicy and pungent, it's of the earth and of the people; and when you eat the earth and eat the sweat of the people that have worked there, it's like my little grandmother says, 'como chile colorado,' like red chile. It goes through your whole system and becomes part of you."*
>
> —DENISE CHAVEZ

Playwright and novelist Denise Chavez hums and sparks with the energy of her characters. Her work is a vibrant tapestry of voices captured in sharp focus—monologues, dialogues, solo arias, and thundering choruses. Like Maxim Gorky, Chavez favors the oppressed and the disaffected: bag ladies, janitors, waitresses, handymen, maids, and ex-cons. With clarity and gentleness, she gives voices to the people we don't see on television.

Denise Chavez was born August 15, 1948, in the dusty bordertown of Las Cruces, New Mexico. She grew up surrounded by an extended family from New Mexico and Texas, neighbors, godparents (called *comadres* or *compadres* in Spanish), and *criadas*, or maids, whom her mother took in from Mexico to help raise her children.

Her parents divorced when Chavez was ten, and she recalls family trips to visit her mother's relatives in a tiny rural town in West Texas. During the long, hot Texas nights, family and friends would drag cots into their backyards to sleep and spend the evening hours eating watermelons and telling elaborate stories. The sound of those voices in the dark—teasing, laughing, and slipping effortlessly from Spanish to English— merged for Chavez with Las Cruces, a place of dust and diesel, heat and wind; but also of profuse purple and blue wildflowers she and her sisters and cousins gathered on the edge of the desert. It was a potent combination, the origin of the spells which later surfaced in her poems, plays, and fiction.

"My internal landscape is the desert," she explains. "I know it very well, I know the heat, I know the lack of rain, and the joy that one experiences when you do have rain." The lion- colored Organ Mountains sharply etching the horizon near Las Cruces, the relentless New Mexico sun, the irrigation ditches that are the lifeblood and playground of a desert city—all of these hover over her stories, sometimes exerting as much sway over the people in her works as any human character.

Chavez's mother, whose family was originally from Chihuahua, Mexico, was a teacher who encouraged her children to excel in school and to read the score of newspapers to which she subscribed. She saved her money to send her daughters to a Catholic school, Madonna High School.

Although Chavez kept a diary from a very young age, it was at Madonna High School that she first discovered theater, which would become her entrance to the world of literature. The nuns encouraged the fifty or so girls to explore their imaginations; and soon Chavez was not only acting in school productions, but writing plays herself.

She fell in love with her drama teacher, a good way to enter any creative endeavor, she laughs; "I played all the female leads, and my friend Ellen Dowling played all the male leads. She was Macbeth, I was Lady Macbeth, she was Creon, I was Antigone, she was Sergeant Duffy in *Sorry, Wrong Number* and I was the little old lady who got murdered. I remember when we were acting in *Macbeth*, it took every ounce of energy for me to not laugh when I'd put my hand on her shoulder and say, 'Bring forth men children only!' "

Chavez was one of a graduating class of twelve from Madonna High School; the girls called themselves "the Apostlettes." New Mexico State University, in Las Cruces, impressed with Chavez's acting, offered her a drama scholarship. She studied there with Mark Medoff and graduated with a B.A. in drama in 1971, then attended Trinity University in San Antonio, Texas, where she received an M.F.A. in 1974.

She continued to spend time in Mexico as a college student, crossing the border to enjoy the nightlife: "We used to love to dance, *corridos* and *rancheras*. We used to go to Juarez and dance and carry on in places like the Noa Noa Lounge or the Caverns—late-night, dingy bars. . . ."

As much as she loved acting, Chavez found herself drawn more to writing scripts; in this, she was bolstered by numerous early successes. Her first play, *Novitiates*, won New Mexico State University's Best Play Award; it was produced while she was still in graduate school, in the Experimental One-Act Play Festival in Dallas in 1973.

Her dramas are peopled with the characters of her childhood, both fictional and real: migrant farmworkers, Catholic saints, teenage toughs. Many have the feel of traditional Hispanic folk dramas, which still flourish in Mexico and rural areas in New Mexico. Chavez acknowledges that she was heavily influenced by those plays, called *los pastores*, and by the traditional Christmas plays, *las posadas*, and the drama of Catholic ritual and the lives of the saints.

Yet Chavez's dramatic studies have allowed her to broaden these Mexican literary forms by adding to them her love for the works of Anton Chekhov and the Italian commedia dell'arte tradition, creating a unique hybrid, folk-street drama. In its scope, her character-based drama may be compared with that of writers who have peopled imaginary communities, such as Faulkner's Yoknapatawpha County or Balzac's *Comédie Humaine*.

Her works can be dark, however, and many of her characters are what she calls "survivors," those who live on the desperate edge of poverty, in prison, on the streets, or fleeing from *la migra* (immigration officials). In this, her plays harken back to precursors such as Chicana playwright Josefina Niggli, who wrote in the 1930s about the Mexican Revolution and the lives of illegal aliens, and who was known for the strength and dignity of her female characters. Chavez strives to avoid a strident, didactic approach and paints her characters, even the less savory ones, with a sympathetic eye—and always a large dose of humor.

In 1975 she began teaching. After receiving her M.F.A., she worked as an instructor for two years at Northern New Mexico Community College, alternating this with teaching at the American School of Paris. Her cosmopolitan experience later resurfaced in a bittersweet story titled "Evening in Paris."

She has always been a prolific dramatist. *The Flying Tortilla Man* was produced in 1975, *The Mask of November* in 1977, and in 1979 a one-act play entitled *Nacimiento* appeared at Albuquerque's Kimo Theatre. She received grants from the New Mexico Arts Division in 1979, 1980, and 1981, and grants from the National Endowment for the Arts in 1981 and 1982. Her poetry has appeared in the anthology *Life Is a Two Way Street* (1980) and *An Anthology of Southwestern Literature* (1977), both of which she edited, as well as in various other publications, including *An Anthology: The Indian Rio Grande* (1977), with essays in *The Americas Review, Journal of Ethnic Studies*, and *Revista Chicano-Riqueña*.

She moved to Albuquerque in 1982 and studied writing with Native American novelist Leslie Marmon Silko and Rudolfo Anaya. Chavez was awarded a creative writing fellowship from the University of New Mexico, where Anaya was a professor of creative writing, in 1982, receiving a second M.A. in 1984. Although she did not abandon drama, she became fascinated with fiction as a new way to channel the chorus of swirling voices in her mind.

One of her most acclaimed dramas, *Plaza*, which presents the lives of working-class people over the course of a single day in a small Hispanic village *zócalo* (square), received international recognition in 1984 when it was performed at the Joseph Papp Festival Latino in New York and several months later at the renowned Scotland Arts Festival in Edinburgh.

Chavez brings to her fiction the highly developed sense of scene, crisp dialogue, and eye for body language, gesture, and characterization she had perfected during her years of study in theater; but through fiction, she was also able to give her characters internal voices and visions. Her work has always been tied to the people and landscape of the Southwest borderlands, flavored with the pachuco English-Spanish code switching common to the Chicanos of New Mexico, Texas, and *el otro lado*, the "other side"—Mexico. Her work thus springs from the oral tradition of the Southwest, and she uses her experience as an actor to provide what rhetoricians might call an oral interpretation of her own work; she has taught this method of playwrighting to thousands of students across the Southwest and in Germany.

One of Chavez's ambitions has always been to bring literature back into the lives of the people, young and old, from all walks of life, who form the backbone of her writing. She has read her work in prison yards and in the lobby of a bank in Houston, Texas; for the Gay and Lesbian Catholic Hispanics; for grade-school children; and for the handicapped. She taught at the Radium Springs Center for Women (a medium-security prison), was an artist-in-residence at the Arts with Elders Program in New Mexico, and spends what she claims is "an inordinate amount of time" reading tabloids from supermarket checkout counters.

"A lot of my writing is done in Laundromats," Chavez says with a smile; "you never know when thoughts are going to be cleared or clarified. . . . You know, I go to Albertson's [supermarket] and I hear things. Or I'm walking down the street and this guy says in Spanish, 'Lala makes me laugh.' I thought, 'Oh, Lala! La Lala,' how we say here in New Mexico: La Mary, La

Becky, La Suzie. I thought, 'La Lala is the name!' I love this character. She turned into a beautician that applies false fingernails at a place called Arturo's Unisex, and she's got Jim, this Anglo boyfriend that is testing out the waters with this wild Chicana, you know?"

In 1984, Chavez married a photographer and sculptor named Daniel Zolinsky, and in 1986 she published her first book of fiction, *The Last of the Menu Girls*. It is a short-story novel structured much like Louise Erdrich's best-selling *Love Medicine*, a series of related short stories which, taken as a whole, forms more than the sum of its parts. The book won the Steele Jones Fiction Award and the Puerto Del Sol Fiction Award. The stories, told through multiple narratives and points of view, center around the coming of age of a young, small-town Chicana who defines herself between both her own Hispanic culture and in the dominant Anglo world as she comes to terms with her sexuality and womanhood.

The magical realism of Gabriel García Márquez and García Lorca is very much present in *The Last of the Menu Girls*, joining the lyric poetics of Rudolfo Anaya and Tomás Rivera. Chavez, however, is particularly interested in the changing situation of women in the patriarchal Hispanic world. Mythotypic women from La Llorona to Diana the Huntress inhabit her fiction as well as her plays.

In *Last of the Menu Girls*, her protagonist, Rocio, sees herself as the Aztec Cloud Princess, her friend Diana as a tragic version of the ancient hunter-goddess, and along with another childhood friend, believes she can someday find out the truth behind the legend of La Llorona, the traditional Hispanic tale of the ghost mother who has murdered her children and is doomed to wander in search of them for all eternity. In one passage, Rocio muses:

> Behind the mirror, eyes half closed, I saw myself, the cloud princess . . . I turned the mirror to the light. The loveliness of women sprang from depthless recesses; I thought, it was a chord, a reverberation, the echo of a sound, a feeling, a twinge, and then an ache. . . . Always there is the echo of the young girl in the oldest of women, in small wrists encased in bulky flesh, in the brightest of

eyes surrounded by wrinkles. There is beauty in hands tumultuous with veins, in my grandmother's flesh that I touched as a child. . . . On my dream canvas my grandmother pats her hands and says, "Someday, someday Rocio you'll get this way."[1]

One drama she is particularly proud of is *Hecho en Mexico* (*Made in Mexico*), which concerns the lives of four maids from Mexico who work in the United States. Here she examines not only womanhood, but the joys and hardships of being dark-skinned in a world dominated by whites, and women in a world dominated by men. In *This Is about Vision: Interviews with Southwestern Writers*, she says of Hispanic culture in the United States, "This has been an oppressed culture and so the oppressed have to oppress as well, and it has usually fallen on women, or those who have darker skin, or the people who are laborers and so on."[2]

In 1988, Chavez became an associate professor of drama at the University of Houston while continuing to travel the country performing readings and holding workshops, eventually returning to her hometown of Las Cruces. She was a founding member of the National Institute of Chicana Writers and a member of the Santa Fe Writers' Co-op. She was also working on her largest project to date—a novel of epic proportions chronicling multiple generations in the lives of two Chicano families in a small New Mexico town.

Face of an Angel, published in 1994 by Farrar, Straus, and Giroux, includes a cast of characters listed in the front of the book numbering nearly one hundred, with subtitles like "Aunts and Uncles," "Lovers," and "El Farol Restaurant Staff." As in *The Last of the Menu Girls*, the main protagonist is a Chicana, this time middle-aged and divorced. And as in *The Last of the Menu Girls*, each short chapter is a vignette, shifting from voice to voice, presenting multiple points of view.

For other Hispanic authors, the significance of a novel centering around an unabashedly Hispanic worldview and full of Spanish-laced English, is enhanced by its acceptance at a prestigious publishing house. Chavez's vision is grounded in the particular, yet offered as universal. This has always been the challenge for Hispanic authors: to find acceptance as writers of more than "local" or "ethnic" literature. "I see myself as a spirit first of all. And then as a woman who happens to be Hispanic and rooted here in the Southwest," Chavez admits. "My voice comes from here and this land gives me strength. But what I am always striving for as a writer is a sense of the universal. I hope that people who read my stories in other parts of the world would be able to sense that this grandmother who's taking her granddaughter aside could be *any* grandmother, *anywhere*."

▲ ❖ ▼ ❖ ▼ ❖ ▲

Chavez is a short, smartly dressed woman with dark hair and intense, flashing eyes; her crackling energy fills a room. Interviewing Denise Chavez is like holding on to a chameleon's tail as it changes colors. She possesses an uncanny ability to shift into a role midway through a conversation, even in midsentence. One moment you're talking with a professor of drama with an international schedule of readings; and the next you're across the table from a fourteen-year-old girl obsessed with tattoos and bai-les (dances). Even her face changes as she swerves into character: her mouth is pursed, her eyebrows wag, and a high whining voice emerges. Less talented adults might be accused of a multiple-personality disorder.

Part of our interview took place in the studios of KRWG-FM, in Las Cruces—in the very building where she earned her B.A. in drama, she says, as we thread our way through its corridors. The rest occurred in her writing room in her home, stuffed with comfortable pillows and books in piles of cheerful disorder. Here one feels the limits of radio in conveying the soundscape where she works and lives. To do so, one would have to include not just her words, but the sound of the sunburned weeds rattling outside her open window; the drill of her sculptor husband, whining away in the distance like a dentist's drill. The ear distinguishes effortlessly among many levels of sound; but on radio these sounds tumble together into cacophony.

Sitting across the table from Chavez and hearing her switch among her gaggle of voices, one is reminded of the personal magic which often characterizes meetings with stage personalities. Chavez is a walking community center, illustrating Whit-

man's line from Song of Myself: *"Do I contradict myself? / Very well then I contradict myself. / (I am large, I contain multitudes.)"*

DENISE CHAVEZ:

There's so much music inside my head; it's jangled and it's magical and mysterious and it comes in and out and it's a very beautiful music. It's the music of many voices, the voices of my ancestors, my mother's voice, the voices of all the women that have come before me that have had no voice.

I often say that my grandmother's voice I can't remember, it's so soft; my mother's voice was tortured, I think, a cry in some sort of way. She suffered deeply. We are in a tremendous time of this outpouring of women's voices—what I hear now are these strong, vital, energetic voices that are like songs. These are women that can communicate and that have a presence, their lives are dramatic, and they have the wherewithal and the ability to communicate.

In many ways, I am the channeler for many voices that I hear, and I feel a commitment and a responsibility. I did not ask to be a writer; it was a gift from God.

[I begin a project] with great fear, trepidation, horror, and prayers! I pray over myself, I pray over my typewriter . . . it takes me a long time to get to the actual words, because I'm thinking through. I will work on it in my mind for months, mull it over, and then I will get to the point where I will maybe [write]. I work in a very organic way. I start from characterization, so I will start with a character, what I call a character sheet, where I describe the character. If I'm working on a particular scene, I will write down the five senses a lot—a master plan of senses and characterization.

I might start off with a genealogy chart. *Face of an Angel* has got an incredible cast of characters, it reminds me of this play that I worked on, *Sí, Hay Posada*, that had about twenty-four characters. I kept sending them out to the bathroom, and I didn't know if I had left somebody sitting on the toilet, or when somebody was coming in.

Sometimes I begin just by drawing a line, a particular place. I begin by drawing what I felt was the character line; some person was convoluted, a wavy, squiggly line. And I begin to try to think of them in abstract ways: color, texture, line movement. Because this is my training as a dramatist.

Sometimes it's a cut-and-paste method, sometimes I put these things all over the wall. I work in a manner that I call "an assemblage of parts," I assemble these pieces, and I start accruing material, and it comes together in this shape, and then I have this mass like a dough, and I kind of knead it and take out what I don't need. I'll finish typing this section, then I'll stop and I'll write awhile. Then I'll refine that, then I'll move ahead and type. So it's like that childhood game: I'll take one giant step and one little baby step and one little scissor step and then I'll eventually find myself someplace.

Landscape in my writing, oh, it's a living presence! I wrote, once, "Stone breasts of horizon moving." I think of that line of a poem of García Lorca's, "Verte desnuda": "to see you naked, is to remember the Earth./ Clean, clear of horses." To see the earth like that, I think that's what we get in New Mexico: it's that panorama, that space of land and to know that in the mountains, you can almost see the outline of breasts, or people, or faces.

Tony Hillerman is a wonderful friend, a very dear friend and a wonderful teacher, and I have learned much from his craft. He's a wonderful master technician, his writing is so clean and smooth and I love his Jim Chee character. He really works hard at his craft and he has always instilled in his students that love of language, the sense of culture and traditions that we have here in New Mexico and the Southwest.

Simon Ortiz—I have loved his writing, his poetry. He has a tremendous gift for capturing so much: sights, sounds, wind, the arid quality of this place, and there's a living presence in much of his work.

Luci Tapahonso is a friend as well. She's such a beautiful person; you must always deal with the spirit of a person. She has such a presence in her readings, such energy and vigor, and such a delicate flame of love that she sends forth. I think that that's what's so beautiful about so many of these people; they are unselfish people, they give of themselves.

Like Rudolfo Anaya, a very dear friend, who I have also had the honor of studying with. He has done more for students of writing and for the state of New Mexico—people will never know how much he has contributed to literature.

And John Nichols, he is a person that is deeply committed politically as well to land rights and water rights and I think that as artists we need to commit ourselves to things like that. I myself am very involved in immigration changes.

Of course, living here in Las Cruces, where my mother was a teacher for forty-two years, I grew up with women who helped us out. They were part of our family, and I'm indebted to these women, these *criadas* (maids), they were never servants, they were part of our family. So I am very deeply committed to changing these immigration laws and to getting away from these boundaries, these invisible membranes that really are so absurd because without the people from Mexico and from other countries, where would we be in this farming community? So I applaud those writers that very lovingly, as John Nichols does, with a great tenderness but also a biting wit and black humor, are able to address issues of environment and a relationship to the earth, to make commitments through their characters, but to do that with a sense of love, not to beat people over the head, but to do it, as Aristophanes did, with a deft hand and much humor.

EXCERPTS

Face of an Angel

My grandmother, Mama Lupita, wants me to become a nun. She often takes me aside and talks to me.

"Priests in the family are a dime a dozen, Soveida. Everybody knows they're *jotos* and *maricones* or lusty goats in search of skirts. What this family needs is a nun. Women's prayers, everyone knows, are more powerful. Any man can give up sex for four years, especially if they get him before he knows what to do with that thing between his skirts. Cassocks, that's what they call them. After that you know what happens. When a woman gives up sex, it's final. Try and sneak sex on a woman, see what happens. Nine months later there's everlasting hell to pay. . . . Every woman wishes she could become a nun. You don't know what I mean yet, *m'ija*, may the Blessed Mother—she was a woman too, don't forget that, so she knows what I'm talking about—may she spare you a drunken man late at night smelling of *chicharrones* and tequila, worse yet, of *frijoles* and beer. *¡Dios mío el gas!* . . . I want to spare you this, *m'ija*, look at me, listen to me. You like to read. Nuns read all the time and no one bothers them. They can be quiet. They don't have no one belching and scratching and making *pedos*, you know, farts, on the way to the you-know-what, *el escusado*. . . . Men cannot be trained. They're wild bulls or *changos:* monkeys, I don't know which. And that's not all. They shed. I could never keep a clean bathtub. . . . Maybe someday women will become priests, ay I won't live to see it, may you live to see it, and if you don't, well then, may another woman live to see it. Me, I never wanted to become a nun. A priest, that's what I wanted to be! May the Blessed Mother support me in this, she knows I would have been a good priest. Ay, we do what we can. So think about it, I mean, becoming AT LEAST a nun."

"Who's El Jester?"

"Me, sonsa! Shit, I'm full of blood. You got some orange juice? I got a thirst you won't believe. Had to go to the farm, way the hell over to Four Points and then back, pick up two dedos, fingers—all I could find was the two—the thrasher probably got the other one, and race back to the car. Y me pegó un asco babes, like you can't imagine, no te imaginas, I got these two bloody dedos on the passenger seat of my TransAm, on my simulated sheepskin, wrapped up in my chamois I had in the back seat. . . . I was like repulsed, mana, to the max! I can tell you babes, it was the longest twenty-five minutes of my whole damn life. When I got to the hospital, there was three, count 'em, three doctors waiting for me by the Emergency entrance with an ice chest. I'd radioed them on my CB. When I saw the ice chest, all I could think of was cold beer, but no way. The chamois was ruined."

"Did you want a Pepsi or a Coke, Joker?"

"Joker, Jester, what the hell. As long as you call me something. It don't matter. I'll take a Coke. So what's your name, babes?" . . .

This was my first meeting with El Jester, as he called himself. His name was really Juan Alfredo Ramos, or Yonny, as his grandma called him, not being able to pronounce the J.

Novena Narratives

Corrine
(An aging, very tough bag-lady. She drags around a big and colorful bag which she empties on the floor. Throughout the scene she will put on clothing from the bag.)

"Antes me importaban las cosas, pero ahora, ssss—I take every day as it comes. Some good, some pretty bad! Like the weather. If it looks like rain or snow, I head down to the Holy Bible Rescue Mission para agarrar mi espacio. I stay there or at the Good Faith Shelter, or one of my other spots. Near the Interstate, that overhang with the old colchón . . . that's my bedroom! Or behind Bennie's La Paloma Bar, by the vents. ¡No te apenes! ¡No sweat! ¡Rain or shine, Corrine got it covered, esa!

(Taking a drink from her wine bottle in the bag.) "I don't want your stupid pity, okay? I got enough problems of my own, you start worrying me about your shag rug and your color t.v. . . . I don't need it, okay? I had a family once . . . kids . . . the whole . . . But don't get me wrong, esa, it's never as good as it looks. I got into writing bad checks. I needed things, you know? I got sent up. That was when they still had the women in the pinta in Santa. Anyway, I was in my 30's csa, and they took it all away—the kids, the house—and then el tonturio went to live with his novia in Belen. They all disappeared. Yeah, I tried to find them, but my family didn't want to have anything to do with me. So I did my

time. Met me my Sophia. Ay, Sophia, Sophia! ¡Que corazo-
nada! We wanted to get married. We did, in our hearts. Later
we got separated; she started seeing somebody else, you
know? So, I said, okay, anyway, I was getting out. Nobody
wanted me the way I was. So I took to the streets. Oh, yeah,
I got me a little, here and there, you know, just enough to
spend a night, take a shower, get some beer. But it didn't
last. I was getting old . . . that was over 20 years ago! Pero
no te preocupes, esa, I got it covered!"

Pauline Mendoza
*(She's a fourteen-year-old girl who's been in the fifth grade
for three years. She's a cholla. She's wearing a red headband,
and spiky wristbracelets. . . . Her hair is fluffy on the side and
long in the back. And she's been stuck in the wall. Her teacher
won't let her talk because she's too jittery, and she talks about
herself. She works on her tattoos behind the screen.)*

"Pauline Mendoza. . . . Las Cruces, fifth grade, fourteen
years old. I'm a freak. . . . Boys, cars, makeup, my red headband, black T-shirts, my leather jacket, my hair cut long in
the back, and short on the sides and front, tattoos. Can I sit
down now?

"I made all the tattoos myself. I'm working on one now.
No you can't see it. Can I go back to my desk now? Okay,
okay, so what do you want to know for anyway? I already
told you what I liked! I don't want to be nothin'! My teacher,
Mrs. Espinosa, makes me sit behind the screen, in the corner, facing the wall. I'm jittery, she says. Hell, so I work on
my tattoos. Nothing better to do. I can't barely read or write.
I'm dumb. I'm a freak. Don't yell at me! Mrs. Espinosa yells
at me. It's embarrassing!

"I've got work to do, okay? Nine times eight? What is it?
Hey, you! Ese! What's nine times eight? Heh, he doesn't know
either. How the hell should I know?

"Yeah, I like my mom. Want me to talk about my mom?
Okay, she's pretty young for a mom. I hate homework!
Thinking? I hate thinking! Maybe I could like it. You want me
to read that book? I can't read the whole thing! Don't you
understand? I'm dumb. I'm a freak. I sit in the corner all the

time. Can I sit down now? I been in the sixth, no the fifth grade, I'm not even in the sixth grade, five years. No, three years, ese, I can't even remember. I'm going to move next year.

"That? Oh, that's my tattoo. No. Oh, okay, since you asked. It's Our Lady of Guadalupe. It don't look like a lady on fire! That's rays of gold, stupid. Don't you know nothing? I just started working on it. Yeah, I told you, I go to church. Why do I like tattoos? I don't talk good. I don't think good. It's something cool. A picture like in a church."

N O T E S

1. *Last of the Menu Girls* (Houston: Arte Publico Press, 1986), pp. 64–65.
2. Bill Balassi, John Crawford, and Annie Eysturoy, eds., *This Is about Vision: Interviews with Southwestern Writers* (Albuquerque: University of New Mexico Press, 1990), p. 164.

JOY HARJO

▲ ❖ ▼ ❖ ▼ ❖ ▲

Joy Harjo, a Native American born in Oklahoma, challenges the prevailing boundaries of southwestern writers. She moves with ease among the various tribes of the region, and her poetry has been influenced not only by her own Creek traditions, but by the Navajo Beauty Way, like Luci Tapahonso, and by Pueblo stories, as in the work of her former partner, Simon Ortiz.

At home in the mesas, mountains, and sage flats of New Mexico and Arizona, her work is grounded in her relationship to the earth, on a physical, spiritual, and mythopoetic level. Like fellow Oklahoman and Native American poet Linda Hogan, Harjo's writing contains a disturbing mixture of darkness and beauty, at once a lament and a moving incantation.

> "Sacred space—I call it a place of grace, or the place in which we're most human—the place in which there's a unity of human-ness with wolf-ness, with hummingbird-ness, with Sandia Mountain-ness, with rain cloud-ness. . . . It's that place in which we understand there is no separation between worlds. It has everything to do with the way we live. The land is responsible for the clothes you have on, for my saxophone, for the paper that I write these things on, for our bodies. It's responsible for everything."
>
> —JOY HARJO

Native American poet Joy Harjo uses her writing to build fragile webs of connection between the past and the present, between Indian and white identities. Her work is an exploration of the landscapes she inhabits as she travels between her tribal world and that of white America.

Harjo's background is a volatile mix of the elements she unites in her poetry and her music. She was born in Tulsa, Oklahoma, on May 1, 1951; her father was Creek, Muskogee, her mother a mix of Cherokee, Irish, and French. To Harjo, the traditional stories and music she heard as a child keep alive long-dead ancestors from both sides of her family.

Her mother's family, like her father's, were victims of the Indian Removal Act of 1830, which forced most of the Cherokee, Creek, Muskogee, and other tribes from the southeastern United States into Oklahoma on the infamous Trail of Tears. To this day the Harjos carry dark memories of that time as well as a few cherished objects which survived what many call a holocaust, passed down from generation to generation. The Trail of Tears is most often associated with the Cherokee, who lost approximately one-fourth of their tribe (eight thousand deaths, according to the latest estimates). Yet along its length, numerous other tribes were included in the forced removals. The Choctaw are said to have lost six thousand persons, or approximately 15 percent of their tribe, and the Creek (Harjo's father's tribe) an incredible 50 percent, due as much to the brutal wars of attrition necessary to force them to leave their homelands as to the rigors of the march itself, followed by disease and outright starvation upon arrival. As incredible as the percentage of the tribes who died is the number who finally survived, and whose legacy of memories, stories, and songs were passed on to their descendants.

Harjo feels these memories as strongly as if she had lived them herself. The ghost of Andrew Jackson, whose militia slaughtered Indians in the nineteenth century, still haunts her. From the stories and memories of those survivors, Harjo's ancestors, she forges a potent weapon: poetry.

From her mother, Harjo claims to have received the gift of music, and tales of outrageous characters: a great-grand-mother who hosted the outlaw Pretty Boy Floyd; another relative who murdered people with a pair of scissors; and her mother's stories of her own childhood partly spent in a haunted house which no one else would live in but which her family, desperately poor, braved. From her mother she also learned the harsh lesson of the grinding poverty in which many Native Americans live, in Oklahoma and elsewhere.

Her father, a full-blooded Creek, grew up in considerable wealth. His father, Marcy Harjo, inherited a tribal allotment of land in Glenpool, Oklahoma, site of one of the largest oil finds in the nation. Harjo's father was born in a twenty-one-room house, but tragedy struck. Marcy Harjo's wife died, the money and land were lost to swindlers, and Harjo's father was sent away by his new, white stepmother to Ponca Military Academy. It was there, however, that he learned to repair aircraft, eventually becoming an employee of American Airlines in Tulsa.

Harjo remembers growing up in the lower-middle-class neighborhood of North Tulsa, an area of mixed races and mixed-race peoples. The shimmering summers of Oklahoma are lodged in her mind, as is the vivid memory of a day when the asphalt by her house actually melted in the sun; to escape the heat, her father often took her cruising the streets of Tulsa in his luxurious Cadillacs (cars he cared for, she recalls without bitterness, sometimes better than he cared for his family) as the radio played Miles Davis—thus began her love affair with jazz. Hers was a music-loving family. Harjo also heard drumming in the southern plains tradition, and her mother singing the heartbreak songs of Patsy Cline.

Her parents separated soon after her younger sister was born, and her mother worked as a cook and a waitress at truck stops and cafés. Harjo's father was rarely present in her life after the divorce, but she recalls the discrimination he suffered, and the derogatory nicknames, like "Chief," which so disturbed him and which today reverberate in her poetry.

Poetry has always played a role in her life. Harjo cites the Bible, in particular the Song of Solomon, as one of her earliest literary influences. She had read the Bible through twice by the time she was ten years old. Her grandfather Marcy Harjo, a Baptist preacher, initiated her into the beauty of the spoken word, as well as the captivating power of the ancient biblical tales. She used to play "preacher" as a child, standing on a tree stump and terrifying the other children with vivid descriptions of hellfire and damnation.

This dynamic imagination helped Harjo adjust to a new life in 1967 at the Institute of American Indian Arts in Santa Fe, New Mexico, a boarding school for Native American high school students. Harjo recalls teachers there who encouraged her and other students to write. Their sources of inspiration and literary models, however, were almost exclusively white— Emily Dickinson and William Butler Yeats were two Harjo especially preferred. It wasn't until she entered the University of New Mexico that she read and met published writers of Native American descent.

In 1968, at the Institute of American Indian Arts, Harjo met Phil Wilmon, a fellow student who became the father of her first child, Phil, Jr., born in 1969. For several years, the three shuttled between Oklahoma and New Mexico, with Joy pumping gas and waitressing, and Wilmon fighting an alcohol problem. They were living in the kind of poverty in which Harjo had been raised, and which she had vowed to overcome. Desperate and uncertain about where to go with her life, Harjo found a job in Santa Fe at St. Vincent's Hospital. She felt a bond with the sick and injured, and sensed a deep need within herself to be part of a healing process, so she decided to become a doctor. Her relationship with Wilmon rapidly deteriorated, and Harjo left him to enter the University of New Mexico's premed program in 1971.

After two semesters, disillusioned with the cold impersonality of her classes and Western medicine's views toward other traditions of healing, she transferred to a fine arts major. A number of her relatives were artists, and Harjo had dreamed as a child of becoming a painter. At a party in 1972, however, she met the first of several Native American writers who would change her life. Simon Ortiz, a poet from Acoma Pueblo in New Mexico and Harjo's first writing mentor, was at the English department of the University of New Mexico, along with noted Native American writers Leslie Marmon Silko, Paula Gunn Allen, N. Scott Momaday, and Luci Tapahonso. Harjo quickly changed her major to creative writing and became a part of the literary explosion taking place within the Indian community at the University of New Mexico throughout the 1970s.

In 1973, Harjo and Ortiz had a daughter, Rainy Dawn. Although her relationship with Ortiz, who was struggling himself with alcoholism, ended soon afterward, Rainy Dawn's birth seemed to spark something in Harjo's life, and she began to focus on poetry. She graduated from the University of New Mexico in 1976 with a degree in creative writing. Then she finally left the Southwest to attend the prestigious Writers Workshop at the University of Iowa, where she received her M.F.A. in 1978, the same year she won a creative writing fellowship from the National Endowment for the Arts. She was only twenty-seven, but a world of recognition awaited her.

Three years earlier, she had published her first collection of poems, *The Last Song*. This is a lyrical, poignant lament, an attempt to make sense of what Harjo calls the "terrible, beautiful history" of her people, a history which she believes is still to be written today. She sees no separation between past, present, and future, or between humans and the earth, and her early poetry incorporates this animism. Through her poetry, she seeks to uncover the connectedness among humans, animals, and landscape; what she calls the "tenuous spirals of memory" reaching backward and forward through time.

Her second book, *What Moon Drove Me to This?* (1980) (whose cover illustration is an original drawing by Harjo) continues her concerns with land and Indian history; but now she had begun to struggle with a personal issue: mixed ancestry. "Mixed-bloods," those of mixed white and Indian ancestry, inhabit a dangerous space. Distrusted for being Indian by the white world, and rejected as white and nontraditional by Native communities, mixed-bloods wear "the face of the enemy" for both cultures. At the same time, they have more mobility (and acceptance) in the dominant culture than darker-skinned Indians, making them the objects of desire, envy, and outright resentment. For Harjo, and many people of mixed race, there is a wrenching price for mainstream acceptance; and an ambivalence about receiving that recognition.

Harjo's later writing has increasingly taken up this contradiction. One poem from *What Moon?*, "The Other Half," tells of the narrator meeting a young man of pure Native American descent at a powwow. The drummers begin a traditional Creek stomp dance song, and the narrator grabs the young man's hand and asks him to dance. He refuses, and she sadly realizes it is her "other half" he desires.

The pain and confusion of such moments endured. In 1978 Harjo returned to the Institute of American Indian Arts in Santa Fe, this time as an instructor, subsequently teaching at Arizona State University in Tempe. At all these schools, she worked with Native American students and probed the duality of her mixed heritage, something that fuels the violence and rage lurking beneath the surface in many of her poems. By the 1980s she had come to grips with her ancestry, harnessing her anger over the past to feed her own creative growth. Her third collection, *She Had Some Horses* (1983), marks a significant break from the previous two.

No less political in content, the book is far less personal. The connecting webs of life, across time and cultures, are here more visible. The *Women's Review of Books* wrote of *She Had Some Horses*, "Harjo's . . . poems are marked by a near-mythic intensity, their effects focused with the accuracy and economy of a burning-glass focusing sunlight."[1] The most haunting piece from this collection is "Woman Hanging from the Thirteenth Floor Window," about an Indian woman who left her reservation in Wisconsin searching for a better life in the harsh urban wastes of Chicago. Harjo wrote the poem after visiting Chicago and realizing the new impoverishment of urban Indians. The poem is not about a single woman, she says, but about many; as she sat at her desk in Santa Fe to write down the verses, almost verbatim, she says she felt their presence watching her.

While her earlier poetry shows the influences of the classic English and American writers that she read—Keats, Dickinson, Shelley—and the burning, prophetic quality of the Old Testament writers, she also found her poems flavored by the new Native American writing emerging at the University of New Mexico. In her invocations to the deserts and mountains, Harjo acknowledges the influence of Simon Ortiz and the ancient chants and songs from which his work springs. The *American Book Review* noted, "In content and stance, Harjo belongs with poets like Carolyn Forche and Audre Lord, though her poems suggest an additional dimension that can only be called spiritual."[2]

Harjo now began to hybridize a number of different tra-

ditions—Creek drumming rhythms, the lyricism of the Navajo
Beauty Way, the larger-than-life mythic quality of the old Bible
stories—into her own unique style. A wide-ranging reader, in
the 1970s she discovered the writings of West African authors,
recognizing in them the similarities joining tribal peoples
around the globe—particularly those colonized by Europeans,
and thus forced to speak two or even three languages. Harjo's
own linguistic development found additional outlet in the language of music, when she had begun to play the saxophone as
a teenager.

Music has surrounded her life. Her mother not only sang
but wrote songs as well, and her father introduced her to the
musical form she would later adopt as her own—jazz. She was
captivated by a music that was itself the hybrid offspring of
different races and traditions.

Several years ago, she formed a band, Poetic Justice, playing an unusual, but oddly harmonious, mixture of reggae, jazz,
and Native American music. She also began setting her poems
to music—or, perhaps, setting music to her poems. Although
her poetic verses have become less structured, she seems to
have adapted the rhythm of the text to the meter of her music.
The chanting of poems and stories to music, so important in
tribal worlds, has been combined with a modern, semioperatic
Sprechgesang, similar to the San Francisco Beat poets' mixture
of poetry and jazz. The result is an entirely original musicality
which becomes more and more apparent in her latest works.
In the *American Book Review* her work was described as "dynamic, charged with restless energy, wailing like the tenor sax
she plays; her poetry is not to be taken sitting down."[3]

Her later poems are less measured and symmetrical, the
verses less formal in structure, longer and more proselike. The
rhythm and repetition of drums and chants pervades these
works, in counterpoint to the intricate, flowing lines of jazz.
Harjo believes that jazz may have been influenced by traditional Creek-Muskogee and Cherokee music. In support she
points to the many escaped African slaves hidden by the Cherokee and Creek and adopted as members of the tribes, as well
as to famous Native American jazz musicians from the 1930s
and 1940s such as "Chief" Joe Moore. Her own grandfather,
Marcy Harjo, she adds, may well have had African blood.

Harjo's interests and talents extend beyond music and the written word. She completed a filmmaking course at the Anthropology Film Center in Santa Fe, and in 1985 authored the script for *Origin of the Apache Crown Dance* for Silver Cloud Video. She is currently writing an original screenplay, *When We Used to Be Humans*, for the American Film Foundation. Harjo finds screenplays are closer to poetry than to fiction. She sees films as a series of images, albeit images in motion, and she looks at her poetry in much the same way.

In 1985, Harjo began teaching as a professor at the University of Colorado at Boulder, moving in 1988 to the University of Arizona in Tucson. The landscape of the desert Southwest played an ever-larger role in her poems. In 1989, she published *Secrets from the Center of the World*, a tightly crafted combination of Harjo's poems with striking photographs of the southwestern landscape by astronomer Stephen Strom. It demonstrates an increasing willingness to experiment with line and form, as well as conveying a feeling of space and freedom. The *American Indian Quarterly* commented, "Joy Harjo has moved to a new place in her writing where the form opens up and associations deepen significantly."[4]

When she first began writing poetry, Harjo says, she was also raising her two children, Phil, Jr., and Rainy Dawn, as a single mother. Her poetic landscape was bounded by the time restrictions and responsibilities of caring for small children and a home. With both children grown, she says, her poetry opened up to the larger world.

In her fourth collection, the award-winning *In Mad Love and War* (1990), her concern for women, especially Native Americans on and off the reservation, is evident. Perhaps the best known poem is "For Anna Mae Pictou Aquash," dedicated to the young Micmac Indian woman murdered, many say by the FBI, for her work with the American Indian Movement.

This volume won Harjo the 1991 William Carlos Williams Award from the Poetry Society of America, the Before Columbus Book Award, the 1990 American Indian Distinguished Achievement Award, the Josephine Miles Award for Excellence in Literature from PEN Oakland, and yet another creative writing fellowship from the National Endowment for the Arts. In

1994, W. W. Norton published her fifth volume of poetry, *The Woman Who Fell from the Sky*.

Harjo currently teaches creative writing at the University of New Mexico in Albuquerque; her current projects include an anthology of Native women's writing, *Reinventing the Enemy's Language*, and a children's book, *The Goodluck Cat*, from Harcourt Brace Jovanovich.

▲ ✧ ▼ ✧ ▼ ✧ ▲

A tall, athletic woman with straight, jet black hair—Joy Harjo's presence has an unmistakable intensity. Her first words, deadpan, were on how as a child, her imagination led her out of her bedroom window to roam the night skies. Despite the half smile that follows, one immediately sees how serious she is. Harjo's world is only partially bounded by the real and the rational. In a quiet, steadfast way, she shifts between facts of Indian history and deeply personal visions.

The day we spoke, she had just moved into a new house and there was a bleariness to her words, as if poured out from under a mess of coffee grounds. She spoke in the studios of KUNM-FM at the University of New Mexico, where she had recently been appointed a full professor. In her manner there was something of the eccentric don who knows the problems and parameters of her subject well—perhaps to the point of impatience with those who don't. To a fellow jazz enthusiast, her response differs dramatically; she is ready to compare notes about reeds and Charlie Parker. At times her jazz career seems to interest her more than teaching. Little separates her saxophone playing and her poetry, two roads to the same destination. Reading poems like "Remember," her voice drops to the edge of audibility, as if she is again that girl staring out the window at the heavens, wondering where she belongs; between sky and earth, Native American or European.

JOY HARJO:

I think every writer probably has one thing that they want, *need* to work out desperately in their writing. It doesn't mean that you write the same story every time or the same poem, but there's always something that follows you around, almost like your shadow. Something that you keep going back to—a home or a landscape that you always return to.

I seem to be dealing with transformation, a way to make sense of a terrible, terrible history, a way to rectify it. I'm dealing with a question of what to do with this terrible, beautiful history and how do I make sense of it, in another time and place? How do I find these connecting spirals? How do I make beautiful sense of it all?

I'm not going to be one of these people that surprises everyone and goes out and shoots people. But I don't know how anybody living at the end of the twentieth century, especially any Native person, cannot have a storehouse of violence, given the persistence of memory. The trick is, what do you do with it? You know, drinking dulls it in some ways, at least for a while, but you can use it—you can use it to run, become a champion athlete, you can use it to write. It's like a gift of fire—a gift you can use to cook with or to burn your house down. It can become a fuel, a very highly combustible fuel. And after a lot of near tragedy, I came to a point where I've decided to let it be my strength rather than to let it destroy me.

Look at this country. Two or three hundred years ago the population of these United States was one hundred percent [Indian]. And now, as I remember the statistics, we're one-half of one percent of the total population.

Given what we see with the Rodney King verdict in L.A., Andrew Jackson is still here. Andrew Jackson is still running in the streets and terribly alive.

I love the mystics—William Blake, Yeats. When I was growing up I read anything I could get my hands on, from my step-father's police-detective magazines to Taylor Caldwell novels I would check out of the library when I was seven, eight years old. I read any Dickens I could get ahold of. I really loved Emily Dickinson's poetry, I used to read her when I was seven, eight, nine years old.

Then in college I discovered the African writers. They're a

tribal people who were colonized, and speak and write in English. I think the tribal world has very different assumptions about how the world works, and time and space, than does the industrialized European.

I feel like in this life that what I'm trying to do is to find a way to speak the English language, which really comes out of another space. I think when Columbus came, he brought with him a certain consciousness—linear time. Linear time is characterized by a beginning and an end. There's always a good-bye.

Linear time establishes a hierarchy. An elementary schoolteacher gets paid less than a university professor even though they work in the most crucial years with children—that's a result of hierarchical, linear time. It emphasizes a past, present, and future, so that you're always proceeding toward something, whereas what I would call spiral time, mythic time, tribal time, is process as opposed to progress. It's a resonant present in which you realize that the past, present, and future are affecting everything, and you understand that what you do at this moment is affecting the past, and also the future.

The landscape is one of the biggest keepers of memory. The earth is the storehouse of memory. Once I was driving up to work with students at Tuba City High [Arizona], and I just drove off the side of the road and started crying. It was, it was beyond anything I'd ever known. It was a time of recognition. It was a moment filled with the failings of human beings in the face of this incredible, astounding beauty, a place where the voices of the stones were larger than anything, as well as the voice of the sky.

I don't think it's just the Southwest—I think everywhere you walk the land could tell you a record of everything that's ever happened. The waves of certain events climb up much the same as heat waves do, and it's not just human memory—I'm talking about memories of the stones, and how they came to be, the memories of the crickets, the memories of the turtles, and so on.

Humans sometimes get fooled—it's why I love Trickster so much, because he/she is so utterly, failingly human. Humans get fooled into thinking that we know everything. Christianity taught that humans were in a hierarchy above all [other] creatures, and that was how Christianity failed. Because in the true scheme of things, or at least the way I've seen, it's not the case.

So memory is something that perhaps Jung called the collective unconscious. It's something that we're all a part of, something like what little I understand of the Aboriginal Dreamtime—the sense of all beings being connected, in terms of a consciousness in which space is no longer a measurement of distance, but space *is* consciousness.

We're walking around like these poor blind moles—I wouldn't even disgrace moles by saying that, because they have their own integrity—but it's strange, we're like Trickster figures bumbling around and walking into each other and into these incredible spaces of myth and story and beauty, and we don't even see them.

I like the Rabbit character in my tribe, the Muskogee people. Rabbit is a Trickster figure. I've been told Rabbit is neither male nor female. I see Rabbit as an androgynous character. The Trickster always crosses lines, jumps from one side to the other, and that's one way we identify Trickster because Trickster embraces the polar opposite of ourselves. Just when we think we have everything figured out, he or she jumps the line, and there we are, forced to deal with ourselves as part of the opposite camp, so to speak.

I feel those ancient stories provide the base, and in terms of the work I'm doing now they're coming to the foreground, but they were never really excluded. I think the contemporary stories become a way of retelling them.

EXCERPTS

What Moon Drove Me To This?

"I Am A Dangerous Woman"

the sharp ridges of clear blue windows
motion to me

[handwritten margin notes: on the edge — suicidal? homicidal?]
[handwritten margin notes: naturalizes technology]
[handwritten margin note: poem]
[handwritten margin note: cutting her]
[handwritten margin note: ? merges window w/what she sees through it.]

from the airports second floor
edges dance in the foothills of the sandias
behind security guards
who wave me into their guncatcher machine
i am a dangerous woman

when the machine buzzes
they say to take off my belt
and i remove it so easy
that it catches the glance
of a man standing nearby
(maybe that is the deadly weapon
that has the machine singing)

i am a dangerous woman
but the weapon is not visible
security will never find it
they can't hear the clicking
of the gun
        inside my head

"It's The Same At Four A.M."

He's half Creek, half plains.
I'm part Creek and white.
"Which part do you want tonight?"
I ask him.

The forty-nine singers are drumming
Creek stomp dance songs on the hood
of someone's car.
I pull his arm
"Com on, let's dance."

But he wants the other half.

She Had Some Horses

"She Had Some Horses"

She had some horses.

She had horses who were bodies of sand.
She had horses who were maps drawn of blood.
She had horses who were skins of ocean water.
She had horses who were the blue air of sky.
She had horses who were fur and teeth.
She had horses who were clay and would break.
She had horses who were splintered red cliff.

She had some horses.

She had horses with long, pointed breasts.
She had horses with full, brown thighs.
She had horses who laughed too much.
She had horses who threw rocks at glass houses.
She had horses who licked razor blades.

She had some horses.

She had horses who danced in their mothers' arms.
She had horses who thought they were the sun and their
    bodies shone and burned like stars.
She had horses who waltzed nightly on the moon.
She had horses who were much too shy, and kept quiet
    in stalls of their own making.

She had some horses.

She had horses who liked Creek Stomp Dance songs.
She had horses who cried in their beer.
She had horses who spit at male queens who made
    them afraid of themselves.
She had horses who said they weren't afraid.
She had horses who lied.

She had horses who told the truth, who were stripped
bare of their tongues.

She had some horses.

[NAMES]

She had horses who called themselves, "horse".
She had horses who called themselves, "spirit", and kept
their voices secret and to themselves.
She had horses who had no names.
She had horses who had books of names.

She had some horses.

[VOICES]

She had horses who whispered in the dark, who were afraid
    to speak.
She had horses who screamed out of fear of the silence, who
carried knives to protect themselves from ghosts.
She had horses who waited for destruction.
She had horses who waited for resurrection.

She had some horses.

[SPIRIT]

She had horses who got down on their knees for any savior.
She had horses who thought their high price had saved
    them.
She had horses who tried to save her, who climbed in her
bed at night and prayed as they raped her.

She had some horses.

She had some horses she loved.
She had some horses she hated.

opposites reconciled.

These were the same horses.

Secrets from the Center of the World

If you look with the mind of the swirling earth near Shiprock you become the land, beautiful. And understand how

three crows at the edge of the highway, laughing, become
three crows at the edge of the world, laughing.

transformation from physical to spiritual world

N O T E S

1. Margaret Randall, *Women's Review of Books*, vol. 2 (Oct. 1984), p. 7.

2. Marilyn Kallett, *American Book Review*, vol. 13 (April–May 1991), p. 10.

3. Ibid.

4. Sidney Larson, *American Indian Quarterly*, vol. 15, no. 2 (Spring 1991), pp. 273–274.

TONY HILLERMAN

▲ ❖ ▼ ❖ ▼ ❖ ▲

Best-selling mystery writer Tony Hillerman has brought the landscape of the Southwest and the Navajo culture into mainstream America's reading. His childhood growing up with Indian people led to a fascination with Native American cultures and prompted him to spend time on the remote reservations of Arizona and New Mexico.

The relationship of Indians with the harshly beautiful high desert country is an underlying force in Hillerman's novels. He uses his fiction to explore the turbulent crosscurrents that occur when ancient Native cultures, traditional Hispanic worlds, and the dominant Anglo society collide.

> *I have a great respect for the Navajo and Pueblo Indian cultures and people. So few Americans think of these cultures as anything except primitive.*
>
> *I would like to show readers these people as they are: as fellow human beings with a culture that is alive and well, complicated and rich. I want them to see this country that is so important to the Navajos and the Pueblo people, their Holy Land. But first and foremost, I like to be a storyteller.*

—TONY HILLERMAN

Tony Hillerman, who has lived all his life in the Southwest and who admits a love affair with the high desert country, is today one of the most widely read mystery writers in the United States and abroad. Translated into German, Dutch,

Swedish, Danish, and Japanese, his works have received awards from the American Library Association, the Mystery Writers of America, and the American Anthropological Association.

Yet none of his best-sellers takes place in a setting even remotely familiar to most Americans. Hillerman's two most famous protagonists are Navajo tribal policemen who patrol the vast reaches of desert and canyonlands that make up the Navajo, Hopi, and Zuni reservations. His secondary characters include witches, shamans, singers, and healers, many of whom speak no English.

His is a world of seasons and magic, of curing ceremonies and ancient cultures, often on a collision course with the Anglo world. Yet virtually everything Tony Hillerman has written for the last quarter century has been a glowing success in that world, both among mystery buffs and the general reading public. What comes as a surprise to many fans is that Hillerman is not himself Native American. He has, however, a special connection to Native folkways that goes back for many years.

Hillerman was born in 1925 in the tiny, and now deserted, town of Sacred Heart, Oklahoma, deep in Pottawatomie County. His father, one of a few whites in town, was a small farmer, sometime postmaster and notary public, and manager of the town's only general store. Nearly all their neighbors were Pottawatomies, Seminoles, and Blackfeet.

The only educational opportunity for the handful of white children was a one-room schoolhouse with a barely literate teacher. Hillerman's parents convinced the next closest school, a boarding school for Pottawatomie girls run by the Sisters of Mercy, to accept their son and a few other local farm boys as students. "We were not allowed in the playgrounds," Hillerman laughs, "and fraternization was strictly verboten. It was an unusual educational experience. It taught you what it was like to be a minority problem. Not only were we white, which was bad enough, but we were also males, which was even worse."

This arrangement lasted through the eighth grade. An avid reader even at a young age, Hillerman regularly mailed off requests to a state lending library for books like *Captain Blood* and *Death on Horseback*. To his chagrin, these were answered with the likes of *History of the Masonic Order in Oklahoma* and *The Conquest of Peru*. Hillerman's childhood friends were mostly Native American boys, and he grew up eating dinner with their families, dating their sisters, and picking up an abiding respect for Native cultures.

His father died when Hillerman was a child. His older brother and he inherited the small family farm. His brother had already enlisted in the air force during World War II, and his mother moved to Oklahoma City, freeing Hillerman for good from the life of a farmer in a dirt-poor corner of Oklahoma. When he turned eighteen, he joined up and shipped out overseas.

Oddly enough, it was his stint in the military that led Hillerman to become a writer—by default. After serving on the front lines in Europe, he received the Bronze Star, the Silver Star, and a Purple Heart, for being severely wounded by a grenade in a battle behind German lines.

Both legs were shattered, and both eyes filled with shrapnel and mud. The legs eventually healed, but his eyes were badly infected, and Hillerman spent several weeks completely blind. For months afterward his eyesight was shaky, and he was unsure he would ever be able to read again. In any case, the eye injury had destroyed his dreams to study chemistry.

As he lay in a military hospital in France, immobile in a body cast with both eyes bandaged, he was contacted by a reporter from the *Oklahoma Daily* who wanted to do a feature story on his Silver Star. She had borrowed from Hillerman's mother several letters he had written from Europe, and she invited him to stop by on his return to the States. When he finally visited her, several months later, she told him he was talented; he should try his hand at journalism. Hillerman promptly enrolled at the University of Oklahoma on the GI Bill, graduating in 1948.

His first writing job, however, was not what he had envisioned. After graduation, he was hired by a tiny advertising agency in Oklahoma City to write early-morning radio commercials for Cain's Age-Dated Coffee and Purina Pig Chow. Each day's commercials had to be snappy, informative, and completely different from the previous day's. According to Hillerman it was the most difficult writing he ever had to do. He lasted just one week.

The following month, he landed the job that would supply him the color and anecdotes which would later surface in his mysteries. He became the police reporter for the small West Texas town of Borger, whose only civic monument, Hillerman recalls, "was a bullet hole in the post office wall where Ace Borger, the first mayor and founder of the town, was shot to death by a dissident policeman. The Texas Rangers had to come in and take over, to try to bring order to the place. Great town to break in as a police reporter. They had every crime in the book, except mopery."

From Borger, Hillerman worked his way up, first to the Lawton, Oklahoma, *Morning News*, then to the United Press International bureau in Oklahoma City, where he married his wife, Marie. In the mid-1950s he was assigned by UPI as a political correspondent in Santa Fe, New Mexico. Once there he became city editor, managing editor, and by his mid-thirties, executive editor of a daily paper, the *Santa Fe New Mexican*.

This was not Hillerman's first time in New Mexico. In 1946, just out of the army, he had worked for a short time as a truck driver. Attempting to make a delivery in a remote area of New Mexico, he became lost and stumbled onto an Enemy Way Ceremony being performed to heal returning Navajo soldiers on a Navajo reservation. His early fascination with Native American cultures and religions was reanimated by the breathtaking beauty of the ceremony.

He began studying the Indians of the Southwest, the Navajo in particular, making friends on the reservations, and learning some of the language. Although he claims his ethnological material is not intended to meet scholarly and scientific standards, according to the *Encyclopedia of Frontier and Western Fiction*, "Hillerman [is] extremely well informed about the customs, rituals, and daily lives of the contemporary Southwest Indians."[1] Even the American Anthropological Association agreed, citing his work in 1990 for its authenticity.

Still, it wasn't until 1963, at the urging of his wife and their six children, that he resigned his editorship of the *New Mexican* to write fiction. He enrolled in the writing program at the University of New Mexico in Albuquerque, where he received his M.A. He taught in the English and journalism departments (which he chaired from 1966 to 1974) at the same time Joy

Harjo and Luci Tapahonso were students there. Rudolfo Anaya was his colleague.

Hillerman chose unusual settings and characters for several reasons. "Initially, I wanted to write the Great American Novel, *War and Peace* in the Southwest." He had no idea if he had any skill at plotting, however, so he chose as a backdrop the Navajo reservation, hoping the relative exoticism would keep readers interested, in case he failed at developing a story line.

He chose the detective story as his genre after studying the works of Ambler, Hammett, Chandler, Graham Greene—and an obscure Australian author named Arthur Upfield, who had created a half-French, half-Aboriginal policeman called Napoleon Bonepart. Hillerman felt the mystery novel was a particularly flexible form, one suited both for entertainment and literature. He was so taken with Upfield's vivid depictions of the Australian outback and its tribal cultures, he decided to attempt a Navajo tribal policeman—Lieutenant Joe Leaphorn.

Hillerman had always been troubled that most Americans are ignorant about Native cultures. Yet in fiction, he had a way to show the aliveness of traditional cultures and the intriguing methods they use in adapting to twentieth-century white America.

Hillerman's Joe Leaphorn is a middle-aged Navajo who has moved for many years in white culture. He is as familiar with it as he is with his own Navajo traditions; through him, Hillerman is able to explore the code switching and culture jumping in which so many Native Americans engage to interact with the dominant Anglo society. The anthropologists, tourists, pot hunters, and the FBI who intrude into that world must be dealt with while maintaining the integrity of the Navajo worldview. The character, Leaphorn, maneuvers between these often-conflicting ways of looking at crime, punishment, and justice.

Despite initial skepticism by publishers, *The Blessing Way* (1970) sold well and received overwhelmingly positive reviews. The quirky character of Leaphorn, the remote setting, and the unusualness of nearly all the major characters being nonwhite enchanted readers and critics alike. "Here's suspense enough for anyone," one reviewer wrote, "but what makes this first mystery by Tony Hillerman outstanding is the wealth of detail about the Navajo. . . ."[2] The *Library Journal* was even more enthusiastic, declaring, "This reviewer has never met a finer, more believable fictional detective than Lt. Joe Leaphorn. . . . Here we have that rarity: a mystery with literary value, one you can recommend to people who don't like mysteries."[3]

And that has been perhaps one of the keys to Hillerman's astounding success as a novelist. His books are read by fans of Western fiction, mystery buffs, readers interested in Native American cultures, and by Native Americans themselves. And in large numbers, they are read by people who otherwise don't read mysteries. His journalistic training shows in the tight, clean lines of his prose, in the fast-moving story line, and in the wealth of details that help bring readers who have never seen the southwestern deserts face to face with red rock mesas, sagebrush, trading posts, and tribal police. While one aim is to teach white Americans about the culture and lives of Indian people, Hillerman is rarely heavy-handed or didactic, and many readers feel as though they have not only read a suspenseful and entertaining work of fiction, but have broadened their cultural horizons as well.

Following *The Blessing Way*, Hillerman wrote a second novel more closely following the standard mystery genre, concerning an Anglo reporter in a midwestern city who stumbles across a story which could destroy a governor's political career. Still, Hillerman was unable to leave his beloved Southwest behind entirely. One of the most highly charged passages in *The Fly on the Wall* (1971) is a manhunt in the rugged mountains north of Santa Fe, the boyhood home of the protagonist, who flees to New Mexico following a murder attempt.

Again, Hillerman's tight, elegant prose, his journalist's eye for detail, and the emotional depth of his story drew the praise of the critics. The *New York Times Book Review* wrote, "Cotton is a model newspaperman who actually talks and works and acts like a newspaperman. . . . The plot also raises basic questions about the philosophy of reporting that are much discussed in city rooms these days. This is a highly credible book full of action, flawlessly plotted."[4] And as with *The Blessing Way*, critics noted that *The Fly on the Wall* was more than just a suspense novel. The *New Yorker* called it "a thriller that is not merely thrilling . . . but also a provocative ethical conundrum."[5]

Hillerman remained fascinated with the Southwest and the world of Native Americans. He returned to that world and to Lieutenant Joe Leaphorn with *Dance Hall of the Dead* (1973) and *Listening Woman* (1978). He had observed, however, that not all Navajos (or Zunis or Hopis) are as deft or comfortable with code switching as he had made Leaphorn. He needed to extend his exploration of Navajo culture to include those a generation younger, who were caught more rigidly between television and the old ways. This was his impetus in creating Officer Jim Chee, who first appears in Hillerman's fourth novel, *People of Darkness* (1980). Like Leaphorn, Chee is a Navajo tribal policeman, but considerably younger and less experienced, both on the police force and in dealing with whites.

Chee differs from Leaphorn in several other important ways. While Leaphorn is definitely a Navajo traditionalist and considers himself such, he is skeptical of many traditional Navajo beliefs, such as the powers of witches, shamans, and mystics. He uses his knowledge of that world to help solve crimes, particularly in interviewing Native suspects and witnesses or noting details that white officers often overlook; but like many modern Navajos, he does not believe in the power of ceremonies or mysticism himself.

In a passage from the best-selling *Listening Woman*, for example, Leaphorn reviews a tape-recorded interview with a blind seer, Listening Woman, conducted by a white FBI agent investigating the murder of a terminally ill man. Leaphorn immediately notes that a number of important facts have been overlooked by the agent that are glaringly apparent to Leaphorn. Listening Woman, Margaret Cigaret, who is a traditional healer, begins to tell the FBI agent about a cave protected by the murdered man which contains several sand paintings. The agent quickly cuts her off, probing for what he believes will be more substantial clues to the man's murder.

Like any Navajo, however, Leaphorn is aware that there should only be a single sand painting existing at any one time. He surmises, correctly of course, that something very unusual is hidden in the cave which the FBI ignored. Leaphorn insists on interviewing the woman himself, although the agent in charge of the case has declared she has no more pertinent information:

"I listened to the tape recording of you talking to the white policeman," Leaphorn said. "But I noticed, my mother, that the white man didn't really let you tell about it. He interrupted you. . . . I came to find you because I thought that if we would talk about it, you could tell me what the white man was too impatient to hear."

Mrs. Cigaret frowned. "The white man didn't think it had anything to do with the killing."

"I am not a white man," Leaphorn said.[6]

Hillerman made his second detective, Jim Chee, on the other hand, not only a believer in the ceremonies, but an apprentice medicine man, a practitioner of the ancient healing rituals. Chee is not particularly comfortable with the ways of white folks and is often amazed by their seemingly inexplicable actions. His struggles to work within (and around) the white man's systems afford Hillerman the chance to illuminate the fragile integrity of Native cultures in the face of a dominant society which devalues them.

In *Skinwalkers* (1988), Leaphorn and Chee are brought together for the first time to work on a case involving ritual murder, witches (skinwalkers), and insurance fraud. The older Leaphorn tests the younger man in the following passage, beginning a kind of paternal, uncle-nephew relationship so important in Navajo kinship structures:

"Was the killer a Navajo?" Leaphorn asked.

Chee hesitated, surprised. "Yes," he said. "Navajo."

"You sound sure," Leaphorn said. "Why Navajo?"

"Funny. I knew he was Navajo. But I didn't think about why," Chee said. He counted it off on his fingers. "He didn't step over the body, which could have just happened that way. But when he walked down the arroyo, he took care not to walk where the water had run. And on the way back to the road, a snake had been across there, and when he crossed its path he shuffled his feet." Chee paused. "Or do white men do that, too?"[7]

Hillerman never forgets that he himself is white, and his Native characters take note of the subtle contempt and discrimination in which some Anglos engage. His white characters are as three-dimensional as his Native ones—neither angels nor devils, sometimes kind, sometimes ignorant, sometimes cruel. Careful to avoid generalizing about Indian cultures, Hillerman is equally reluctant to romanticize or exploit them.

Though many Native Americans resent white authors who they feel use their culture to sell books while perpetuating romanticized visions of "the noble Redman," Hillerman's novels are actually taught in Navajo and Zuni reservation schools. His knowledge of, and obvious respect for, Native peoples have gained him a loyal following among the tribes of the Southwest. In 1973, the students at Zuni High School voted to ask Hillerman to be their commencement speaker, an honor he regards as more important than winning the Edgar Allan Poe Award, which he received in 1974 for *Dance Hall of the Dead*. The Navajo Nation has elected him to their Special Friends of the Navajo Nation Society.

Some critics have wondered whether Hillerman has betrayed the Navajos by his detailed descriptions of rituals; but Hillerman points out that Navajos are willing to talk about most aspects of their culture with respectful outsiders. The taboo about revealing sacred things, he notes, is strictly a Pueblo trait.

Other critics have noted how Hillerman's work has bridged the gap between pop novel and literature. One critic wrote of *Skinwalkers* that Hillerman was creating "fiction of the highest caliber—tight, elegant writing, vivid characters, a hauntingly beautiful sense of place."[8] And about *Coyote Waits* (1990), the *Boston Globe* wrote, "The plot is tightly and elegantly constructed, the characters compelling, and the sense of place breathtaking."[9]

Major elements in such positive reviews are Hillerman's absolute familiarity with the Southwest and his believable characters, based on a keen ear for dialogue and gesture. With a reporter's resourcefulness, he draws his vivid details of daily life not only from Native American friends, but from the Window Rock telephone directory, his Navajo dictionary, books on Anasazi pottery, and encyclopedias of edible plants of the Rocky Mountain region. For accurate speech patterns, he reads the minutes of the Navajo Tribal Council meetings. As an

Oklahoma country boy, Hillerman says, he feels more comfortable sitting on a porch with a Navajo friend discussing sheep than conversing with college professors at an academic gathering.

Hillerman captures with equal precision the flowing formality of the Navajo language; the staccato rhythm of English spoken by those whose first language is Navajo; the clipped, jargon-filled speech of the professional FBI agent; and the soft rural drawl of characters like his white storekeeper, McGinnis.

As one critic noted, "Hillerman's characters are not just there to provide dialogue for a story that dances along. . . . Leaphorn and Chee each have a past they remember, a present they puzzle over, and a future they anticipate with mixed feelings."[10] The *New York Times Book Review* wrote that "the author continues to prove himself one of the nation's most convincing and authentic interpreters of Navajo culture, as well as one of our best and most innovative modern mystery writers."[11]

▲ ❖ ▼ ❖ ▼ ❖ ▲

One of the best places to interview a writer is, of course, his study. There the books lining the shelves provide constant, continuing inspiration. There one has a built-in guarantee of isolation from disturbance (else how would he ever finish his work?). Hillerman's study, ironically enough, was located on Texas Street in Albuquerque—ironic because, though Hillerman grew up not far from the Texas border, his work is ultimately New Mexican. New Mexico as a state has always looked with suspicion on its larger, well-heeled neighbor. Natives often quote an old saying: "Poor New Mexico. So far from God, so close to Texas."

In the forty years since Hillerman moved to New Mexico from Texas, many (but not all) of his works have concerned New Mexico: in his M.A. thesis on quirky incidents in the state's history, in tour guides for Fodor's, and on audio cassette.

As one might expect, his office is a colony of books, many authored by friends, especially those in a writers' circle he has favored for the last fifteen years, including Norm Zollinger, novelist, and Roger Zelazny, science fiction author.

Hillerman claims that he cannot forecast plots; yet in our in-

terview he drafted one spontaneously for what would become Thief of Time. *As he spoke, his office chair would squeak, particularly when he rocked forward in emphasis as he asked hard questions of his characters' motivations. His answers directed the book's dramatic action. Always, the reader's interest comes first. By keeping his sights on readers (recognizing the stiff competition for their attention from television) Hillerman, like Terry McMillan, crafts fast-reading popular literature which often ends up on the nation's best-seller lists despite his deliberately esoteric settings. The considerable authenticity of his Indian characters and locales has helped right a century of distorted and disrespectful portrayals.*

TONY HILLERMAN:

I've always been class-conscious. I've always identified with the underdog, the bottom of the social-economic spectrum, because those are the kind of people I grew up with. When I see the Navajo who are really impoverished, I just see my relatives, my family, my friends. You know, they're my kind of people.

From a relatively young age, I've always been interested in religions, plural—in people who allow a belief in the metaphysical to affect the way they live. That interests me, intrigues me. Well, among the southwestern Indian cultures you see that vividly. Makes it difficult for a Navajo to live off the reservation, affects the way Zunis behave, and so forth.

Leaphorn and Chee, both in their different ways, are loners. They're outsiders. They never really fully cooperate with the FBI, even though they're supposed to. They sort of look on the white man's law as all very well as long as it makes sense to them, and as long as it doesn't violate the much higher law which is the Navajo way of life.

Chee came along in my fourth novel. I had been troubled by the fact that I had made Joe Leaphorn too old, too sophisticated, too wise in the white man's ways to do what I wanted to do, which was to tell the story through the eyes of a young

Navajo—a very traditional Navajo who was still curious and amazed sometimes by the way of the white man.

I've never been able to outline a plot, and I've tried, because it seems common sense that you should outline a plot. The book I'm working on right now, for example [*Thief of Time*], it's going to concern a murder.

The murdered person will be an anthropologist who is going to be a woman. I might change it, but I think she's going to be a woman who's an authority on Anasazi pottery and is working at Chaco on a contract with the Park Service.

It's going to concern pot hunters, and the Southwest swarms with them, who make money on the side by looting unexcavated ruins, digging out the pots, and selling them. Now some of these pots are worth forty or fifty thousand dollars. I've got Sotheby catalogs here that are full of them.

In the second chapter, the victim has disappeared. The victim has also herself been accused of being a looter, a stealer of pots. So, my Navajo policeman, Leaphorn in this case, the older man, is going to be intrigued by a couple of incongruities that I'll introduce in the second chapter. I'm not exactly sure what they're going to be yet.

Everything's got to be logical. It's got to be reasonable. Would this woman do this? Does this make sense? Why wouldn't X simply pick up the phone and make a call instead of getting in her car and driving somewhere? I'm always testing it, what I'm doing against what I think would really happen under the circumstances.

By the time I finish the second chapter, which may be tomorrow if things go well, I will know where I have to go with the third chapter. Now that is a very unscientific way to write a mystery novel, but it's the only way I've ever been able to do it.

It seems to me that the world of fiction is alive and well. My eye is caught by a book called *New Hope for the Dead* by a Miami hard case named Charles Willeford who is writing Miami sociology in the form of the novel. He is grabbing you with a fascinating character and a fascinating story. The whole book is rich with the meaning of this polyglot Miami culture. I'm sure the *New York Review of Books* would drop dead before they would review it, because it's not one of the anointed elect writing it.

What I really mean is that to have an interesting novel, you have to have interesting people. Now a lot of people simply find it difficult to get interested in whining, self-indulgent, self-pitying, upper-middle-class white folks who want to write about the pain of being young and rich. It's hard to get intelligent people interested in that.

[Western writing?] It's a hard definition to get into. What is "regional" writing? Is everybody except New York writers "regional"? (laughs)

One western writer is the guy who writes about the mythic West. A good many great storytellers have done it. Then you have another kind of western writer, like Max Evans, who writes about the real West in books like *The Rounders*, about the cowboy of 1975. And then you have Leslie Silko, who writes *Ceremony*—a Laguna Indian who writes a mainstream novel which simply happens to be about Laguna Indians.

Then you've got Roger Zelazny, who's internationally known, who writes science fiction. He writes about the West, but in the twenty-third century.

The only thing that might tie [western writers] together is the landscape. High desert country. This area, where the air has finally risen up out of the heavy, wet air of the Gulf, and you're in clear air, and your altitude is high, and you have cool nights, and you can see a thousand miles.

The colors are gray, and blue, and red. It gives you these tremendous skyscapes which you don't have in the flatlands. These immense clouds which stir my spirit.

The landscape puts you in perspective—a very small human in a very large landscape. It's not a land on which you can easily make a living, where you could eat, where you could survive if you didn't have any help.

Whatever is out there when you're looking out your window in New Mexico, there's a lot of room, emptiness, a landscape not made to human scale—the empty space, the big sky, the beauty, the isolation, the golden eagles, the mountains way back over there.

EXCERPTS

Listening Woman

The thunderhead that promised a shower to Tuba Mesa in the morning had drifted eastward over the Painted Desert and evaporated—the promise unfulfilled. Now another, taller thunderhead had climbed the sky to the north—over the slopes of Navajo Mountain in Utah. The color under it was blue-black, suggesting that on one small quadrant of mountainside the blessed rain was falling. . . . The Hopis had held a rain dance Sunday, calling on the clouds—their ancestors—to restore the water blessing to the land. Perhaps the kachinas had listened to their Hopi children. Perhaps not. It was not a Navajo concept, this idea of adjusting nature to human needs. The Navajo adjusted himself to remain in harmony with the universe. When nature withheld the rain, the Navajo sought the pattern of this phenomenon—as he sought the pattern of all things—to find its beauty and live in harmony with it.

Now Leaphorn sought the pattern in the conduct of a man who had tried to kill a policeman rather than accept a speeding ticket. . . .

Leaphorn got up and stretched. He thanked McGinnis for the hospitality and said he would go to the sing. He used the Navajo verb *hodeeshtal*, which means "to take part in a ritual chant." By slightly changing the guttural inflection, the word becomes the verb "to be kicked." As Leaphorn pronounced it, a listener with an ear alert to the endless Navajo punning could have understood Leaphorn to mean either that he was going to get himself cured or get himself kicked. It was among the oldest of old Navajo word plays, and McGinnis—grinning slightly—replied with the expected pun response.

"Good for a sore butt," he said.

Talking God

Talking god and his retinue were close now and High-hawk was no longer singing. He held something in his right hand. Something metallic. A tape recorder. *Hataalii* rarely gave permission for taping. Chee wondered what he should do. This would be a terrible time to create a disturbance. He decided to let it ride. He hadn't been sent here to enforce ceremonial rules, and he was in no mood to be a policeman.

The hooting call of the Yeibichai projected Chee's imagination back into the myth that this ceremony reenacted. It was the tale of a crippled boy and his compact with the gods. This was how it might have been in those mythic times, Chee thought. The firelight, the hypnotic sound of the bells and pot drum, the shadows of the dancers moving rhythmically against the pink sandstone of the mesa walls behind the hogan.

Now there was a new smell in the air, mixing with the perfume of the burning piñon and dust. It was the smell of dampness, of impending snow. And as he noticed it, a flurry of tiny snowflakes appeared between him and the fire, and as quickly disappeared. He glanced at Henry Highhawk to see how the grave robber was taking this.

Highhawk was gone.

The Dark Wind

"Somebody lost a boot," he said.

Even from where he stood, at least fifteen yards further down the trail, Albert Lomatewa could see that nobody had lost the boot. The boot had been placed, not dropped. It rested upright, squarely in the middle of the path, its pointed toe aimed toward them. Obviously someone had put it there. And now just beyond a dead growth of rabbit brush which crowded the trail, Lomatewa saw the top of a second boot. Yesterday when he had come this way, no boots had been there.

"Stay away from it," Lomatewa said. "Stay right here. . . ."

Beyond the second boot, the path curved sharply around a weathered granite boulder. Lomatewa sucked in his breath. Jutting from behind the boulder he could see the bottom of a foot. The foot was bare, and even from where Lomatewa stood he could see that there was something terribly wrong with it. . . .

He turned and walked back to where his guardians were waiting.

"A dead Tavasuh," he said. Literally the word meant "head pounder." It was a term of contempt which Hopis sometimes used for Navajos and Lomatewa chose it deliberately to set the tone for what he must do.

NOTES

1. *Encyclopedia of Frontier and Western Fiction* (New York: McGraw-Hill, 1983), p. 160.

2. *Saturday Review*, March 28, 1970, p. 40.

3. W. H. Farrington, *Library Journal*, May 15, 1970, p. 1860.

4. Newgate Callendar, *New York Times Book Review*, Nov. 7, 1971, p. 26.

5. *New Yorker*, Sept. 25, 1971, p. 142.

6. *The Joe Leaphorn Mysteries: Listening Woman* (New York: Random House/Wing Books, 1989), p. 402.

7. *Skinwalkers* (New York: Harper & Row, 1988), p. 63.

8. Jonathan Kellerman, back cover, *Skinwalkers*.

9. Martin Nolan, *Boston Globe*, July 8, 1990, p. 73.

10. Mitch Finley, *Christian Science Monitor*, July 11, 1990, p. 13.

11. Robert Gish, *New York Times Book Review*, June 24, 1990, p. 12.

LINDA HOGAN

▲ ❖ ▼ ❖ ▼ ❖ ▲

Like Joy Harjo, Chickasaw writer Linda Hogan weaves together the beautiful and the terrible. Her poetry and fiction grapple with the reality of mixed blood so common in the cultural polyglot of the Southwest, and with the tragic history of Native Americans and the loss of their lands.

The landscape, animal spirits, bat medicine, and traditional tribal cultures compete in Hogan's writing with the technological onslaught of the twentieth century. Her bittersweet realizations about her mixed heritage echo in the works of Hispanic writers such as Alberto Rios and Denise Chavez.

> In my left pocket a Chickasaw hand
> rests on the bone of the pelvis.
> In my right pocket
> a white hand. Don't worry. It's mine
> and not some thief's.
> It belongs to a woman who sleeps in a twin bed
> even though she falls in love too easily,
> and walks along with hands
> in her own empty pockets
> even though she has put them in others
> for love not money.
>
> —LINDA HOGAN[1]

Of Linda Hogan's first novel, *Mean Spirit* (1990), *Newsday* wrote, "Extraordinary. . . . If you take up no other novel this year, or next, this one will suffice to hold, to disturb, to enlighten and to inspire you."[2] The unnerving juxtaposition of the disturbing and the inspirational characterizes all of Hogan's poetry and prose. The result has been called everything from modern, post-tribal literature to North American magic realism, but always it is haunting and mesmerizing.

Hogan was born in Denver, Colorado, on July 16, 1947, and her childhood was a mix of Chickasaw traditions (passed on through her father and uncle) and the transitory homelessness typical for military families. She attended schools in Oklahoma, Colorado, and in Germany, where her father was stationed. She graduated from high school in Colorado Springs in 1965. The struggle to straddle these varying worlds successfully, and to come to grips with an ancestry both Indian and white, informs Hogan's work.

Much of her childhood was spent shuttling between Colorado, where her favorite uncle, Wesley, was one of the founders of the Indian mutual-aid society, the White Buffalo Council, and Oklahoma, where the rest of her relatives and most of the Chickasaw still live. The history of the Chickasaw ties Hogan to the rich grasslands of the red dirt hill country where Hogan's tribe was forcibly resettled. Exiled from their traditional homelands in Alabama and Georgia by the Trail of Tears (with Cherokee, Creek, and other southeastern tribes), the Chickasaw's legacy demonstrates the amazing resilience of a people who managed to find the sacred in the strange, rolling plains of the West.

For most of the transplanted tribes, however, times were hard in Oklahoma. Despite receiving allotments of land from the government, the Chickasaw today are virtually a landless tribe. Many lost their allotments to swindlers during the oil boom years of the 1920s, when whites would often marry into the tribe in order to gain possession of oil-rich Indian lands. Hogan says there is some evidence that her great-grandfather may have done exactly that. Her father's family managed to hold on to a final remnant of their allotment, farming and raising cattle, until the dust bowl days of the Great Depression finally forced Hogan's grandfather to give up the last of their land and cattle.

Hogan's connection to the earth, and to animals as both

physical and spiritual beings, comes in part from her family and in part from the traditions of the Chickasaw, who acknowledge a firm spiritual connection between humans and animals, and between women and turtles in particular. Her father kept pet turtles even while in the military; and her grandmother had a giant tortoise with whom, Hogan says with a smile, "she communicated. We were sort of a turtle family." One of her most famous poems, from her 1978 collection *Calling Myself Home*, is entitled "Turtle" and was inspired by the large snapping turtle that lived in a "tanque" (an old French spelling still common in rural Oklahoma for a word meaning water hole or pond) at her grandmother's farmhouse. The animal was a powerful spiritual presence; she felt "the pupil in the eye of the water."

Her grandmother's Oklahoma farmhouse centered Hogan's childhood. Her grandmother raised chickens, her grandfather was a wild bronc rider, her father trained horses part-time, and one uncle is a farrier. The abundant animal life and the reverence it inspired among her elders are a continual strand in the web of Hogan's writing. Along with the horses, chickens, and turtles that meant home, Hogan's work buzzes with insects, birds, snakes, bats, and the variety of animals to be found roaming the backwoods and fields of rural Oklahoma.

The merger of animal spirits and oral literature began on the back porch and parlor of her grandmother's farmhouse. It was there that young Linda nightly listened to jokes, songs, and tall tales under the clear, bright southwestern sky. The important community activity of visiting neighbors in the isolated rural hill country often meant sitting by the stove or on the porch of an evening and swapping tales.

Hogan's grandmother was the powerful female center of the family circle. At the Chickasaw girls' school, from which she graduated in 1904, one of the necessary refinements of girls was the mastery of music. Hogan's grandmother played the piano and the violin, veering effortlessly from classical music to ragtime, country fiddle, and gospel depending on her audience. She gave music lessons to supplement what she earned from her chickens. The piano was a favorite family gathering place, though Hogan laughingly claims not to have inherited any of her grandmother's musical talent despite a brief foray with the clarinet in her high school marching band.

What she did inherit was her grandmother's, father's, and uncle's gift for storytelling and love of language. "We are metaphor-thinking people in my family," she recalls. She would be so overwhelmed with the back-porch tales that she would hide in the bathroom and write down what everybody would be saying. "These stories were incredible, and I didn't want them to be lost."

The stories did not all have happy endings. Many passed on the dark history of the Chickasaw people and the more recent tragedy of loss, often via outright theft, of the pitiable allotments of land left to those survivors of the Trail of Tears who arrived finally in Oklahoma. Her father's family, like many Chickasaw, lost their allotment through bank foreclosures and shady land deals during the Great Depression. That land is today the site of the Ardmore Airport. "I remember when my father would describe what was there. We'd be looking at this paved-over land where some of my relatives were working as janitors. My father would be telling me, 'This is where the pasture was, and this was the lake. . . .' " What the banks didn't get was often swindled away during the frenzied oil-rush years that rocked Oklahoma and Texas.

Part of her need to bear witness to this tragic history was nurtured by her uncle Wesley's organizing projects in Native American communities in Colorado. Not only was he a founder of the still-active White Buffalo Council, which helped Indian people find housing and work in Denver, he regularly took young Linda to powwows. He made sure she knew she was part of a larger Indian community. At these powwows she first encountered the amazing variety (and vitality) of the North American tribes. She recalls being mesmerized by the keening, high-pitched singing of the northern plains peoples, so different from the softer songs of the southern Indians.

She also became sensitized to her mixed ancestry and to the complexity of racial issues within the Native world. The Chickasaw have a long tradition of mixing both with other tribes and with whites, dating back to prerevolutionary times; however, the results of these crossings have not always been peaceful. Hogan's grandmother was disowned for marrying a very dark-skinned Chickasaw man by her great-grandfather—the same man, according to family legend, who married a Chickasaw woman and became part of the tribe in order to grab Indian lands. This white great-grandfather had hoped that his daughter would marry "up" to a lighter-skinned Indian, or even a white man.

As for herself, Hogan admits having felt pressured among other Native Americans to prove herself an Indian in compensation for her light skin. She feels equally uncomfortable when whites assume that because she is not a pure-blooded Native American, she is somehow more like them than darker-skinned peoples. "There are differences within [Native American] communities that are sometimes really hard for people to deal with. In terms of blood quantums—and I hate that term, that Bureau of Indian Affairs term—there are trust issues involved, and fear. We have fear of each other. We have fear that we're not going to do the right thing. We have fear that what we do is going to result in more destruction, in more disintegration in our [Indian] communities."

Hogan does not see Indian culture as either destroyed or frozen in time. Rather, for her, it is dynamically evolving; and the Chickasaw's history of mixing makes them an apt example of that growth. "There's this ability to take in a great variety of different materials. There's nothing that's virginal, that's strict [so that] in one area you could say 'this is Chickasaw' and nothing else can come in. One time I saw a man wearing a southern plains headdress at a powwow. Someone told him that he was a Chickasaw man and that was not his traditional thing to wear, and he said, 'Well, I'm a Chickasaw, and I'm wearing it, and I guess that makes it Chickasaw!' "

This hybridization is not confined to Chickasaw culture, Hogan is quick to point out. Evolution and adaptation occur throughout Native America. She points to the northern Chippewa jingle dresses, the skirts of which are decorated with tiny bells fashioned from the tin lids of snuff cans (a tradition itself recent to the northern tribes), which she first observed in Minnesota. On her return to Colorado, three years later, the women dancers there were wearing jingle dresses, which have now become popular as far south as Oklahoma.

Hogan began writing in her early thirties, and attended a variety of community colleges as an older student, working as a waitress, secretary, nurse's aide, and library clerk, before receiving her M.A. in 1978 in creative writing from the University of Colorado, where she is currently a professor. Her first collection of poetry, *Calling Myself Home* (1978), was allegorical and autobiographical—a map of an internal journey back to her past. For many Indian people, the search for one's self begins with the return home, she says; while for Anglos the search to find identity often means leaving home.

cf. Animal Dreams.

Hogan has been a prolific poet. *Calling Myself Home* was followed by *Daughters, I Love You* (1981) (dedicated to her two adopted daughters, Tanya Thunder Horse and Sandra Dawn Protector, both full-blooded Oglala Lakota) and *Eclipse* (1983). Native American scholar Kenneth Lincoln writes of *Eclipse*, "Hogan crafts phrases of common speech and weaves the lines in natural idioms. . . . Her poems offer a careful voicing of common things not yet understood, necessary to survival. . . ."[3]

Two years later her fourth collection of poetry, *Seeing through the Sun* (1985), won the Before Columbus Foundation Book Award. Critic Robert Berner in *World Literature Today* wrote of Hogan's 1988 collection, *Savings*, "Her poems reveal a profound sense of the price we pay for alienating ourselves from our origins in the natural world. . . . Linda Hogan is a major poet of her generation."[4]

Honors started coming her way. She won a grant from the National Endowment for the Arts and the Minnesota State Arts Board to spend three years in Minneapolis teaching at the University of Minnesota and volunteering at one of her favorite pet projects, a wildlife rescue clinic specializing in raptor rehabilitation, work which she continues in Colorado.

In 1990, Hogan published her first novel, *Mean Spirit*. Selected by the Literary Guild, it is a haunting story of the disintegration of Oklahoma's Osage tribe as their world is torn apart by the frenzied search for oil on Indian land in the boom years of the 1920s. Based on an actual series of murders of Native Americans in Oklahoma during that time, *Mean Spirit* examines the tragedy through the lives of two Osage families, beginning with the deliberately unsolved killing of an oil-rich Indian woman named Grace Blanket.

White men determined to possess the wealth of oil began marrying Indian women to become the legal owners of their allotments; if the women refused to marry, false marriage certificates were filed and the women, like Grace Blanket, would then die in mysterious accidents, their lands passing legally to the hands of their "husbands." The plots grew to include the secret purchase of life insurance policies on Native Americans with land, and forged wills. The allotments of all the victims passed to white developers, and the FBI was eventually called to investigate a conspiracy which extended from the sheriff's department to the governor's office. All but one of the murders chronicled in *Mean Spirit* actually occurred.

Hogan explores not only the brutal racism which prompted such cold and calculated killings, but also the divisions which erupted within the tribal communities: between full- and mixed-bloods; between traditionalists desperate to preserve the old ways and younger Indians who believed the only way to survive was to modernize; and between those who trusted their white friends and neighbors, refusing to believe the killings could be the result of a conspiracy, and those who wished to end all contact with whites.

The bitterness and sense of betrayal from those dark days live on in Hogan's work. She acknowledges, "I carry the history, and a lot of it is because of the telling of stories—the telling of history [that's] been passed down to me. I've carried my father's anger and frustration from the things that he experienced. . . . I carry them as if they were my own. And that was the driving force behind *Mean Spirit*—the need to speak this story and to, in some way, bear witness to what I know."

The *Los Angeles Times Book Review* saw in *Mean Spirit* "North American magic realism: in the same way Gabriel García Márquez and Isabel Allende examine their political history with a conjurer's eye, Linda Hogan has wrapped wonder and magic around some brutal American truths. . . . She carves a vast tragedy down to a size and shape that will fit into a human heart."[5]

Throughout the novel, her prose borrows the rhythms of her poetry, spare and powerful, combining the frightening with the lyrical. Hogan herself acknowledges her debt to modern poets and writers, from Kenneth Rexroth to Audre Lord, and especially to Chippewa author Louise Erdrich, whose experimentation with voice, storytelling, and the novelistic form in *Love Medicine* inspired Hogan to venture out from poetry into commercial fiction.

In 1991, Hogan published another collection of poetry and short fiction entitled *Red Clay*. "Half of this collection is prose," noted one critic, "woven together with history both personal and tribal. Like the poems, these stories burn with emotion and a great sense of truth. . . . This book will be appreciated beyond the usual number of poetry/essay readers. Highly recommended."[6]

By the mid-1990s, Hogan's work had won the recognition many writers dream of: fellowships from the National Endowment for the Arts and the Guggenheim Foundation, a full professorship at the University of Colorado. In 1993, she published a collection of poetry, *The Book of Medicines*; in 1995, two titles of hers appeared: *Solar Storms* (a novel, Scribner's) and *Dwellings* (essays, W. W. Norton).

▲ ✧ ▼ ✧ ▼ ✧ ▲

Linda Hogan was interviewed at the threadbare studios of KGNU-FM in Boulder, Colorado. Barbara Kingsolver was also interviewed there that day. The pair of writers met in the hallway: both women were in their forties, on book tours, and at the height (so far) of their careers.

Hogan was just finishing interviews about her first novel, Mean Spirit; *she had the road-weary writer's slump, from being asked to explain too often why she wrote her book. (At times, such questions seem to call for the author not only to explain her work but to justify it, a task some find tiresome.) By contrast, her talk with "Writing the Southwest" focused on her earlier poetic works, chapbooks written a decade earlier, some of which were, by this point, near strangers to her. Despite occasional hoarseness, she read through these poems—many of which take up the theme of mixed-blood identity.*

To the casual eye, Linda Hogan's Chickasaw ancestry might not reveal itself. A woman of medium height, with short auburn hair and a creamy complexion, she could pass for Caucasian—until she reads her work. In even cadences, in a surprisingly hushed voice, her poems evoke a world of animal spirits and shamanism. One quickly hears the passion for nonhuman species that led Hogan to work at an animal shelter for injured wild birds and support environmental action groups.

Moving to a discussion of Mean Spirit *and the tragic expropriation of her Chickasaw tribe's lands, Hogan's voice rings with anger—but also with compassion. She wonders aloud about the dark greed that caused outsiders to marry Native American women only to collect insurance and land upon their deaths. Her preoccupation with Indian history was somehow that of the zoologist, puzzled by the foibles of the species. For her, writing is a kind of caretaking activity, similar to defending the habitat of animals from human encroachment.*

LINDA HOGAN:

People always think of Oklahoma as the dust bowl, but it's really a very rich land. It's a very beautiful, and in comparison to the other places I've lived, a strange and almost surrealistic landscape. The colors are intense. I'm sure there's a scientific reason for it, you know—why, when the sun sets, the light is so red for so long and the way it lays across the land.

I do think there's tension between urban and rural Indian people, and I think a lot of it comes from different needs and from the different experience of living in an urban environment versus the rural environment. A lot of times it's very frustrating for reservation people when relatives come from the city who have not had the same kind of experiences and want to be traditional, want to be a certain kind of person that they are not.

And one of the hardest things for us in the city is dealing with the stereotypes about ourselves. How do we identify who we really are? And feel good about our Indianness? I think more than other minority groups, our stereotypes are very confining for Indian people.

If you read some of the people that are not Indian people,

like Lynn Andrews and Carlos Castaneda, you would think that everyone spends all day thinking about the sacred in everything they touch and everything they do. Which is really not the case, because many people are so hurt and so broken that just getting through a day, getting enough food for your family is an issue. As in *Mean Spirit*, where the young men want the sacred so much that they kill an eagle [for] the sacred eagle feathers. . . . They do not understand that the living eagle is more sacred than the feathers. There is a split in the search for spirituality that takes place in ways that are somehow dissociated from spirituality.

For people in my generation, we've been through this, and the thing is, how do you keep going? How do you plod on? How do you continue to do your work with the smallest amount of despair possible?

I know when a poem is working [when] I feel it physically. When it's ready, a line will come . . . and the hair will stand up on the back of my neck. Fiction is a different kind of thinking. It's more linear. A poem is like weaving—you get inside and you resonate with it. With a story, there has to be movement that goes outward and goes on. There's no way I could have told the story [of *Mean Spirit*] in poems.

[*Mean Spirit*] is set in the 1920s in Oklahoma. It's based on Osage history, although I've changed some of the history for fictional purposes. The novel begins with the murder of one of the most oil-rich Indian women in the area—Grace Blanket. . . . All the murders that take place in the novel, except one, are true-to-life, real murders. I did quite a bit of research on the legal history of what had taken place there. The murders actually began in 1918. They were originally the murders of American Indian women who had oil. They were killed by non-Indian men who went in, many of them, with the intention of marrying an Indian woman and somehow getting rid of her so that they would inherit the land, according to the United States law. Some of them stayed around long enough to have children as well, so they could inherit their children's allotment lands. But as the conspiracy grew, it also became a life insurance conspiracy where people would buy a life insurance policy on another person who could not pay them but who owed them money, and then they would have that person murdered.

One of the main characters, Stace Redhawk, was actually based on an Indian FBI agent from Pine Ridge, South Dakota, who went in posing as a medicine man to investigate. At that time there were more FBI agents in that one area in Oklahoma than had ever been in the entire state of New York. . . . But the attitude was—and has always been—that the Indian people there were somehow in the way of progress and were disposable. There really wasn't a lot of guilt or remorse.

On my good days I think that poetry is an act of caretaking for me. On bad days, I think it's probably a very useless activity. But I live to do it, and I could be doing something much worse with my life. I think it's a little dishonest for me to think that in the 1990s poetry can change the world. I do think it changes people's minds, and I do think it changes people's hearts.

EXCERPTS

Calling Myself Home

"Heritage"

From my mother, the antique mirror
where I watch my face take on her lines.
She left me the smell of baking bread
to warm fine hairs in my nostrils,
she left the large white breasts that weigh down
my body.

From my father I take his brown eyes,
the plague of locusts that leveled our crops,
they flew in formation like buzzards.

From my uncle the whittled wood
that rattles like bones
and is white

Juxtaposition of nurturing and destructive imagery.

Not a consistent heritage.

simile — negative or positive.

and smells like all our old houses
that are no longer there. He was the man
who sang old chants to me, the words
my father was told not to remember.

receives forbidden knowledge

From my grandfather who never spoke
I learned to fear silence.
I learned to kill a snake
when begging for rain.

ironic

three negative actions

hardship, poverty, harsh environment.

Stanza begins "then goes "blue," to "brown" and to "black."

And grandmother, blue eyed woman
whose skin was brown,
she used snuff.
When her coffee can full of black saliva
spilled on me
it was like the brown cloud of grasshoppers
that leveled her fields.
It was the brown stain
that covered my white shirt.
That sweet black liquid like the food
she chewed up and spit into my father's mouth
when he was an infant.
It was the brown earth of Oklahoma
stained with oil.
She said tobacco would purge your body of poisons.
It has more medicine than stones and knives
against your enemies.
That tobacco is the dark night that covers me.

leaves out "from"

Why does she get the most space?

simile — recalls 2nd stanza

tactile imagery recalls memories, "covers" her, "colors" her.

recalls the white breast image — She is colored by her heritage.

— odd simile, comparing tobacco to food.

metaphor

metaphor

She said it is wise to eat the flesh of deer
so you will be swift and travel over many miles.
She told me how our tribe has always followed a stick
that pointed west
that pointed east.
From my family I have learned the secrets
of never having a home.

— need to travel, escape?

?

has memories instead, stories, oral heritage

nourishment/food: bread, crops, food, eat the flesh of deer.

— memories are tactile, sensory.

— Heritage is mental, is a way of understanding the world. It's conflicted and contradictory.

Daughters, I Love You

"Blessing the Children"

Blue curves of our ears
are filled with a bird
moving branches.
The smell of pine and water,
touch of light on skin
taste of air and bread.

Children, the wind in leaves
feeds fire
gives you dreams
and words
to move your lives.

Rain comes down.
Light. Odor of pine.

I make tobacco prayers for you
woven along a string.
I sweat. The third time
light came in
a spider sat before me.
It blessed
these children and us.
I thought I heard it speak
and its voice was the clean wind.

Returning home
a doe and fawn
cradled in black leaves.
Look, little ones
all the places are holy.
Everything blesses us.

[Handwritten annotations:]

who is audience?
where are they?
Who is "our"?

why blue? Cold day?

open vowel sounds reflect "open" ears

how can ears be filled with an image? Yet, they are also filled with the other senses — all but hearing. Thus, nature speaks to us.

lack of punctuation merges the senses.

Addressed to children again, lack of punct, emphasizes unity

action

nature (wind) is nourishing and generous, stimulating the imagination which can promote action.

positive connotations

consonance

Very short stanza. Crystalizes these images. Each is separate. Each is clean.

both description of hard hand its raining, and of the light

children

animal speaks (like the wind above.) Nature is personified.

could be these or kids returning home.

addresses the children again.

good connotations

image of mother/child echoes relationship of speaker/audience

connects children & us.

goes from specifics (wind, trees, deer) to the general. Thus teaches children how to understand

Addressed to children. Has a magical, vivid, inventive quality that might hold kids' attention

☆ Poem's language is simple.

Mean Spirit

In Watona that autumn the temperature dropped only by a few degrees. The leaves that had not been eaten away by hungry bag worms turned red. There was a hint of fall in the air, a slight odor of decay, but the hot weather had not broken. . . .

Up the road from Grace's sunburned roses, was an enormous crater the gas well blowout had made in the earth. It was fifty feet deep and five hundred feet across. This gouge in the earth, just a year earlier, had swallowed five workmen and ten mules. The water was gone from that land forever; the trees dead, and the grass, once long and rich, was burned black. . . . These bruised fields were noisy and dark. The earth had turned oily black. Blue flames rose up and roared like torches of burning gas. The earth bled oil. . . .

That night, after the men who buried John Stink went to their beds tossing and turning . . . the mongrel dogs at the gravesite whined and pawed away at the earth. One dog scratched a hole in the ground. Another pushed a stone away from the mound, and from inside the grave, John Stink felt the rock thump earth. He began to work his arms out of the ropes that held him . . . he moved earth, until finally one of his hands found its way through to air where it was licked by the happy dogs.

The dogs were the only witnesses to the miraculous return of John Stink. They were overjoyed that their master rose up from the grave, and when the old man's pockmarked face emerged, they yapped and licked him, and with their aid, Stink managed to pull himself out of the coffin. . . . He examined himself. His hands were raw, the thick nails broken. He was dressed like a ghost, all right, in a winding sheet.

He examined the opening he climbed through. It was, indeed, too small for the emergence of a mortal man. He sat on the ground in the midst of his dogs and tried to remember what had happened. . . .

So this is what death was like, he thought, as he wrapped the white sheet tighter around his naked body. Out of habit more than anything else, he started out for his home up on Mare Hill above the golf course.

The dogs, who couldn't tell the difference between ghosts and mortals, wagged their tails and followed Stink home. He was surprised that he still wanted a cigar.

N O T E S

1. "The Truth Is," *Seeing Through the Sun* (Amherst: University of Massachusetts Press, 1985), p. 4.

2. *Newsday*, back cover, *Mean Spirit* (New York: Ballantine, 1990).

3. Kenneth Lincoln, introduction to *Eclipse* (Los Angeles: University of California American Indian Studies Center, 1983), p. vi.

4. *World Literature Today*, Autumn 1989, p. 723.

5. Barbara Kingsolver, *Los Angeles Times Book Review*, Nov. 4, 1990, p. 3.

6. Louis McKee, *Library Journal*, March 1, 1992, p. 91.

BARBARA KINGSOLVER

▲ ❖ ▼ ❖ ▼ ❖ ▲

Kentucky native Barbara Kingsolver, like John Nichols and Edward Abbey, has become inextricably linked to outsiders' perceptions of the Southwest. Yet in the tradition of Joy Harjo and Linda Hogan, Kingsolver's work bridges gaps between divergent communities: East and West, rural and urban, Native American, Anglo, and Hispanic. And like African-American novelist Terry McMillan, she is committed to illuminating the lives of the oppressed and the silenced, particularly working-class women.

Drawing on both the southern literary renaissance and the stark beauty of the Arizona desert, Kingsolver weaves together these apparently unrelated forces. As desperate and wrenching as the lives of many of her characters are, Kingsolver's vision is always one of hope and ultimately redemption, through the power of individuals, families, and communities.

We crossed the Arizona state line at sunup. The clouds were pink and fat and hilarious-looking, like the hippo ballerinas in a Disney movie. The road took us through a place called Texas Canyon that looked nothing like Texas, heaven be praised for that, but looked like nothing else I had ever seen either. Rocks stacked on top of one another like piles of copulating potato bugs. Wherever the sun hit them, they turned pink. The whole scene looked too goofy to be real. We whizzed by a roadside sign on which I could make out a dinosaur. I wondered if it told what kind of rocks they were, or if it was saying that they were actually petrified dinosaur

*turds. I was laughing my head off. "This is too much," I said
to the Indian child. "This is the best thing I've seen in years."
Whether my car conked out or not, I made up my mind to
live in Arizona.*

—Barbara Kingsolver[1]

Barbara Kingsolver burst onto the American literary scene
in 1988 with a first novel, *The Bean Trees*, described by one
critic as "an astonishing literary debut."[2] Rumors about her
personal life circulated. Some assumed she was Native American,
the persona she sardonically calls "Soaring Barbara"; others
thought that she had lived all her life in the Southwest.

Kingsolver was born in 1955 in the naval hospital at Annapolis,
Maryland, but grew up in the small town of Carlisle, in
rural eastern Kentucky. Her father, a physician born and raised
in this region, turned his back on the money to be made in
large metropolitan hospitals. Instead, he returned to his rural
roots, becoming a farmer and general practitioner in a county
where few people could afford to pay him. As a result, Kingsolver
recalls, she and her brother and sister often wore hand-
me-downs, a source of ridicule during her high school years.

The homey flavor of farm life and the small, stark tragedies
of small-town America are often combined in Kingsolver's work
even in urban settings—gardens flourish in tiny backyard plots
in tight-knit communities afloat like islands in a sea of concrete.
Kingsolver's novels are alive with plants, plant imagery, and
animals of all sorts. "Living in the middle of an alfalfa field was
an important influence," she laughs. "I grew up noticing where
things come from and where they go—in the sense of seed and
compost rather than heaven and hell. I think the whole way I
look at the world was formed on a farm."

Her hard-eyed pragmatism about those living on the edge
of poverty—whether in Carlisle, Kentucky, or Tucson, Arizona—is
woven through her books, as is a love for the arts.
Music, which Kingsolver saw as her ticket out of rural Kentucky
life, surrounded her as a child. Tiny, isolated Carlisle was
too far from any major city to receive many radio broadcasts,
but the musical tastes of Kingsolver's parents ranged freely
from Debussy and Ravel to the Weavers and Pete Seeger. Be-

cause television was outlawed in their home, she spent hours lying on the living room floor listening to records as her father challenged her to describe what the music made her think of.

This early love of music continued as she attended DePauw University in Indiana on a music scholarship, studying classical piano. Kingsolver recalls, "I studied music there for a couple of years and realized eventually that the job opportunities for classical pianists were limited. Maybe eleven per year could get a job in the United States and all the rest of us would end up playing 'The Shadow of Your Smile' in a hotel lobby somewhere. I decided that really wasn't where I was headed."

She changed her major to a more practical one in evolutionary biology, but her college years influenced her in ways other than her choice of careers. She remembers her shock at being ridiculed for her Kentucky accent, and how she scrambled to make up for what she saw as her shameful lack of acquaintance with popular culture, what everyone else seemed to have learned from television and radio. "In Indiana, that hotbed of cosmopolitanism, everyone thought I 'just talked so funny.' Complete strangers would stop me on the sidewalk and ask me to pronounce 'hair' and 'all.'"

Kingsolver was far from alone. As Bobbie Ann Mason told the *New Yorker* recently, "Like many Kentuckians who leave the South, I have experienced the shame these images impose on us. They make you deny your language and your story and accept as authority others' view of you. In the Sixties, when I moved to the Northeast after college, I met people who made me feel that my accent was uncouth, my tastes deplorable, my political and cultural opinions naive."[3]

Kingsolver's family was atypical of rural Kentucky, where most of the children she went to school with "knew exactly where they were headed—towards pregnancy or farming, depending on gender." Her parents urged her to read, to excel at school, and more importantly, to write.

"I'd been keeping a journal since I was eight, and writing was always the thing I used to mark the time and make sure it didn't slip by me unnoticed. But it never crossed my mind that I'd be a writer when I grew up, because I didn't really think of writing as a profession. I didn't think of books as having been written by people like me, or even people unlike me. I just knew books were these wonderful, disembodied things that somehow arrived in my hands by way of the bookmobile."

After her B.S. in ecology, she lived in Europe, struggling from job to job with no particular goal in mind. Eventually, she ran into trouble renewing her work visa and decided on a whim, in 1977, to return to the United States and live in the Southwest—for no reason, she claims, other than that she had never been there.

She enrolled at the University of Arizona in Tucson. After finishing her M.A. there, she was hired by the university as a scientific writer. Although the subject matter was somewhat dry—algae production in sewage plants and growth rates of bacteria—her first writing job provided the opportunity to polish her skills; she also developed the habit of writing every day, whether she felt like it or not. This experience, she believes, was the solid foundation upon which she became a professional author, able to make a living, as only a handful of writers in the United States can, producing poetry, short stories, and novels.

Kingsolver began writing short stories around 1983, although she claims she never had any real intention of publishing them. She traces the creation of these early stories to the influence of the great short story writers of the Southern Renaissance, Flannery O'Connor and Eudora Welty; and indeed, the quirky, odd, yet realistic characters Kingsolver creates reflect the works of these women. "They taught me about telling a story, and telling the darkest, most awful truths with a punch line. You can't forget to laugh, ever, because if you do, then you'll just curl up and die."

Another strong influence on Kingsolver's fiction is the work of Doris Lessing, whom Kingsolver admires for writing about "the color bar and the gender bar." The writing of women, and women's ways of perceiving the world, has deeply informed her work. She says, "In high school, I learned that there are three great themes in literature: man against man; man against nature; and man against himself. So it was all 'man' and it was all 'against'; and yet so much of my life has no 'against' in it. It's mostly 'with.' I'm usually figuring out how I can get something done with the help of somebody else, and that is not one of the great themes of literature. I know that because it wasn't on the blackboard in Miss Harney's class. I thought you could only write stories about men killing whales or going fishing all by themselves.

"But Doris Lessing wrote about women whose goals in life were not to escape from connectedness with humanity but to become connected, and to find a way not to lose themselves at the same time. I think that's what a lot of women write about—connectedness instead of againstness."

During the 1970s, Kingsolver's friends urged her to circulate her work. It seemed like the logical next step, and she soon had a short story, "Johnny Rose," accepted by the prestigious *Virginia Quarterly Review*. Even more surprising, Kingsolver says, they sent her a check. Now she felt she was a writer.

She began publishing articles in a number of scientific journals and magazines, including the *Smithsonian*. In 1983, as a stringer for the *Tucson Weekly*, she covered the bitter and sometimes violent Phelps-Dodge copper-mining strike in southern Arizona. She soon became obsessed by the strike.

Union locals at five mines had banded together to strike Phelps-Dodge (one of Arizona's largest mining companies), not for higher wages but for safety in the mines and for medical care for the miners' families. Phelps-Dodge Copper vowed to break the unions, no matter what the cost. The isolated company towns in southern Arizona, because of their economic dependence upon the mines, represented the weakest links in the union chain.

Within two weeks of the beginning of the strike, Phelps-Dodge had obtained an injunction against the miners, making it illegal for them to form a picket line. It was a devastating blow to the miners because, Kingsolver explains, "If you can't hold the line, the strike is broken." At this point, however, something happened that neither the unions nor Phelps-Dodge had anticipated. The wives of the miners—traditional Hispanic women who had told Kingsolver that they didn't even leave their houses without their husbands' permission—re-formed the picket line themselves.

For two long years, these self-proclaimed housewives "held the line" in a drama straight out of the pages of Zola's *Germinal*. Because there was little other work in the mining communities outside of Phelps-Dodge, the men were forced to travel to other towns, often to other parts of the state, to find jobs. Their wives continued to defy not only Phelps-Dodge and its replacement workers, but the governor of Arizona, the National Guard, the Guard's Huey helicopters, even tear gas assaults.

The profound growth she witnessed in these women inspired *Holding the Line* (1989), which remains one of her favorite books. After six months, a Phelps-Dodge officer made his now famous remark, "If we could just get rid of these broads, we'd have it made."

"But they couldn't get rid of the broads," Kingsolver says. "These women had suddenly discovered what they were put on this earth to do, and that was to scream obscenities at officers of the law on the picket line, and, incidentally, to keep their towns and their communities intact and alive."

Over the course of two years, Kingsolver returned every week or two to interview the same seventy women. "And by the end of that strike, you can believe they were not asking their husbands' permission to leave the house anymore. Their husbands were ironing their own shirts." The whole scenario was straight out of the film of the New Mexico mine strike, *Salt of the Earth*.

Phelps-Dodge eventually succeeded in breaking the unions. The replacement workers, eligible to vote on representation after one year of employment, voted the union out of Phelps-Dodge. By this time, however, the company had lost so much money fighting the strike that it was forced to close many of the mines. But the women would never look at their own lives in quite the same way again: "I just figured somebody had to write a book about it and maybe that would be me."

Kingsolver sold the idea for *Holding the Line: Women in the Great Arizona Mine Strike of 1983* to a literary agent but continued to work as a stringer to make ends meet. With thousands of hours of taped interviews to organize, she wouldn't finish the project until 1989; but in the meantime she had a child and wrote a novel. During her pregnancy in 1986, she suffered almost continually from insomnia. The result of those sleepless nights was her highly acclaimed first book, *The Bean Trees* (1988).

When she finished the work, in her ninth month of pregnancy, she called the agent who was representing *Holding the Line*, apologizing for not having finished the project. Kingsolver asked her if in the meantime she would like to look at *The Bean Trees*. The agent agreed.

"So I sent it to her and she called me back at six o'clock in the morning two days later and said, 'Yes, Barbara, it's a novel and we're going to auction it.' So I promptly went into labor and they were calling me in the hospital with bids. Within twenty-four hours I became a mother and a novelist and life has never been the same since."

The Bean Trees echoes Kingsolver's own move west. Her heroine leaves the poverty of rural Kentucky for Tucson, mirroring the great American tradition of searching for a new life on the western frontier. Yet Kingsolver's work is definitely not traditional. As the *New York Times Book Review* wrote, "Her book is a strange new combination: branchy and dense, each *novel of* of its stories packed with microstories, and yet the whole as *oppositions* clear as air. It is the Southern novel taken West, its colors as translucent and polished as one of those slices of rose agate from a desert rock shop."[4]

Kingsolver's collection of short fiction, *Homeland and Other Stories* (1989), her second novel, *Animal Dreams* (1990), and her book of poetry, *Another America* (1991), brought critical success: "A writer of rare ambition and unequivocal talent," wrote the *Chicago Tribune*.[5] Critics have noted Kingsolver's debt to Doris Lessing; the *Women's Review of Books* wrote of *The Bean Trees*, "In style and vision, she has written a book all her own, and with a deep female consciousness that feels like bedrock when put up against some of the preachier, more explicitly feminist works."[6] Yet throughout the praise for *The Bean Trees* and her other books, some faulted them for their explicit political intent.

Kingsolver responds, "When I write a novel, I'm not thinking, Now how can I get political themes into this? I just write the novel. It grows out of the world I live in. And the world I live in happens to be full of sexism and racism and screwed-up immigration policies and people who use power against other people in unjust ways. If I lived in another world I would write an entirely different kind of novel.

"But I don't write the novel and then go back and see where

I can work in child abuse or Native American rights. Those are simply the things that I walk through every day, things that inform my hand as I construct theme and character and plot."

What Kingsolver walks through are, sadly, things many American women must also endure, though few write about them so trenchantly. Rape at knifepoint by a stranger appears not only in her poem "1044" (the police radio code for rape), but symbolically in her novels. One critic notes, "*The Bean Trees* is about invasion. Invasion, not as it is probed and theorized about by political thinkers, psychologists, or academics. Invasion as it is experienced by middle America. And not middle-class America, but real middle America, the unemployed and underemployed. . . . Two related versions of invasion, the sexual invasion of a child's body and the political invasion of a nation's sovereignty, come together and unfold in this story of ordinary people who understand both realities as they touch their own lives."[7]

Yet as harsh and devastating as the realities of Kingsolver's books can be, they are never without hope. The roots of her idealism go back to her father, whom she credits for preferring what is right, rather than what is most profitable. This lesson was reinforced by her experiences in the 1960s. She says, "I consider myself the very tail end of the sixties generation. I got to college just in time to go holler and yell and watch someone else burn down the ROTC building. We got out on the street and we yelled, and then what do you know? The war ended and Nixon resigned, and what could be better in terms of sheer reinforcement of this idea that you can have an effect on your surroundings?

"I see people coming up behind me who seem so disenfranchised, who seem positively convinced that nothing they could ever do would make a difference, but that's not me. I feel just the opposite. If I see something wrong I have to fix it, whether it's a leak in my bathroom or a lawbreaking government. I don't have a choice."

Her concern for political developments in Central America led the author in *Animal Dreams* to take up the cause of Sanctuary workers: those risking prison to smuggle political refugees into the United States. The heroine of *Animal Dreams* is a Chicana M.D. who becomes an outsider in her hometown (a recurring theme in Kingsolver's works). She takes a job as a schoolteacher and educates her young charges about struggles both in Central America and among their Indian neighbors.

In Kingsolver's view, too many nonfiction writers—and their readers—do not appreciate what is required to write respectfully about Native American culture:

"To write the scene about the Pueblo in *Animal Dreams*, I did several things. I read everything in the library about the ethnography, history, and culture of that Pueblo. Then of course I went there and saw those dances, and talked with people to whom those dances were important. . . . I know what those deer dancers looked like because I was there. I saw them. I have no idea what that young woman was thinking as she stood in the black dress in the snow, barefoot. I have no idea how those men felt when they became deer."

Similarly, *Pigs in Heaven* (1993) turns around an emotionally charged battle for custody of the Native American child abandoned in *The Bean Trees*, using the same characters as that earlier novel. "I only wish I hadn't made the baby Cherokee," she told "Writing the Southwest." "Cherokees have one of the most complex laws regarding adoption of any tribe."

After a series of Indian-Anglo confrontations, the child, Turtle, inspires a surprising network of alliances which end in her rightful adoption. Kingsolver's extraordinary attention to detail reveals how deeply authenticity is part of her political vision.

"That's a confusing word, 'political,' " Kingsolver reflects.

"What does it mean? I think I finally figured it out during the Gulf War.

"Some friends of mine wanted to set up a table in a shopping mall and distribute information on some of the less pleasant and cheerful aspects of the Gulf War, and the administrators of the mall said, 'No, you can't do that.' And my friend said, 'Well, why not? Those people over there are setting up tables every day passing out yellow ribbons and bumper stickers that say, "We kick Iraqi butt." And the administrators of the mall said, 'Well, yes, they can do that because what they're doing is a public service and what you're doing is political.'

"So, bingo! I understood exactly why my work is called political. It's not a public service. It's reminding people what's the matter, and that maybe they ought to think about that."

Kingsolver has been forced to think about "what's the matter" and about invasion in other ways. Between 1983 and 1986, the FBI conducted a vast investigation of more than three hundred human rights and community organizations in the United States. Although in 1988 the FBI admitted that its suspicions of international terrorism were without merit, they had touched Kingsolver's life forever.

"Among the groups and individuals who were investigated were the Maryknoll nuns, the Quakers (those renowned terrorists), the National Education Association, and me. I got a call at work one day at the University of Arizona. This fellow introduced himself and said, 'I'm investigating you for suspicion of international terrorism.' And I said, 'Wait a minute, aren't you guys supposed to be subtle?'

"But apparently they weren't. They tapped our phone, and occasionally when I was talking, a male voice would break in and say, 'Could you repeat that? I didn't get it.'

"It is kind of hilarious, but it is also infuriating because gathering secret information was so conspicuously not the point. The point was to intimidate me and frighten me out of doing the things I was doing—community organizing and educating people about U.S. foreign policy in Latin America. It made me really mad, and so I took my feeble revenge on the FBI by writing a poem about that investigation."

▲ ✣ ▼ ✣ ▼ ✣ ▲

Standing in front of her house in the mountains west of Tucson, not far from the winter home of Frank Waters, Barbara Kingsolver is not an imposing figure. She looks trim but rumpled, in worn jeans, with shoulder-length dark brown hair with russet streaks. As she shows us around the grounds, her step has a bounce that comes from more than her cardinal red, high-top sneakers.

Our interview took place in the studios of KUAT-FM at the University of Arizona in Tucson. Behind the microphone, she is composed. She delivers rehearsed anecdotes with a trace of won-

der in her voice—*her voice rises at the end of her anecdotes with a lilt that suggests the true professional, struggling to maintain freshness in the face of familiar questions.*

She comments that she has never before read in public the poem, "1044," concerning a rape. She often can't get through it without choking up. Asked if she was willing to allow its broadcast, she says, quietly: "Yes, otherwise I wouldn't have published it."

Chatting over lunch at a vegetarian restaurant, she allows how the pressure of meeting the public on book-signing tours is exhausting her.

"In principle, I am opposed to publicity. What bothers me is how people feel that they know you. They assume they know a part of your life when they don't at all, no more than you know them. People have asked me if I have a hot Apache boyfriend— right!"

What propels readers to pack book signings of their favorite author? More than celebrity seeking, it's an ancient laying on of hands, the way the reading public today completes the experience of literary art: by touching the artist.

Kingsolver is a quick study and, like most writers, quick to catch an allusion or challenge received wisdom. She speaks expansively of her involvement in the book trade, including the performances at the American Booksellers Association meetings of her rock band, the Rock Bottom Remainders. (The band also includes Amy Tan and Stephen King). She has become a publishing insider and a star, in publishing's cyclical fascination with the American Southwest. Still, she believes in her right to privacy, away from the eyes of even passionate readers.

EXCERPTS

Another America

"On the Morning I Discovered My Phone Was Tapped"

On the morning I discovered my phone was tapped
I sat behind all the locks in my house

and remembered what was stolen,
remembered the time I saw an animal's belly
slit open in front of me.

If you have nothing to hide,
they say.

I counted every time in a month
it had touched my mouth:
to talk to my mother, my sister,
the doctor who knows my uterus,
a friend with cancer,
the man whose hands
touch me when I sleep.

If you have nothing to hide,
they say,
then a man with a special badge will come.

The simplest things have uses beyond conception.
I am told that agents of my country
train agents of other countries—mainly small
and far away—in the use of the telephone:
two of the wires are cut and attached
one to the tongue,
one to the genitalia.
This is an effective way of learning secrets.

If you have nothing to hide,
they say,
a man with a special badge will come
to your house, and watch you undress.

If I am to live in a house where even my skull
has windows, and men probe
the soft parts of my brain for potential crimes,
I would rather give my secrets
than have them stolen:

* * *

First, I am not fastidious.
My house is ruled at night
by hard brown beetles
that crawl from wet crevices in the plumbing.
If my yard had mice I would ask them in.
I know this. I have left food
uneaten for days,
because of hungry eyes in a newsprint photograph.

Second, I am sometimes terrified of ridiculous things,
especially at night,
and yet I am naked when I sleep.
Wrapped in a fever of sheets
I talk to the newsprint faces,
hurry to catch up to them over stones
in the roads of small and distant countries.
In clutched handfuls
I hold out the coins of my birth
in exchange for theirs, as if these currencies
were of equal value.

Third, I am not repentant.

The Bean Trees

When I drove over the Pitman Line I made two promises
to myself. . . . The first was that I would get myself a new
name. I wasn't crazy about anything I had been called up to
that point in life, and this seemed like the time to make a
clean break. I didn't have any special name in mind, but just
wanted a change. The more I thought about it, the more it
seemed to me that a name is not something a person really
has the right to pick out, but is something you're provided
with more or less by chance. I decided to let the gas tank
decide. Wherever it ran out, I'd look for a sign. . . .

And so what I promised myself is that I would drive west
until my car stopped running and there I would stay. But
there were some things I hadn't considered.

Animal Dreams

The snowy plaza was marked with a single line of tracks: in the center of the white square stood a tall young woman in a black dress that hung from one shoulder. Her other shoulder was bare. Her waist, her upper arms, and wrists and her buckskin moccasins were all decorated with garlands of colored yarn, fur, and sleigh bells; at the crest of her head was a tuft of white eagle down. . . .

Then deer arrived from everywhere. They were men and boys with black shirts and leggings, white kilts, and deer antlers. Their human features disappeared behind a horizontal band of black paint across the eyes. They moved like deer. They held long sticks in front of them imitating the deer's cautious, long-legged grace. . . .

"Who's the striped guy?" I asked Lloyd.

"Koshari," he said. "A Kachina. He has to do with fertility. His home's in the East." . . .

"I thought a Kachina was a little doll."

"That's right."

"And also a person dressed up?"

"Yep. And a spirit."

"A spirit with a family and a mailing address?"

"That's right. When the person dresses up a certain way the spirit comes into him and into the doll if it's made right."

"Okay," I said. . . .

One of the hunters had drawn his bow and shot an invisible arrow into a deer. It gave an anguished shiver, and then the other hunters lifted its limp carcass onto their shoulders.

"I've seen Jesus Kachinas too," Lloyd said. "I've seen them hanging all over people's houses in Grace."

Now there was a thought to ponder.

NOTES

1. *The Bean Trees* (New York: Harper & Row, 1988), p. 35.

2. *Cosmopolitan*, March 1988, quoted in *Contemporary Authors* (Detroit, Mich.: Gale Research, 1992), vol. 134, p. 289.

3. Mason, Bobbie Ann, *The New Yorker*, Nov. 1, 1993, p. 50.

4. Jack Butler, *New York Times Book Review*, April 10, 1988, p. 15.

5. Melissa Pritchard, *Chicago Tribune*, Aug. 26, 1990.

6. Margaret Randall, "Human Comedy," *Women's Review of Books*, vol. 5, no. 8 (May 1988), pp. 1, 3.

7. Ibid.

TERRY MCMILLAN

▲ ❖ ▼ ❖ ▼ ❖ ▲

Writers often refer to a tri-cultural Southwest: Anglo, Hispanic, Native American. A few acknowledge often overlooked African-American influences in Indian cultures, as Joy Harjo does earlier in this volume. But many are unaware of the contributions to this region made by those of African descent as ranchers, soldiers, and homesteaders in the nineteenth century, and as more modern settlers.

Like many other writers, best-selling African-American novelist Terry McMillan has followed the great American migration westward. Her work is representative of the rapidly growing black population in such southwestern cities as Denver, Phoenix, and El Paso.

McMillan is known for her dialogue, and for bringing new readers to popular fiction reflecting contemporary African-American experience. Like that of Denise Chavez and Barbara Kingsolver, McMillan's work has the freshness and dynamism of characters set in a racially mixed society.

> At fifteen years old, all I was concerned about was what I was going to do with that thirty-two dollars I was getting as my paycheck. I had no fantasies about being a writer. First of all, back then I didn't know that I even had any role models. I didn't know about any black writers when I was fifteen—none. I didn't even know what it was I wanted to do with my life. All I knew was that I was going to college—by hook or by crook, I was going.
>
> —TERRY MCMILLAN

Terry McMillan has become one of the most popular U.S. writers of the 1990s. Critics associate her with an emergent genre in American literature—black feminist fiction—and her three best-selling books, *Mama*, *Disappearing Acts*, and *Waiting to Exhale*, have generated public enthusiasm beyond anything her publishers expected.

Though prizes and sales figures cannot truly account for McMillan's popularity, they are one indication that black readers have found a popular voice in her work. *Mama* (1987) received a Before Columbus Book Award, like the work of Joy Harjo and Linda Hogan—but this book has sold over 300,000 copies. Of *Disappearing Acts* (1989), 450,000 copies have been sold, with film rights optioned by Metro-Goldwyn-Mayer Pictures. Yet it is *Waiting to Exhale* (1992) that has turned the publishing world on its ear. The book has been devoured wholesale by black America, selling 700,000 copies in hardcover with forty weeks on the *New York Times* best-seller list. Paperback rights, purchased by Pocket Books after a frenzied three-day auction, went for an amazing $2.64 million, one of the most lucrative book deals of its decade.

What has surprised publishers, and pleased the author immensely, is that the bulk of these sales are to African-Americans, a group regarded by the publishing industry as a poor market for fiction. McMillan claims it is her characters—ordinary blacks speaking with authentic voices, dealing with everyday survival—which draw an audience who might not otherwise purchase fiction.

The startling realism of McMillan's fiction is grounded in her life. The oldest of five children, she was born in Port Huron, Michigan, in 1951. She barely knew her father, who died when she was sixteen. Edward McMillan spent several years in a sanatorium fighting tuberculosis. When he was home, episodes of excessive drinking, violence, and abuse forced McMillan's mother, Mamie Tillman, to divorce him and raise her children alone in economically depressed northern Michigan.

The inspiration for Mildred Peacock, the title character of *Mama*, Mamie Tillman waged a daily struggle to feed and clothe her family. Working as a maid, and later in a factory for Ford Motor Company, Tillman's strength and ferocious belief in her children drove McMillan to obtain the education that would prove her salvation. In 1985, she wrote a short story called "Mama Take Another Step" in an attempt to come to grips with the things her mother had done to raise five children alone. "I just couldn't understand how she'd pulled it off," McMillan says, shaking her head. "So I wrote this story which stopped where she made the decision to leave an abusive marriage. That was the end of the story."

She read the piece in front of a writing group, and they said, "Ah! That sounds like the first chapter of a novel."

"Novel?" McMillan had answered. "I don't know how to write a novel. I'm struggling with a short story, okay?"

The group would not take no for an answer, insisting that they had to know what happens to Mildred Peacock.

"She leaves the guy," Terry told them, but the group said McMillan could not leave them hanging. What happened to Mildred, now a single mother? Ideas rolled around inside her head, to the point where she admitted that she knew the story wasn't finished.

Ironically, it was her family's dire economic situation that led to McMillan's intellectual awakening and her discovery of literature. To help support herself and her four siblings, McMillan, fifteen, found a job as a page at the public library. While shelving books, she came across two that were to change her life.

The first was a biography of Louisa May Alcott. McMillan recalls her amazement at entering the world of a white family that also suffered through poverty and a young white girl who worked to support her family.

The second was a book that caught her eye: on the back cover was a black man. Surprised that an African-American could have a book published, McMillan nevertheless assumed that whatever the man had to say could not have been as well written as the writing by the white authors assigned in school; so to cover her embarrassment for him, she quickly shelved the book without reading it. She remembered the author's name, though—James Baldwin.

Two years later, at seventeen, with her new high school diploma in hand, she moved to Los Angeles, California. The first class she enrolled in at the local community college was "Vocabulary Building"; the second was "Afro-American Literature." From there she never looked back from the world of books. She transferred to the University of California, Berkeley, where she earned a B.A. in journalism in 1978. There she signed up for her first writing class, taught by African-American poet Ishmael Reed. Reed became her mentor, publishing her first short story, "The End," in the *Yardbird Reader* in 1976. She was twenty-five years old.

In 1978, after friends and relatives urged her to find a more remunerative means of expressing her creativity, she started studying for a master of fine arts in film at Columbia University, while working in a book publishing job. She completed only twenty-six credit hours, however, before dropping out, amid a stress-related drug and alcohol problem.[1]

By the early 1980s, she had her life back under control; certain that filmmaking was not her calling, she began writing days and working nights as a legal secretary. Amid all this, she gave birth to her son, Solomon, in 1984, and completed her first novel. *Mama* was published in 1987, but the publisher, Houghton Mifflin, hesitated to promote a first book by an unknown author. Characteristically, McMillan refused to accept this fate. Working full-time and caring for her infant son, she researched publishing and promotion strategies. After work she sent out over three thousand letters to critics, reviewers, and bookstores and offered to do readings promoting her new novel.

Despite her publisher's dour expectations, *Mama* sold over three hundred thousand copies. In 1988 McMillan won a National Endowment for the Arts fellowship.

Critics have compared *Mama* to Alice Walker's *The Color Purple*, citing its unsentimental saga of an economically deprived African-American woman who finds the strength to leave an abusive relationship.[2] Her work might be more closely related, however, to the woman Walker herself calls her "spiritual godmother," Harlem Renaissance author and historian Zora Neale Hurston.

Like Hurston's best works, McMillan's writing resonates with the sound of real black voices and the razor-sharp lyricism of black vernacular. As in Hurston's 1937 masterpiece, *Their Eyes Were Watching God*, McMillan's characters use cutting humor on the daily horrors of racism, sexism, and poverty.

It's a "laughing to keep from crying" approach, to shrink one's troubles to manageable size.

Many readers feel as though the people in McMillan's books are sitting across the kitchen table from them. This realism reached a peak in her second novel, *Disappearing Acts*, chronicling the two-year love affair between Zora, a college-educated music teacher, and Franklin, a mostly unemployed construction worker who had dropped out of high school. The *Washington Post* called it "one of the few novels to contain rounded, sympathetic portraits of . . . black men and women as something more than the relationship between victimizer and victim."[3]

Her sensitive portrayal of a male character examines the devastating effects of racism and poverty on relationships between black men and women and echoes the works of Ralph Ellison and Richard Wright. Issues of class, education, and economic security play a major role. And as in Wright's *Black Boy*, Franklin's blunt, first-person narrative forces the reader to come face to face with the myriad ways racism spawns frustration, rage, and self-hatred in black men; the result can easily be violence, often aimed at black women. Like Richard Wright, McMillan pulls no punches. Her portrait of Franklin is stark and unrepentant, and yet vastly sympathetic.

The book spawned controversy on many fronts. Some African-American men felt betrayed by what they considered a harsh portrayal of black males, a criticism often leveled at Alice Walker's treatment of male characters in *The Color Purple*. McMillan responded that she wrote a single character in *Disappearing Acts*, not a representative for the entire black race. Other critics disapproved of her characters' use of profanity, a charge she scoffs at. "The language that I use is accurate," she told *Publishers Weekly*. "That's the way we talk. And I want to know why I've never read a review where they complain about the language that male writers use!"[4]

The book also resulted in a $5 million lawsuit filed by Leonard Welch, the father of McMillan's son, who claimed the portrait of Franklin in *Disappearing Acts* libeled him. The case was decided in McMillan's favor, but it contributed to the controversy and hype surrounding her second best-seller.[5]

The novel also contributed to the end of her relationship

with Houghton Mifflin, the publisher of *Mama*. She explains that Houghton Mifflin wanted her to rewrite her manuscript telling the entire story from Franklin's point of view, rather than the alternating first person she uses to show the reader the events as interpreted by both Zora and Franklin. They objected in part, she says, to Zora's voice. "When my editor told me Zora sounded kind of preppie, I said 'Look, she's not barefoot and pregnant, living in the projects and getting her ass kicked. I cannot apologize because some of us have been to college, okay?' "[6]

The by-now shaky relationship came to an end when Houghton Mifflin demanded to see a completed manuscript of *Disappearing Acts* before making an offer. McMillan's agent presented the finished chapters to Viking, which bought the manuscript two days later.

A no-holds-barred look at black male-female relationships, as well as the binding power of friendships among black women, drives McMillan's third and most successful novel to date, *Waiting to Exhale*. This is a character study of four African-American women of differing economic classes and educational backgrounds, all living in Phoenix, Arizona. As in *Disappearing Acts*, McMillan has occasionally been criticized for making some of her characters, particularly Savannah in this novel, sound "white." At the same time, some critics objected again to her use of profanity. Charles Larson, a professor of literature at American University, wrote in a *Chicago Tribune* review that reading *Waiting to Exhale* was like "listening to four foul-mouthed standup comedians—all of them lashing out blindly at men. . . ."[7] This raises an issue important to McMillan, and to African-American literature in general today: linguistic pluralism.

McMillan acknowledges that her characters do not always speak in the snappy, streetwise dialect of *Mama*, insisting that they are an accurate reflection of black life today. Many African-Americans in the 1990s are college graduates and the children of college graduates, she points out. Their speech, their jobs, the cars they drive, and the neighborhoods they live in reflect the rapidly changing lifestyles of young black professionals.

Not everyone in the black community, particularly the

scholarly and literary African-American intelligentsia, has been pleased with McMillan's work. She has been dismissed as a black Danielle Steel, writing sales-driven popular literature.[8] *Belles Lettres: A Review of Books by Women* says of *Mama*, "The novel has no . . . outstanding or magical literary quality that might elevate it to the level of entertainment or rapture."[9] McMillan admits her writing is not particularly scholarly or literary in the classical sense; nor, she feels, must it be. Her aim is to tell stories she herself would like to read. Her books are deliberately accessible. The fact that black readers are buying her books in record numbers is more important to her than accolades in literary-critical circles.

In 1987, McMillan and her son moved to Laramie, where she taught fiction at the University of Wyoming. She has lectured across the United States and in London, and been interviewed on National Public Radio, PBS, "Good Morning America," and "The Oprah Winfrey Show."

In 1988 she accepted an appointment at the University of Arizona at Tucson, where she taught for four years. One of her greatest disappointments, she says, is that she has had only two African-Americans in her creative-writing classes. She believes it is time for black students to have the courage to major in art or literature, instead of the "safe" areas of medicine or business.

She moved in 1992 to a wealthy suburb of Oakland, California, with her son, giving up teaching in order to write full-time and pursue what has become one of the most pressing goals in her life—bringing the writings of other African-American authors onto the literary landscape.

One of her more tangible steps toward this goal was to edit an anthology, the first in seventeen years dedicated to contemporary African-American fiction. *Breaking Ice* (1990) featured established writers, up-and-coming authors, and the young unknowns passed over by white publishers and editors. For McMillan, it became a most important project, one she hopes will inspire young black writers with a legacy for generations to come.

She is currently working with Ron Bass on a screenplay for *Waiting to Exhale*. Her new novel, *A Day Late and a Dollar Short*, will be published in 1995.

▲ ✧ ▼ ✧ ▼ ✧ ▲

Terry McMillan was interviewed at her house in the low, eucalyptus-scented hills east of Oakland. She lives in a neighborhood, Blackhawk, on a ritzy block cut into a hillside. As she led me through her large downstairs living room, awash in the colors of the bright paintings she has collected, we struggled to find a room where hammering from nearby remodelers would not dominate. We ended up conducting the interview in her bedroom, a large airy room with speakers built into the walls and a lavish bath decorated in white and black. Throughout our session, gray doves cooed in the background from a perch on a yellow flowering tree outside her window. The cooing lent a gentleness to our conversation about the rough life in the streets of many African-American youths.

McMillan, wearing a yellow T-shirt and sweatpants, propped herself up on the edge of her bed. As she spoke about her literary aspirations and the difficulty of finding serious literary recognition, she became quite animated. One could imagine her bounding up after the interview to jog into the nearby hills. She was by turns patient, as she accommodated the need for quiet of the recordist, and reflective, as she recalled her experience reading classic African-American authors. Reliving her determination to find a publisher and an audience, she revealed the iron-in-the-soul quality which allowed her to find the organizational and spiritual resources to overcome persistent rejection.

By the end of our session, discussing young African-American writers and how some publications seem closed to their work, McMillan flailed at journalists and those who dismiss her work as "sociology": "I don't write sociology, I write people's lives. My stories are about survival. They are about how people get from one moment to the next, one year to the next, they're not all final, everything's not wrapped up, nice and neat."

TERRY MCMILLAN:

I started reading in college, I mean seriously reading; but I got a job when I was fifteen working at the public library and I really think *that* affected me.

I was going to college, my mother told me, "Because you're not going to grow up like that"—get on welfare, have a house full of babies. These people had made some really bad choices, early on. They responded to what happened to them, and they didn't seem to realize that they could make things happen, or alter their reality in some way.

I was the first one in my family to go to college. I went to Los Angeles City College, and when I got there to register I saw this Afro-American lit class, and I said, "They have a whole class with nothing but black writers in it?" So I took the class, and that was very liberating for me, reading Jean Toomer, Countee Cullen, Frederick Douglass, Langston Hughes, Zora Neale Hurston.

I started becoming familiar with our history as a people in a lot of different ways: through slave narratives, poetry, and also through fiction. That's how I found out where we came from, our history in this country, and to get it in such a lyrical way, with imagery, was really overwhelming. It opened up something in me that I wasn't aware of at the time. I think I gained a lot more respect for black people, because everybody used to talk about us as people, and we grew up believing that black people were lazy.

I said, "Damn, why didn't somebody tell me this when I was growing up?"

And that's how I learned just how much ignorance [costs] —the price is very high. I'm glad that I found out at eighteen, you know what I'm saying? Basically, I ended up having to educate myself, and I still am. But it freed me. I didn't know how much power you could have as a person.

Richard Wright used to scare me. His work is so dark, and it weighed so much. He is up there with Thomas Mann, *Death in Venice*, all that kind of stuff. Even though I knew it was exquisite writing, where I had just come from was dark, you know? I was [saying], "Shit, give me some light."

I think that's one reason why I [read] Ring Lardner and Langston Hughes. I think that has a lot to do with why there's so much humor in my work. Things can be bad, but there's got to be a little light.

I think my strength lies in dialogue. I'm a pretty good listener, so far at least (laughs). I think of catching the nuances, the way people talk. My narrative is weak. That's why you don't find very much of it in my books. And probably never will. I like to think that one of my strengths is that I tell realistic stories. I tell stories about people in real-life situations.

There's no way in the world I can capture the essence of all the lifestyles and the perils of African-Americans. There are some of us out here who are dealing with corporate America. That's an altogether different kind of struggle, stress, and peril. But economics is still high up there on the list.

I've been criticized in some ways for that. Especially some critics who want to say "Well, she's writing about a serious subject matter here, it's not fluff, it's not fantasy," but because of the *language* I use, and because my prose isn't all eloquent, not full of metaphors, they don't know quite how to categorize me. Plus, because I sell a lot of books, some of them don't want to consider me a literary writer. I'm writing about stories, I just don't write like Katherine Anne Porter, Jane Austen, Virginia Woolf, Toni Morrison, or Alice Walker. I've got my own voice and my own style.

Toni does things that I'll never do. The way she weaves myth and magic realism—I don't do that, and I'm not going to even try. I don't want to, because that's not the way I tell a story. But I'm glad she's out there. And the same with Alice— what she does with history, what she discovers about human nature, and particularly African-Americans, and women. I respect [all that]. I love why they do what they do, because I understand it, and I am really grateful for the fact that all of our voices are, in fact, different.

* * *

Because of what happened with *Waiting to Exhale*, publishers said, "Hey, gee whiz, look at all the people buying this little black girl's book. She's making a shitload of money. Do we have any [other] black writers?" So now they're all scrambling, and of course there'll be a backlash; there always is to every so-called trend, but it may at least enable some writers to get attention who I think deserve it.

White people basically set what they call standards for literature and good fiction. They're the ones who define it, they're the ones who determine the whole structure. And if you don't fit into their little slots, then they don't know what to make of you.

[Some] people out there don't care about black people, therefore they don't care about [black] stories or the people who inhabit the stories.

They could really spruce up *The New Yorker* if they put some stories in there by some Native Americans, Asian-Americans, and African-Americans—maybe more people would read the magazine. But you won't be reading many stories by black writers in *The New Yorker* or the *Atlantic Monthly*. *The New Yorker*'s a white magazine, and they publish stories about white people, in very white situations, and I think that's really dreadful.

EXCERPTS

Mama

She sat at the kitchen table and started going through a stack of envelopes that she had already shuffled and re-shuffled in order of importance over the past few weeks. It didn't make a difference. Most of them were going to have to go unpaid. Bills. The coal bill. The gas bill. The light bill. The water bill. The garbage man. The insurance man. The washer and dryer bill. The house note. Groceries. Lunch money. Special field trip money. Gym suit money. School books. Notebook paper. Tennis shoes. Sunday shoes. The dentist. Popsicles. . . .

"Here's the mail," Bootsey said, handing it to her. . . .

Mildred went through the envelopes quickly, tossing aside the ones she didn't want to look at, and then she came across a letter from her oldest brother, Leon. He lived in Phoenix. What would he be writing me for? she wondered. . . .

Mildred let the thought pass when she got to the part where he suggested she consider selling the house and moving out to Phoenix. He said there were better job opportunities out there for colored people, the weather was hot and dry all year long, which meant hardly any mosquitoes, the kids might meet some civilized children instead of those hoodlums running loose in Point Haven, and above all else, Mildred might meet a stable and loveable serviceman with a pension and she might even consider getting her high school diploma.

She folded the letter and put it back in the envelope, letting her fingers crease it over and over again. She could hear the furnace clicking on. Heat, Mildred thought. Wouldn't need no furnace in Arizona. She walked over and flicked off the switch.

Disappearing Acts

Franklin:

I do know I can be a pain in the ass, but that's my nature. I just like to test people, see what they made of, where they coming from. I got discharged from the navy because of my temper, lack of cooperation. Couldn't carry out, let alone follow, orders. And didn't give a shit. Didn't wanna go in the first damn place. A black man got enough wars to fight at home. . . . Everybody thought it would do me some good. But how can taking orders from the white man, killing people that ain't never done nothing to me personally, do me some fuckin' good? It took me two years to get out.

My whole family disowned me. If I was white, I probably woulda been disinherited. . . .

Zora:

    . . . I'm not into interrogation. I prefer to wait and see if the image he projects lives up to the man. And vice versa. Let's face it: All men are not husband material. Some of 'em are only worth a few nights of pleasure. But some of 'em make you get on your knees at night and pray that they choose Door Number One, which is the one you happen to be standing behind. And it's not that I haven't been picked before. Because I have. They turned out to be a major disappointment. Some of 'em just weren't ready. They wanted to play house. Or The Dating Game. Or Guess Where I'm Coming From? or Show Me How Much You Love Me Then I'll Show You. . . . I told them that this wasn't high school or college, but the grown-up edition of life. . . . So now I'm taking off the blindfolds and doing the bidding myself. After a while, even a fool would get tired of bringing home the TV and finding out it only gets two or three channels.

Waiting to Exhale

Savannah:

    I have tried being honest, telling them as diplomatically as I possibly could that they just weren't right for me, that they shouldn't take it personally because there was somebody out there for everybody. Which is how I became "the bitch." . . . I wanted to tell all of them to come back and see me after they grew up or got some serious counseling. Unfortunately most men are deaf. They hate advice. Especially if it's from a woman. They get defensive as hell if you so much as suggest that there's a few things they might try doing that would truly please you. "Fuck you," is what they ended up saying to me, because they didn't want to be *told* what I liked or needed; they preferred to guess. Well, I'm here to tell you that at least seventy-five percent of the ones I've met were terrible guessers.

Robin:

After he leaves, I feel this incredible sense of relief. I have energy for days. . . . I take my car to the car wash and start the ninety-mile drive to Tucson, with the top down and the music blasting. . . . I pass through the Gila Indian reservation and, as usual, wonder where they all are. I see fields of cotton and think it's ironic that it's Mexicans now who pick it. The mountains that are far away look like someone painted them into the sky. The one that's right here, Picacho Peak, makes me want to stop the car and climb up to the top. One day I will. . . . By the time I get to Orange Grove Road, I know I've been trying too hard to make myself not think about what I'm thinking about. For the last eighty miles, I've been trying to appreciate how breathtaking nature can be, how beautiful Arizona is.

NOTES

1. Esther B. Fein, *New York Times*, July 1, 1992, p. C1; Kim Hubbard and Liz McNeil, *People*, July 20, 1992, pp. 93–94.

2. Esther B. Fein, *New York Times*, July 1, 1992, p. Cl.

3. David Nicholson, *Washington Post*, Aug. 27, 1989, p. 6.

4. Wendy Smith, "Interview with Terry McMillan," *Publishers Weekly*, May 11, 1992, pp. 50–51.

5. Ibid.

6. Ibid.

7. Charles Larson, quoted by John Bondreau, *Los Angeles Times* (Washington Edition) June 19, 1992, p. B10.

8. *The New Yorker*, Nov. 13, 1989, p. 147.

9. Kamili Anderson, *Belles Lettres: A Review of Books by Women*, vol. 3, no. 1 (Sept.–Oct. 1987), p. 9.

JOHN NICHOLS

▲ ✢ ▼ ✢ ▼ ✢ ▲

Like Edward Abbey, John Nichols has become identified with the Southwest and with a style of writing at once highly polemical and infinitely readable. His classic novel, _The Milagro Beanfield War_, has brought the complex and highly charged social relations of New Mexico to the attention of the world; yet like Barbara Kingsolver and Denise Chavez, even his most passionate political works are filled with generous doses of humor and compassion.

Nichols brings his readers face-to-face with the more unpleasant aspects of rapid development in a largely rural region. Nichols has been called a modern-day Steinbeck, and like Terry McMillan and Arizona writer Alberto Rios, his characters inhabit the racial, cultural, and class borderlands that divide and define the American Southwest.

> _"I've always believed, if you're involved even in a very small struggle—in some sort of infinity in a grain of sand—in your local neighborhood, that every action has universal implications. I believe if I struggle for the rights of an acequia in Taos, New Mexico, that the ripple effect [will spread] from that tiny struggle."_
>
> —JOHN NICHOLS

John Nichols has grown from an irrepressible prep school graduate to a southwestern legend and a symbol for Hispanic-Anglo cultural crossings. His New Mexico Trilogy, _The Milagro_

Beanfield War, *The Magic Journey*, and *The Nirvana Blues*, developed a cult following over the last decade, and the filmed version of *The Milagro Beanfield War* has brought New Mexico's cultural conflicts to the attention of the world. Nichols is one of a handful of Anglo writers fascinated with the contemporary situation of rural Hispanic life in the Mountain West. His novels have widened public understanding of the fragile relationship between land development, water rights, and tourism.

The cultural and ethnic mosaic for which Nichols is known is found in his own background. Born in Berkeley, California, on July 23, 1940, Nichols grew up largely on the East Coast. In Mastic, New York, on the south shore of Long Island, he played in a house which belonged to his family for over two hundred years (now a history museum). For games of "cowboys and Indians" he used flintlock rifles fired by his ancestors in the Revolutionary War and dressed up in uniforms worn by other forebears in the Civil War. Nichols's great-great-great-grandfather, William Floyd, was a Revolutionary War general who signed the Declaration of Independence for the state of New York.

His paternal ancestors were sea captains and whalers out of New York and Salem, Massachusetts. One unfortunate relative was actually executed during the famous Salem witch trials, as documented in *The Witch's Breed*, written by Susan Pulsifer, a paternal great-aunt. (The Pierce-Nichols house in Salem has also been converted into a museum.)

Nichols's mother was the granddaughter of Anatole Le Braz, the French poet, writer, and historian from the Brittany region, known for his haunting stories of the peasants and fishermen of the Brittany coast. Though raised in Barcelona, Spain, she identified herself as entirely French. She died when John was two.

John Nichols's parents had married in Paris, but moved to the United States while his father attended the University of California, Berkeley. His father speaks several languages, and often sang his son to sleep with Russian lullabies. Susan Pulsifer also wrote a half dozen other books, including one on the history of the Nichols family. His paternal grandfather, for whom Nichols is named, was a noted herpetologist, ichthyologist, and ornithologist, the author of numerous scientific articles, and curator of fishes at the Museum of Natural History in New York. Nichols grew up stalking birds and other wildlife with a camera and memorizing proper scientific names from his father, who supplied the museum with specimens.

Learning in a structured academic environment proved more difficult, however. He drifted among schools from California to New York and Virginia. In 1954, he was sent to Loomis, a private school in Windsor, Connecticut, where, according to Nichols, he distinguished himself as the third-worst student in his class. At graduation his grades were so low he had to be voted through. Fortunately, he excelled in football, track, and hockey, and for the latter he was accepted to Hamilton College in upstate New York on a full scholarship. Always, he wrote on his own, turning out stories imitating Damon Runyon and Thomas Wolfe, Hemingway, and Steinbeck.

Ironically, it was his involvement in athletics that helped launch Nichols as a political novelist. Although he had written stories since he was sixteen, none was socially conscious. At Hamilton College, all white and all male, Nichols became more attuned to class and racial prejudice. During his sophomore year, he was injured in a hockey game and spent three weeks in traction. He seized that opportunity to write a novel on racism in the American South. "I was going to Herndon High School in rural Virginia, which at that time was all white and highly segregated, when *Brown v. Board of Education* went down in 1954," he recalls. "The next day all my friends [came] to class carrying potatoes with razor blades stuck in them, with baseball bats, chains, switchblades, brass knuckles—determined to beat away any black kids that might try to integrate that school. That was a very powerful experience in my life."

Nichols took that firsthand experience and combined it with the actual murder several years later of Emmett Till, a black teenager lynched in Mississippi for speaking to a white woman—a tragedy which helped spark the civil rights movement. The result was a two-hundred-page novel called *Don't Be Forlorn*. Although it was never published, it launched Nichols into the literary form with which he would build his career as a writer.

Nichols graduated from Hamilton College in 1962 and moved to Spain, where he lived with his grandmother in Barcelona. There he wrote his first published novel, *The Sterile Cuckoo* (1964), a deceptively simple story about a love affair between a boy and girl at a small college in upstate New York. The work was rejected by thirteen publishers, but with characteristic stubbornness, Nichols submitted it to yet another. The novel was accepted, published, and immediately snapped up by the Literary Guild, then turned into a film by Alan Pakula, starring Liza Minelli.

Almost overnight, at the age of twenty-four, Nichols was catapulted to fame. He took an apartment in New York City and wrote his second published novel, *The Wizard of Loneliness* (1966), which was also turned into a movie.

Nichols lived in New York until 1969, rediscovering his concern for social issues and becoming deeply involved in the Vietnam protest movement. He wrote four more novels during that time, all highly political works, and all rejected by every publisher to view them.

In frustration, Nichols, his then-wife Ruby, and their three-year-old son, Luke, moved as far away as possible from New York. They deliberately chose Taos, New Mexico, as their destination, a place Nichols felt to be as close to the Third World as possible, and therefore more reflective of how the majority of people in the world must live. The choice of New Mexico was influenced by what Nichols calls "the most fabulous summer I'd ever had in my life."

At the age of seventeen, he had found a summer job in Taos, New Mexico, plastering an adobe house belonging to the brother of a farmer Nichols worked for in Virginia. It was his first introduction to the unique Hispanic culture of the New Mexico highlands, and he recalls being enchanted by old folk songs played on fiddles and guitars at the home of a neighboring Hispanic family, and by the sight of women, dressed in traditional black usually seen only in Spain or Mexico, replastering the ancient Ranchos Church.

For the last six weeks of that summer, before he returned to Loomis for his senior year of high school, Nichols found employment in the remote mountains outside of Portal, Arizona, first working at a research station run by the Museum of

Natural History in New York, studying a rare beetle, then fighting forest fires in the Chiricahua Mountains on the Arizona-Mexico border. His fellow firefighters were mostly Chicanos and Mexican nationals. For a young man fascinated with traditional cultures and the grandeur of nature, the American Southwest was a paradise to which he was fated to return.

At the age of thirty, however, after less than a year in New Mexico, he was no longer the boy wonder of the American literary scene. By November of 1972, his marriage was failing and he was broke, unemployed, and barely able to pay the $78.32 monthly mortgage on his four-room adobe house. He and his wife heated with wood, used an outhouse, and got by without a car.

On the verge of giving up writing altogether, Nichols decided to take one more shot. For the two previous years he had researched land and water issues for *The New Mexico Review*; now he thought he'd turn his material into fiction. He envisioned a novel which, like the previous four, would deal with racial and environmental issues, but with a twist. Instead of angry, polemical prose, Nichols decided to try tempering his message with humor. He took a job as a dishwasher at a local restaurant during the day and followed a lifelong habit of writing at night. He finished the first five-hundred-page draft of *The Milagro Beanfield War* in five weeks, took three weeks to correct it, and another three weeks to type it. He then sent it off to his publisher, who promptly purchased it for ten thousand dollars. A total of four months had passed from the time he wrote the opening sentence.

The success of *The Milagro Beanfield War* (1974) was followed by the second novel of the New Mexico Trilogy, *The Magic Journey* (1978). Like *Milagro*, this book holds true to Nichols's passionate concern for land and the people who must make their living on it. *Harper's* said, "*The Magic Journey* is a plausible history of exploitation, lush with eccentric characters, with myths, legends, ghosts, and revealing shards from the past four decades, all carried by a Dickensian narrative exuberance."[1]

Set in the fictional town of Chamisaville, loosely based on Taos, it started out to be the story of a small-time "miracle" which leads to the tourist development of a tiny, rustic village.

"When a dog-racing track is placed on Pueblo Indian land, financed by the Mafia," Nichols explains, "the destructive exploitation of the village is complete. So I wrote draft after draft of that book, trying to make the jump from 1930 [when the so-called miracle occurred] to 1970 in thirty pages." He soon discovered that the intervening forty years required explanation. "I wound up writing a three-hundred-page introduction to a four-hundred-page novel," he laughs. "I couldn't figure out any other way to do it." It remains one of his favorite novels.

The Magic Journey was followed by a nonfiction essay entitled *If Mountains Die* (1979), a highly praised work combining Nichols's prose with photographs by William Davis. The *New York Times Book Review* noted, "This is not simply a picture book. Mr. Nichols has written a vivid account of . . . his neighbors' struggles against the incursions of building, overpopulation and traffic. . . . This is a moving, entertaining and beautiful book."[2] It was Nichols's first venture into what would become his passion, environmental writing; however, he continues to produce works of fiction.

A Ghost in the Music (1979) is one of his most autobiographical works and is exemplary of the idiosyncratic path his stories travel on their way to completion. Begun in 1965, it was based initially on the journey taken by a young couple whose marriage is failing. Like Nichols and his former wife, they sail on a lobster boat carrying bootleg rum to a dry island off the coast of Maine. The captain of the boat, based on Nichols's lobsterman uncle (David Pulsifer, also a rumrunner), is a symbol of what Nichols sees as the destructive misdirection of creative energy. As Nichols continued to rewrite the novel over the years, it evolved into the story of a final week spent together by an estranged father and son in a small New Mexico town. It is the father, Bart, now a movie producer rather than a lobsterman, who is a self-destructive whirlwind of creativity locked into the hard-drinking, macho image he feels is the only proper role for a real man.

Like much of Nichols's work, the book received mixed reviews. The *Washington Post* compared it to the works of Jerzy Kosinski and William Saroyan and wrote, "Nichols provides painful insights into people whose concept of affection is to keep talking on the telephone after the other party hangs up.

. . . [His] finale makes the Bart-Marcel relationship speak for fathers and sons loving each other everywhere. . . . Nichols may still write another best seller. But he'll never do a better job of capturing how it feels to love someone who doesn't stay around to be loved."[3] Critic Al Barozzi, however, blasted *A Ghost in the Music*, claiming the plot was weak and calling Bart "a totally unsympathetic character, in no way did he come alive and produce any emotion in this reader. . . . Nichols' talents have failed him, and the final product is shamelessly uninspired."[4]

The response to *A Ghost in the Music* was typical of reactions to much of Nichols's work—readers seem to either love it or hate it, with no middle ground, and sales of his books have been mixed: *The Milagro Beanfield War* has become a cult classic while *A Ghost in the Music* and *The Nirvana Blues* (1981), the final portion of his New Mexico Trilogy, found fewer readers.

In 1980, Robert Redford became interested in directing a movie version of *The Milagro Beanfield War*. The same year, Nichols had worked with Konstantinos Costa-Gavras on the script for *Missing*, which garnered four Academy Award nominations and won for best adapted screenplay. It was Nichols's first harsh introduction to the world of Hollywood. He realized too late that, through various complicated negotiations, the Writers Guild had arbitrated him out of screen credit for the script. The movie won him recognition in Hollywood, however, and in 1981, at Robert Redford's request, he traveled to Utah to Redford's new Sundance Film Institute to discuss a rewrite of Nichols's script for *The Milagro Beanfield War*.

It was, Nichols claims, "one of the most embarrassing moments of my life." The script was read and evaluated by a number of actors and directors, including John Shea and Alan Alda. Nichols was certain his script was a disaster. He approached Redford afterward, asking if it could be salvaged. Redford assured him the script was fine and that he could probably make a movie from it as it was. "I just sat there," Nichols laughs. "I thought, I don't believe this. Either there's something very intrinsic that I don't understand about movies, or Robert Redford is nuts! It turns out there's something very intrinsic that I don't understand about movies."[5]

Filming for *The Milagro Beanfield War* was finally completed in 1986 after numerous fits and starts, including one sample script produced by another writer which revolved around the premise that the main character, a Chicano farmer, is unable to tell the difference between peas and beans and so accidentally plants an entire field of peas, not realizing his mistake until harvesttime. Like the novel, the movie was a limited financial success but quickly became an underground cult classic.

In 1987, Nichols published *American Blood*, a dark, violent novel centering around the return of a Vietnam vet and his desperate psychological struggle toward a new life in rural New Mexico. *An Elegy for September*, published in 1992, performs an about-face and chronicles, in understated prose, a love affair between an older writer and a nineteen-year-old college student who worships his work.

Nichols's ability to produce prose of such varying styles results, he believes, from his love of art. "I've been influenced by a lot by painters," he explains. "I love muralists like Diego Rivera, huge panoramic painters like Brueghel, Hieronymus Bosch, Jan Van Eyck, which obviously has been influential on books like *The Magic Journey*, *The Nirvana Blues*, or *The Milagro Beanfield War*. On the other hand, I've always been torn between wanting to write *War and Peace* and wanting to write *The Great Gatsby*. I like working on things that feel tight as well as things that have 250 characters or a thousand-page manuscript."

Nichols today devotes more of his energies to nonfiction on environmental issues, particularly the farmers and ranchers in northern New Mexico who are squeezed out by developers promising economic prosperity. To date, Nichols has published five such books: *If Mountains Die*, *The Last Beautiful Days of Autumn* (1982), *On the Mesa* (1986), *A Fragile Beauty* (1987), and a book-length environmental prose poem called *Keep It Simple* (1992), illustrated with Nichols's own photographs.

The literary evolution of Nichols's work is toward simplification, a paring down of prose to the bare essentials. From the overflowing exuberance of *The Milagro Beanfield War* to the Hemingwayesque spareness of *An Elegy for September* and *Keep It Simple*, his writing has become cleaner and more personal. The *Chicago Tribune Book World* wrote "there used to be writers that cared about people. . . . Proletarian writers they were called. . . . Nichols, now, seems almost alone upon this inherited terrain. . . . He has all of Steinbeck's gifts, the same overwhelming compassion for people, plus an even finer sense of humor, and the need to celebrate the cause and dignity of man."[6]

Early Nichols may be read as an American realist in the tradition of Dreiser or Norris, but with the comic bent of Robert Benchley or Ring Lardner. As the years have passed, he and Tony Hillerman have come to be regarded as the leading Anglo novelists of New Mexico, with interests in deep ecology, southwestern regionalism, and Hispanic nationalism. These themes center on the ability of diverse groups in the Southwest to coexist.

Nichols's works of the 1980s, particularly his nonfiction pieces, harken back to the literary and conservationist traditions of his New England ancestors, especially writings of Emerson and Thoreau. Nichols has found his Walden in northern New Mexico. The naturalist streak, the art of close observation of the natural world, became the impulse to find infinity in a small New Mexican town. Nichols turned a naturalist's eye to the environmental degradation of the Taos region. In this, he returns to the tradition of American Romantics, with their near-mystical relationship with nature.

Though *Walden* concerned itself with the search for an independent lifestyle in harmony with nature, Thoreau also maintained a connection to the larger political currents of his day and was involved in abolition and antiwar activities. In his opposition to the Mexican-American War, which he saw as an expansionist landgrab by southern slaveholders at the expense of the region's Hispanic inhabitants, Thoreau was actually fighting the same battle as Nichols—struggling against the encroachment of Anglo culture in the Southwest—only a century earlier.

Nichols is profoundly engaged in charting writers' responsibilities, politically and socially. An inveterate petition signer, Nichols joined Rudolfo Anaya on the panel on censorship for the National Writers' Congress in 1981. His interest in politics is not casual. He is fond of quoting German poet Heinrich

Heine: "A poet should have on his casket not a wreath, but a
pistol to show that he was a faithful private in the liberation
struggles of humanity." Yet these harsh words convey only the
passion and not the gentleness and steadfast commitment that
motivates someone to remain a political idealist–activist for
nearly a half century. His political inspiration recalls the old
New England hymn which asks, "Shall I be lofted to the skies,
on flowery beds of ease, when others must strive, to win the
prize?"

▲ ❖ ▼ ❖ ▼ ❖ ▲

*John Nichols was interviewed twice for this book, both times
in Albuquerque at KUNM-FM. The first session followed a visit to
the cardiologist over the weak heart of this active, sandy-haired
author. He told a characteristic story about the deep gashes in the
front of his pickup: years ago a Hispanic neighbor and he were
hunting for firewood. They had their day's haul and were heading
home when they came upon one more tree they were too tired to
chop down; so Nichols, at his friend's urging, just pushed it over
with his fender.*

*John Nichols could be dismissed as a bundle of cultural con-
tradictions: a prep-school boy from New England who went to a
prestigious college, yet settled in the southern Rockies, far from
the corridors of power; a writer of national fame at age twenty-
four who left New York and the center of publishing to start over
in what he thought of as a small Third World country, New Mexico. Nichols is staunchly radical, self-conscious of the political situation of his art, and a gentle man easily imposed upon.*

*In addition, Nichols is a musician. He was deeply influenced
by the acoustic blues tradition and by singers such as the blind
Reverend Gary Davis. Nichols met Davis and other guitarists in
Greenwich Village, as he dragged his guitar from hootenanny to
coffeehouse in the 1960s. Nichols's first career aspiration, he con-
fides, was to be a folksinger.*

*In the studio he waxes characteristically passionate about pol-
itics. He is unabashedly partisan, but able to see the other side
of arguments.* American Blood, *his Vietnam novel, offers extraordinary sympathy to the plight of the grunt in Vietnam—the very
group that Nichols in his twenties tried so hard to prevent from*

shipping out in the first place. His political intelligence is clearly humanistic, inspired by his wide-ranging reading habits. Yet behind an almost meek demeanor, an imperious streak occasionally emerges: Nichols was once observed trying to convince a complete stranger not to shoot his snapshot vertically, a practice which the photographer in Nichols cannot abide.

Nichols's second interview occurred while he was a Visiting Writer in the English department at the University of New Mexico. He walked across the campus to the radio station from his office, where, for the first time in twenty years, he was teaching a creative-writing seminar and another, of his own devising, "The Writer in Society."

In person, one finds few signs of the cult novelist whose work is closely followed in Germany and Japan. He is an unassuming man, every bit as happy chording blues tunes on the piano in the studio while the engineer changes tapes as he is discussing his fiction.

Nichols's passionate engagement carries over into scarcely less ideological issues, such as whether he can be considered a "southwestern writer." He is quick to insist that he, like most authors, strives to write about universal subjects for a universal audience. He sees the label of the southwestern writer as something which reduces an author's status by rendering him "regionalist." Yet few who read the passages on the next few pages will doubt his profound connection to the southwestern landscape, the mesas, the sweeping vistas, and the craggy brown mountains behind his house in Taos.

JOHN NICHOLS:

All my life I have only felt comfortable in social situations where there was a great *mezcla*, a mixture, of races and cultures and languages. I love being in an area where there's also a mixture of classes. Most of my life—who knows why—most of my sympathies always seemed generated toward the working class and to the nature of the struggle to right the inequalities that exist on earth. I never felt comfortable with the privilege that I was raised in.

In 1965, I became very aware of the Vietnam War after taking a trip to Guatemala. The trip really changed my life. It was only for a couple of months, I was visiting a friend on a Fulbright grant, but I was shocked by the terrible lives that the Guatemalan people were leading and by the obvious fact that much of their misery was a direct result of the policies and the government of the United States.

I wanted to develop some kind of polemical art, art with a social conscience, art that wasn't just entertaining but would proselytize people to change the nature of how they acted on the earth. For many years the books I wrote were geared toward trying to teach Americans that they had to get out of Vietnam. They also were involved with the environment, trying to teach people that we have to stop destroying the earth. So, the kinds of books I finally managed to publish when I got to New Mexico were essentially the kind of books that I began to write when I was still living in New York City, but I didn't have the skills at that time to bring it all together.

When I got to Taos, a small town, curiously, things were revealed to me, or were opened to me in a way that they really weren't in the big city. Everything is so exposed in New Mexico because of the space, the lack of trees, the wideness, and that includes the people. I often tell folks that I learned more about New York City by living in Taos, New Mexico, than I ever did living in New York.

We live in a country that has a long and distinguished history of political writing, going back to Thomas Paine and Jefferson, moving up to people like William Dean Howells and John Steinbeck. Bertolt Brecht, the famous German poet and writer and playwright, once said: "Young man, reach for a book, it is a weapon."

I spent a lot of my life feeling that it was useless to be a writer in the United States, that really I should wind up spending my life on the barricades instead. Finally, when I was about thirty-two years old—and I had been writing at that point for about fifteen years—it hit me, lightning bolts out of heaven, that literature, as well as most other aspects of culture, is often one of the most polemical, important parts of political struggle all around the world. I don't know why it took me so long to realize that, probably because I was raised in a country that taught me that art and politics don't mix. Nevertheless, if you get outside of the borders of the United States, you realize quickly that the definition of being a writer is to be a political human being. I think that's the reason that most of the great writers in our hemisphere—Latin America, Central America, and Mexico—spend, or have spent, most of their lives in exile: simply because the definition of literature in their countries is that it is a political act.

I suppose any artist just simply uses the topical and local as the springboard toward what's universal. Any artist, whether it's Tolstoy writing about Russia, Philip Roth writing about New York City, William Faulkner writing about some area of the South, or John Nichols writing about New Mexico—they're all writing about small towns, maybe, but it's all universal.

New Mexico is not a middle-class, bourgeois American state, it's much closer to the Third World. New Mexico is a state where a very small percentage of the population controls a very large amount of the wealth, where there is a large minority—in fact a majority-minority population in the north, which nevertheless works for minimum wage or less. Eighty percent live at the poverty level or below it.

I remember after *The Milagro Beanfield War* came out a number of local people would come up to me and say, "How could you know so much about our culture after only living here for two years before you wrote the book?" And my response is usually that 85 percent of the book is universal, that I knew it before I ever got to New Mexico.

I often begin on a one-sentence premise, you know: A thirty-five-year-old unemployed Chicano handyman cuts water illegally into a half-acre bean field and all hell breaks loose. And then I just type "Once upon a time."

There are as many true stories as there are people to tell those stories. What the culture does with stories, whether it mistreats or exploits stories, is something that is not, I think, for any artist to be able to control. It's very difficult for an artist, particularly one who receives some kind of recognition, to then control the "pizzafication" of that recognition which this culture automatically bestows. If artists wished to avoid that particular dilemma then they would simply refuse to create.

With *The Nirvana Blues*, again, I was broke, and so I did a treatment of the book I was going to write, and the publisher would not give me an advance because they said it sounded like a stupid novel. What's funny is, I planned to write a novel that took place over a year and the structure of the book was going to be predicated on the structure of building a house. I had that all plotted out quite carefully and then I sat down to write the book, and a few months later I was on page six hundred, and I'd only gone from a Saturday night to a Tuesday morning and I realized I was never going to get to the building of the house.

After about the fourth or fifth draft of *The Nirvana Blues*, I had a book which had very little shape whatsoever. I was interested in satirizing everything I could think of, from the Me Generation self-absorption of est, Scientology groupies to the Erica Jong myth of the "zipless" screw. I had this amorphous mass of pages, and so I finally said, "I've got to put some kind of structure in here just to get people to turn pages," which is when I imposed on the novel the hero trying to make a buy of half a kilo of cocaine, in order to get the money to buy the land to build his house.

I'm always aware that my first drafts may be ten drafts away from the finish of the book, but it's the most important draft in that I get a whole lot of pages, I get some kind of structure, I get something to play with. It's like creating clay in order to then start shaping it into some form that works.

I've been influenced by almost everything I've read, whether it was Dickens, Émile Zola, Victor Hugo, John Steinbeck, or Ernest Hemingway.

Magical realism? I've read a lot, and the world seems to be a place where there's an awful lot of magical realism going down. I mean I've watched people crawling on their hands and knees across stones to the Virgin of the Pilar, the big post in the cathedral in Zaragoza, and press their lips against this marble column that has this huge indentation on it from centuries of being kissed by people who believe in God. Now if God and the Bible isn't magical realism I don't what is, you know?

On a purely pragmatic level, movies are the only way I've ever been able to earn a living. I've published eleven books and even have eleven books in print, but I don't think that the royalties from all those books in print over the years amounts to five thousand bucks a year, if that. I've worked on about seven or eight movies, all of which I've been proud to work on, that were heavily political, and it always startled me that people were actually willing to pay me money.

By 1982 I'd written about five drafts of the script [for the screenplay of *The Milagro Beanfield War*] and nobody was excited about anything that I'd done. I was dropped from the picture and I thought that it was over. Then, in 1985, I received a script written by a guy named David Ward, who scripted *The Sting* for Redford. And they said this picture was going to be on again, and what did I think of this script? I read the script and did not think very highly of it at all. It was predicated on the assumption that a farmer in northern New Mexico, José Mondragon, plants a field of beans, but by mistake!

He doesn't realize that they're peas all during the gestation period of these plants, until finally he gets all his neighbors together to go out and harvest this crop, and somebody realizes, "Oh my God, it's peas, not beans!"

You can imagine how I felt.

The process [of writing] is that things percolate for a long time. I get an idea, I make notes on the backs of envelopes and I throw them into a cardboard box, I type them up every now and then. And after a while various themes and ideas and instincts, in fact, not very focused instincts, begin to float around about a book. I get emotions about what I'd like to accomplish. I usually just focus on two or three one-sentence premises on what the book's going to be about. And after a while, it all nags and nags and I feel that there's a book there because I feel that in my vague concept about the material, there's an awful lot of energy that can be shaped into something worthwhile.

Then finally, I put off and I put off and I put off actually starting it because my life is so complicated, I have no time whatsoever, and would have even less time when I sit down to write a novel. So I put it off for days and months and maybe years until finally, I make a decision, You're a real jerk! You can't put it off any longer, and then I just close my eyes and hold my nose and I jump off the cliff.

Once I begin the process of writing a first draft of a book, though, I have one cardinal rule, which is you make a decision to do three pages or five pages or ten pages a day, and you hold to that decision every day, seven days a week, four weeks a month. I can't stop the momentum, because that's too debilitating. Once I begin the momentum, I've got to carry it out each day because in that way, the book manages to carry itself also, however awkwardly.

When I began writing *A Ghost in the Music*, I had a self-conscious literary metaphor of meaning underlying my reasons for writing it. I wanted to write something about the tragedy of creative energy in our country: it seems that one of the great lies in our arts is that the artists and poets, et cetera, should all drink themselves to death and commit suicide or jump off bridges, that self-destruction was considered creative.

On a wider level, of course, I was very conscious about North America, the United States, as having been given this utterly virgin land to experiment with rather late in history—with all the opportunities to create an unbelievably wonderful society—and instead look at what we're doing.

My grandfather grew up in a world where there was only what? A billion people, a billion and a half people. Everything that we've ever talked about before as to conservation areas or protecting the earth or setting aside national parks, is no longer relevant. We've got five and half billion people on the globe; it's going to turn into ten billion people, what, in the next forty years? When people talk about environment nowadays, you have to include every acre of the globe. You have to include the incredible disasters of urban areas and inner cities. You have to recognize that four-fifths of the planet, including the planet's surface area and the planet's populations, human and natural, are essentially already living in a form of Armageddon or apocalypse. Human societies have broken down, animal societies have broken down, the atmosphere is breaking down, the forest system is breaking down, the oceans are starting to break down.

Obviously when we begin to talk now about solutions to this problem, we've got to talk about entirely revamping, re-educating, changing the societies as they exist today, and whether you're a capitalist or a Marxist, you have to talk about radically altering the theories that drive your philosophies because none of the old ways work anymore.

EXCERPTS

The Milagro Beanfield War

All his life Amarante had lived in the shadow of his own death. When he was two days old he caught pneumonia, they gave him up for dead, somehow he recovered. During his childhood, he was always sick, he couldn't work like other boys his age. He had rheumatic fever, chicken pox, pneumonia three or four more times, started coughing blood when he was six, was anemic, drowsy all the time, constantly sniffling, weak and miserable and—everybody thought—dying. At eight he had his tonsils out; at ten, his appendix burst. At twelve, he was bitten by a rattlesnake, went into a coma, survived. Then a horse kicked him, breaking all the ribs on his left side. He contracted tuberculosis. He hacked and stumbled around, hollow-eyed, gaunt and sniffling, and folks crossed themselves, murmuring Hail Marys whenever he staggered into view. At twenty, when he was already an alcoholic, scarlet fever almost laid him in the grave; at twenty-three, malaria looked like it would do the job. Then came several years of amoebic dysentery. After that he was constipated for seventeen months. . . .

Amarante limped, coughed, wheezed; his chest ached; he spat both blood and gruesome blue-black lungers, drank until his asshole hurt, his flat feet wailed; arthritis took sledgehammers to his knees; his stomach felt like it was bleeding; and all but three of his teeth turned brown and toppled out of his mouth like acorns. In Milagro, waiting for Amarante

Córdova to drop dead became like waiting for one of those huge sneezes that just refuses to come.

The Last Beautiful Days of Autumn

I live for autumn. All year long I have reveries of those cool, beautiful days to come, and memories of Octobers past. It's the most alive, the most heartbreakingly real season in my bones. I love the chilly winds and dying leaves and the first snow flurries that sweep intermittently down this lean valley. I adore the harvest smells around me, of ripe and rotting fruit, of the last alfalfa cutting. Nervous horses with their heads raised, flared nostrils tautly sniffing arctic odors, make me feel like singing. And I long for the gorgeous death of that high-country season when the mountains pulse with the pellucid varnish of winter whiteness, and the spears of a million bare aspens—only moments ago bursting with resplendent foliage—create a soft, grey smirrh across jagged hillsides. . . .

I live in a beautiful high country valley.

On the eastern side of Taos the Sangre de Cristo mountains rise up to thirteen thousand feet. West of town, the broad sagebrush mesa is bisected by a magnificent narrow crack in the Earth, the Rio Grande Gorge. The heart of Taos area is productive, wet, verdant. Dozens of irrigation ditches and their many smaller veins branch off of nine major streams, forming an arterial system that sustains a dwindling number of small fields and farms. . . .

Okay, so it's autumn, time for work, and I'm steaming along strong on a novel. Sometimes, in the wee hours, I take a break, make coffee, sink my teeth into an apple, flick on the radio, and read the paper. . . . The wind is howling outside, but I'm snug in my disorganized, comfortable kitchen, listening to Merle Travis sing: *"If You Want Your Freedom PDQ, Divorce Me C.O.D."*

The Nirvana Blues

... Chamisaville was so unbalanced and disoriented, people did not know if they were dreaming or awake. . . . A small sand cloud piloted by a confused trade wind, floated over the valley, depositing fine layers of grit. On the day it arrived, a galactic seer, Mojo Shir Bud, hit town, and, experimenting with astral projection, immediately went into a trance atop the plaza police pillbox, freed his soul from his body, forgot how to reel it back in on its silver cord, and keeled over dead as a doornail, becoming the first known case of "death by meditation" in the southwestern United States. Eight hours later, the town manager, Kenneth Eagleton, almost lost his own life under equally weird circumstances. Early that morning, he had treated his head with a "dry-look" hairspray. Around noon, when he lit a cigar after dining in the La Tortuga, with the young lawyer, Bob Moose, and the Mayor, Mel "Sonny" Christiansen, his hair exploded into flames, and only some fast moves by the Mayor, who doused him with a pitcher of dry martinis, saved the town manager's life. Hardly had Kenneth recovered, than insult was added to injury when a lanky freak wearing a red cape and a chartreuse ski mask walked into his office and nailed him in the kisser with a lemon meringue pie. . . .

An Elegy for September

It was raining again. She'd invited him over to her room at the foundation and they had built a cedar fire and snacked on graham crackers and chamomile tea. He sat in a chair by the window, gazing into the storm while she touched the bow to her violin and played the sweetest music he'd ever heard, a high forlorn melody that broke his heart. It seemed very important not to watch as she played. He had no wish to disturb her in any way that might break the spell. So he remained stationary while raindrops splashed against the window and tree leaves fluttered in the wind.

NOTES

1. Jeffrey Burke, *Harper's*, vol. 257, no. 1539 (August 1978), p. 89.

2. Doris Grumbach, *New York Times Book Review*, June 10, 1979, p. 18.

3. Joel Swerdlow, "Father and Sons on the Brink," *Washington Post Book World*, September 9, 1979, p. 6.

4. Al Barozzi, *Best Sellers*, vol. 39, no. 8 (Nov. 1979), p. 283.

5. John Nichols, speaking at Salt of the Earth Bookstore, Albuquerque, New Mexico, April 16, 1988.

6. Norbert Blei, *Chicago Tribune Book World*, quoted in *Contemporary Authors* (Detroit, Mich.: Gale Research, 1982), vol. 6, p. 368.

SIMON ORTIZ

▲ ✣ ▼ ✣ ▼ ✣ ▲

Like many writers in this series, from Ed Abbey to Luci Tapahonso, Pueblo poet Simon Ortiz's poetry resonates with
images of the desert landscape: arid plains, wind-carved rocks,
immense expanses of porcelain blue sky. Ortiz's focus is on
language, and how the stark beauty of the desert can be made
to sing with rhythm and verse. His poetry is rooted in the ancient oral traditions of the Acoma tribe, but it branches out
into the realities of modern life, urban and rural, in the new
Southwest.

> *Beneath the cement foundations*
> *of the motel, the ancient spirits*
> *of the people conspire sacred tricks.*
> *They tell stories and jokes and laugh*
> *and laugh.*
>
> —SIMON ORTIZ[1]

Native American poet Simon Ortiz grew up in Acoma
Pueblo, believed to be the oldest continually inhabited settlement in the United States. Many of the thick-walled adobe
buildings date back to the dawn of this millennium, some even
earlier. The main pueblo, known as the Sky City, sits atop a
flat-topped six-hundred-foot mesa which rises sharply from the
desert floor some seventy miles west of Albuquerque, New
Mexico. Until the late 1930s, the only way to the top was by a
narrow series of hand- and footholds carved into the sheer

rock wall of the mesa and worn smooth by countless generations of Acoma.

For many European-Americans, a cultural identity, a language, or a body of stories that has survived a thousand years
is difficult to imagine; but for Ortiz, this cultural continuity nes-
tles at the heart of his poetry. To date, Ortiz has published
eleven books of poetry and one of short stories; his work has
been reviewed widely in Native American publications, including *Wicazo Review* and *American Indian Quarterly*. He is one of
the few American Indian poets to have been published nation-
ally (by Harper and Row).

Ortiz sees himself as born on a cusp, when his tribe was
balanced "on the edge of something new." Born on May 27,
1941, as a young child his life was shadowed by World War II,
when many of his relatives left Acoma to join the army or find
work in California or Chicago. The old ways of the Pueblo were
in flux.

Ortiz's father worked for the Santa Fe Railroad line for most
of his life. His parents lived in Acoma Pueblo's second village,
below the mesa top, McCarty's. (In traditional Pueblo fashion,
the house, built of traditional hand-hewn stone by his father,
actually belonged to Ortiz's mother.) The railroad, the major
source of knowledge and goods from the outside world, ran
just two miles north. In addition to bringing the outside world
to Acoma, it took Acomas to the outside world.

In the Native Southwest, Ortiz says, jobs like his father's in
the early half of this century were a trade-off. The railroads
laid tracks through the Pueblos, often taking the best and most
fertile farmland (because it was also often the flattest), then
offering the men jobs in return. As a result, traditionally agrarian Pueblos grew increasingly less self-sufficient and more de-
pendent on paychecks from the outside. Railroad jobs were
mostly unskilled, labor-intensive positions with poverty-level
wages and few opportunities for advancement. Yet there was
little other work to be had in rural New Mexico.

Ortiz's father was moved several times by the Santa Fe line
while Ortiz was still in elementary school, to Arizona and then
briefly to California. Ortiz and his mother followed, but they
always returned to Acoma. From the winding curves of the
narrow two-lane road leading to the pueblo, the fluted stone

walls of the mesa thrust abruptly from the sandy, high-desert floor dotted with gray-green sagebrush and low juniper and piñon trees. The vast expanse of sky and sand stretches to a jagged horizon of distant mountains to the north. Just east of Sky City stands a second formation, Enchanted Mesa, the top of which can easily be viewed from Sky City. It is said to be inhabited by the ghosts of a lost pueblo, trapped there when a violent rainstorm caused an entire wall of the mesa to collapse, destroying their precarious handhold access trail.

The physical landscape of the pueblo and its age-old cultural and social ties are the threads that bind Ortiz's poetry and stories. His earliest memories are of the voices of his clan and parents singing together these threads from the cloth of Acoma's vibrant oral tradition.[2] Ortiz's mother was a traditional Acoma woman, a potter and elder of the Eagle clan, the clan to which, according to Pueblo tradition, her children belong. She honored the responsibility of her position as a clan elder, ensuring that her children were familiar with their history and traditions. "I remember the silence of the Southwest," Ortiz says, "and music was a mixture of my father singing and my mother speaking songs and stories—sounds of an elder generation—and the railroad which rattles, rumbles, east and west, constantly, north of my mother's house."

To Ortiz, Pueblo oral tradition is more than folktales passed from one generation to the next: "It embodies the ceremonial, social life that has been kept within the continuum of the Acoma people," he explains. "It includes advice and counsel, those things told to you by your elders to ensure that you are living responsibly, to ensure that the relationships among family members are correct and according to Acoma ways of life.

"There are also children's stories, and stories that are historical in nature and look at the Spanish colonization. These types of stories are very much a part of how [white] America is seen by Acomas. There are many stories that provoke thought, speculation, that provide insight into how that other way of life works, stories which tell very clearly what the role of an individual is in Acoma and what the role of a person is in the whole scheme of life in the universe."

This living oral tradition, adapting and absorbing elements of outside cultures, is quite different from the one Ortiz learned

in Anglo schools, where Indians and their cultures, if acknowledged at all, were presented as artifacts of "the vanishing
race." On the contrary, Ortiz views his traditions not as frozen
in time before the arrival of Europeans, but as a synchronizing
process of adapting realities of life in the twentieth century to
a uniquely Native vision.

In the early 1950s, he recalls, he would huddle next to his
brother and both of them would listen intently to his older
sister's radio, which could pick up country-and-western stations from Del Rio, Texas, and rock and roll from Shreveport,
Louisiana. The broadcasts, he says, were "like a signal coming
from Mars, a voice from another world. They were also the
connection that really indicated the changes that were taking
place."

Ortiz's father embodied this cross-fertilization of culture.
His father was a singer in the ancient Acoma tradition, an elder
of the Antelope Society, but he also loved the western tunes
of the 1930s: "He would sing railroad songs, folk songs, Jimmie
Rodgers, set into the context of the Acoma cultural life. It was
a part of that indication of change."

When Ortiz was six years old, he began attending McCarty's
Day School, administered by the Bureau of Indian Affairs. Here
he learned English and came to grips with the enormity of the
world outside Acoma. Ortiz recalls it as exciting, but frightening, to go to the BIA school. Speaking any Native language was
forbidden and punishable with whippings; but he looked forward to knowing other children from remote corners of the
Pueblo.

The best part was learning to read. As a child, Ortiz was
such a diligent listener, and occasional eavesdropper, that his
father teasingly called him "the reporter." Learning to read
and write in English unlocked a world of knowledge about distant and exotic places.

In the fifth grade, Ortiz moved to one such place—the
macabre-sounding, mostly Anglo, Skull Valley, Arizona, where
his father had been transferred by the railroad. The family
lived there for only one year, but Ortiz never forgot the railroad's substandard housing—often no more than old boxcars,
without electricity or running water. It inspired him to begin
questioning life, socially, politically, and personally—and it in-

spired him to write. His first piece of poetry (a Mother's Day poem) was published in the Skull Valley school newspaper.

After a final year at McCarty's Day School, Ortiz was sent to St. Catherine's Indian School in Santa Fe, New Mexico, the same school his father had attended and from which he had repeatedly run away. Up to the 1950s, federal policy was to send Native American children to boarding schools far from their homes and families, in hopes that physical separation would destroy the social and cultural bonds tying them to the reservations and "integrate" them into white society. It was the job of these boarding schools to turn Native American children into what on the reservations are called "Apple Indians"—red on the outside, white on the inside.

At boarding school in the 1950s, Ortiz first took his writing seriously. He kept a journal into which he incorporated poems, song lyrics, and fragments of stories. He was a voracious reader and daydreamer, imagining himself, he admits sheepishly, a famous writer, "a kind of Acoma Hemingway."

Although he was temporarily embarrassed when his journal was discovered by a nun—only girls were supposed to keep diaries, Ortiz laughs—by the time he finished high school, he had decided to become a writer.

He studied writing at the University of New Mexico and the University of Iowa, working occasionally at the uranium mines near Acoma. The mines and the poignant symbolism of machines wrenching ancient rocks from beneath a pueblo to make the most powerful bombs on earth were especially compelling. Ortiz turned to this uneasy juxtaposition for his first poetry collection, *Naked in the Wind* (1970). This was followed six years later with the acclaimed *Going for the Rain* (1976), and then by *The Good Journey* (1977). Critic Don Byrd called these works "a powerful and moving record of a Native American who is an alien in his own land. . . . Ortiz gives us some of the most complete articulations to be found in English of that consciousness which swells in proximity with the eternity which ritual makes manifest."[3]

His works have been critically well received. Ortiz has been called one of the country's most important Native American poets. Yet, Byrd insists, "Ortiz should not be read as a specimen Native American or an anthropological curiosity. He is, above all, an American poet and a very good one, [writing] lines . . . envied by any poet."[4]

Ortiz's poetry glides effortlessly from the world of the Acoma Antelope Society, to the glass and steel of L.A. International Airport, to his mother's living room in the house his father built for her from hand-hewn sandstone, where she loves to watch "As The World Turns" and "Monday Night Football," rooting for her favorite football team—the Washington Redskins.

These startling cultural juxtapositions are made all the more sharp by the precision of Ortiz's language. Words are for him potent sources of change and remembrance. Although he writes in English, he sometimes frames his poems first in the Acoma language, or imagines them spoken by friends, family, or acquaintances, multilingual speakers whose speech is informed by the rhythms of multiple Indian languages as well as Spanish and English.

The irony of this patchwork of languages, especially against the backdrop of the whippings administered to Native children in BIA schools, is something Ortiz acknowledges. "You have to recognize the political nature of language, the political nature that can limit us. Yet language has a kind of neutrality at its very essence. When I look at creative literature as language, and language as energy, I don't see a contradiction."

The language of the Acoma reflects the landscape of the desert in which they live and to which they are tied in a spiritual sense. "My audience, in my early work, was the land," Ortiz recalls. "It was a giving back to the land that voice that it had given me." The harsh beauty of the Southwest moves Ortiz to "a certain linguistic outlook that has a sense of economy, of breathing in a certain way, a sense of rhythm that evokes not grandiosity as a response, but rather taking very great care."

And to this desert land Ortiz addressed his first poems: "The landscape is one vast, engulfing, enclosing place for me. The far mountains, blue in the distance, the canyonlands, red, brown, orange, yellow. The plateaus of semiarid vistas, out there, but also inside.

"Our literature refers to landscape, colors, the dryness of the land, the images of blue skies that wait like me for rain to come from the West; then seeing the land transformed when the rain does fall. These kinds of environmental influences bring about inspiration."

This responsibility of giving back the power of language to the land, and to the people who live on it, inspired Ortiz to become a teacher. Beginning in 1969, he taught at a half dozen institutions: the Rough Rock School in Arizona; briefly at San Diego State University in California; then back to the Southwest and the Institute of American Indian Arts in Santa Fe; Navajo Community College in Tsaile, Arizona. Since 1982, he has lived in Portland, Santa Fe, and Tucson, while working as his tribe's translator and editor of the Pueblo of Acoma Press. Today he spends much time traveling to local schools, speaking to the children, often in their native Acoma tongue, and trying, as he believes all poets should, to "demystify language."

Among his stints teaching creative writing was one at the University of New Mexico in 1972. There he met the young poet Joy Harjo, with whom he lived and eventually had a child, Rainy Dawn, in 1973. Their relationship brought together two prominent poetic voices and created a subtle exchange of writing styles which strengthened the work of each. It was a time of enormous growth, politically and artistically, in Native American communities, and the height of what is often referred to as the Red Power Movement, documented in fellow New Mexican Stan Steiner's seminal work, *The New Indians*.

This Indian civil rights movement paralleled the Hispanic self-determination struggles taking place in northern New Mexico and much of the Southwest, where Chicano leaders such as Reyes Tijerina seized control of small towns to protest the sale and taxation of their land grants to outside Anglo developers, and Cesar Chavez galvanized migrant farm laborers into demanding higher wages and safer working conditions.[5] Red Power activism, which culminated in the bloody confrontations at Wounded Knee in Pine Ridge, South Dakota, took the form in New Mexico and Oklahoma of safeguarding traditional hunting rights on Native land, such as the right to hunt out of season and without state licenses. (This same struggle was in its infancy at the Taos Pueblo when Frank Waters took it up in the 1940s with *The Man Who Killed the Deer*.)

Caught up in this rising tide, along with fellow Indian writers and scholars such as Leslie Silko, N. Scott Momaday, and Paula Gunn Allen (all of whom passed through Albuquerque and the University of New Mexico campus in this period), Ortiz researched Indian history, leading to the publication of *From Sand Creek* (1981). "Sand Creek" refers to a location in southeastern Colorado where, in 1864, six hundred Southern Cheyenne and Arapaho people, two-thirds of them women and children, were massacred by Colonel John M. Chivington and his volunteers of the Colorado militia. In Ortiz's words, it is "a long poem which looks at victims and victimizers." In this work Ortiz melds history and literature into an evocation of the tribulations of the past and their lessons for the Native American future: "That Dream shall have a name after all/ and it will not be vengeful/ . . . it will rise in this heart/ Which is our America."[6]

Also during the 1970s began Ortiz's battle to overcome alcoholism, a disease which had also plagued his father. In 1974, after returning from teaching at San Diego State University, Ortiz entered a detox program in Albuquerque, in an effort to cement his deteriorating relationship with Joy Harjo. Although their relationship ended soon after, Ortiz now considers himself a recovered alcoholic, and the experience left him with a particular compassion for the homeless, reflected in poems such as "Every Word, Everything," written in Portland in 1989, whose ghostly refrain is a street person's lament: "Help me, help me, help me."

In 1992 he published *Woven Stone*, a major compilation of three volumes of poetry, *Going for the Rain*, *The Good Journey*, and *Fight Back: For the Sake of the People, for the Sake of the Land* (1980) with an extensive introduction linking the works. According to critic Harold Jaffe, the poems in this volume "convey hope and the vision of a people whose traditions are the foundation of the soul of this land called America. Highly recommended."[7]

After and Before the Lightning was published in 1994. It charts a winter (the time between the prairie thunderstorms of autumn and spring) Ortiz spent teaching at the Rosebud Lakota Sioux Reservation in South Dakota, site of the Wounded Knee massacre. The work contains both poems and prose, weaving together the harshness of a northern plains winter with the equally difficult political realities facing its Native peoples. Leslie Marmon Silko calls *After and Before the Lightning* "a masterpiece, a symphony composed of poems of celebration and prayers for survival in America's prairie winter of the soul."[8] Terry Tempest Williams writes, "The poetry of Simon Ortiz is wind, rain, light. . . . He reminds us what we have lost, what we love, and what we must recover to see the world whole, even holy. The wisdom, the power of his language and the force of his life bear witness to the full range of human emotion."[9]

Together, Ortiz's poems are brief stories which form an epic of endless travel throughout an America burdened with a feeling of being lost at home. His vivid characterizations of people and places are accounts of a man synthesizing his cultural background with visions of a larger, ominous world.

Though Ortiz describes the darkness and destructiveness of America, he remains optimistic. The powers of language and myth that he has always known are still here. As Harold Jaffe commented in *The Nation*, "the cumulative impression [of *From Sand Creek*] is, admirably, not of gloom and despair, but of a renewed faith in the prospect of relationship with the land and solidarity among the dispossessed."[10]

In recent years, Ortiz's poetry has turned from Indian history to documenting Indian people's worldview and to the long-range implications of environmental degradation of Indian lands. Many have already been strip-mined and scarred until the land (and the folkways it sustained) is as downtrodden as the homeless in Ortiz's poem.

His work today, he comments, is directed at "that great mass of people who I think need to be reaffirmed of their humanity. Kind of a tall order, but what's a poet for?"

▲ ✧ ▼ ✧ ▼ ✧ ▲

At the time of our interview, Ortiz had just arrived from working with urban Indians in Portland, Oregon. He possesses a quiet but unmistakable power; it glides with him across the room, with his springy boxer's step. His squarish shoulders and silver-black hair are rather typical for a Pueblo Indian his age. He dresses modestly and carries himself gingerly. His ego is pushed out of site as he talks; for he often represents his tribe, which is also his family and his oldest friends. Though Ortiz lectures frequently across the West, he returns to the Southwest like a bird in winter.

It's probably impossible for non-Indians to realize fully the conflicts modern Native American artists face. The more successful they become, the more conflicted, from balancing family, tribal, and professional responsibilities. As a traditionalist—someone who keeps up with his ceremonies and rituals, even if he can't always attend—Ortiz's obligations persist even if he is teaching thousands of miles away from the Acoma reservation. With so few men in the tribe, every absence is noted. Many North Americans maintain a satisfactory family balance after moving across country from family and friends. Imagine how different this would be if they had to return every month or season for a medicine sing.

Ortiz relishes his role as a senior Indian writer, having taught at countless workshops and seminars. Encouraging young authors and directing them to editors and publishers are daily activities. Above all, though, he is a storyteller. As he tells a tale of an old man hunting in the mountains, he becomes an old uncle with the children gathered around. His rich voice jumps from the sonorous to the squeaky as he acts out the parts. His flat, sun-lined face, surprisingly like that of a northern European, flickers with passion when we turn to the difficulty of finding models for young Indian writers—particularly in his own era. His voice tightens until it has an intensity just short of piercing. The interview ended, he stands up slowly, shaking out a cramp from sitting too long in an airplane and in the studio, and heads out west, back to Acoma, Sky City.

SIMON ORTIZ:

Everything is story, in the sense that the tradition out of which poetry and song comes is like the story of the life of a people. That is, the culture survives because of the story of its birth, and goes on into its development and to the end of a cycle.

One's personal life, for example, begins with birth although one's personal story is only a continuation of a larger story.

Story is important in that it's a kind of lifeline that connects the individual back to that larger story.

Poetry is a part of that story as a form of the oral tradition. The oral tradition lends itself very well to the narrative form of story, and poetry is certainly included within it, say in prayer and song. [There is] a sense of spirituality, a sense of being connected so inextricably and forever to that whole general story of life as we live and know and practice it.

Poetry is essentially story and language, language being an energy that forms us and at the same time the essence of how we come into being. Poetry, a part of language, then, is a part of this story of how we come into being and how we perceive and express that being.

The oral tradition insists upon the affirmation of life. Western culture's written literature is a kind of definition of life rather than the essence of life. Oral tradition, which is the source of myth (and of the spiritual reality that all life is) is quite different.

Mythology is more than just legends or tales, it's literature that has a spiritual dimension, that includes that creative source that is of mythic proportion.

"Uncle, tell us a story," people would say. "Tell us about the time you went to the mountains to hunt."

And the old man, Page, would say, "Well, I don't really want to; I don't have any stories."

"Please, Uncle," they would say.

So he would tell.

"When I was getting older, I went to the mountains to go hunting," he said. "I was getting blind and they didn't really want me to go, but I said that I would be the cook, so they let me go along.

"Well, when we got there and set up our camp, the younger men went off to hunt, and they told me to stay behind and cook and pray and keep the camp, because I couldn't see very well.

"So I did that for a while, but then I thought to myself, I'm not that old and blind yet. I can still go out and hunt.

"And so I went out. I went to the north a little ways, looking on the ground and looking into the oak thicket to see if the deer were there waiting for me. I looked and looked, and pretty soon I saw some tracks. I looked closely and they were big."

"How big were they, Uncle?" the people would ask.

"Oh, they were this big."

"You sure they weren't bigger?"

"Well, okay, bigger. They were this big," he would reply.

"So I followed the deer tracks along and I would sing, and take out from my cornmeal bag, the meal. And I would put them with precious stones and my prayers in the tracks of the deer up ahead, which I knew was waiting for me. And I would tell it, 'Please, deer, please wait for me. I'm getting old and I can't see very well. You have to wait for me up ahead.'

"So I went along and I got to a certain point and I had to go down to this oak at the bottom of a hill. I went down very carefully and I could hear something moving around in there.

"I said, '*Oh-hoy*, I can hear you in there. Thank you for waiting for me.'

"And so I prepared myself one more time and said my proper prayers, and I looked into the thicket and I saw this thing moving toward me. I lifted my rifle to shoot and looked for a vital spot, and this animal looked at me, and it was a pig, not a deer.

"Well, I decided it was going to be my pig anyway. '*Cochino*,' I said, 'you will have to be my pig today!' And I shot it and I dressed it and along my way back to camp I picked up my precious stones."

When I first began to see myself as a writer, there really were no Native American writers. When I first became conscious of the specific use of words in writing, I was a writer, because I simply stepped into that energy that language is, with a love for language, and a writer is a writer before he uses language on paper, simply by his love for something beyond the love for language.

I didn't really have any Native American influences before I decided I would be a writer. Hemingway, Faulkner, Whitman, Sandburg, Theodore Dreiser—realists like Hamlin Garland, Steinbeck, Sinclair Lewis—were my models. Later on, in the 1960s when I became aware of Native American writers, I looked for them, but we were all more or less contemporaries.

N. Scott Momaday, the Kiowa novelist and poet who is only a few years older than I am, was a student at the University of New Mexico. Jim Welch, Leslie Silko, we all came along about the same time. We were interdependent models for each other.

I believe that I might also be following the traditions of other poets that I admire, Pablo Neruda, Ernesto Cardenal, writers who voice an appreciation and respect and love for life and land and people to inspire them, as well as criticize, to point out certain elements that need to be pointed out.

A consciousness leads [southwestern writers] to share identifiable images, metaphors that could only be southwestern geographically. There is an interface, a struggle, that affects us all. The Southwest is essentially still a colonized, colonial territory. John Nichols, with his own work, tries to bring out this idea that the land here and the lifestyle that has been lived for thousands of years must resist the more destructive changes brought by Western expansionism, including the railroads, land developers, uranium exploitation by Los Alamos and Sandia National Laboratories, and planning for purely economic profit.

EXCERPTS

Woven Stone (A Good Journey)

"A New Mexico Place Name"

In this case, American history
has repeated itself.
It is too easy to stop itself.

COCHITI CITY

The crux is a question
of starving or eating.
An unfair question, surely
but who of the people

will not find it necessary
to ask?

Salas, of the old city,
points his finger
toward the

CITY

off to the right,
pointing to where
there is a sacred place.
"Right there," he says,
a halting in his voice,
"right there,"
and a bulldozer rumbles
over the horizon
of the hill unto that place.

This year a model

CITY

is being sold by salesmen
from Southern California.
Sometimes I think
that history will come
to know no one
except its salesmen.

Going for the Rain

"Hunger in New York City"

Hunger crawls into you
from somewhere out of your muscles
or the concrete or the land
or the wind pushing you.

It comes to you, asking
for food, words, wisdom, young memories
of places you ate at, drank cold spring water,
or held somebody's hand,
or home of the gentle, slow dances,
the songs, the strong gods, the world
you know.

That is, hunger searches you out.
It always asks you,
How are you, son? Where are you?
Have you eaten well?
Have you done what you as a person
of our people is supposed to do?

And the concrete of this city,
the oily wind, the blazing windows,
the shrieks of automation cannot,
truly cannot, answer for that hunger
although I have hungered,
truthfully and honestly, for them
to feed myself with.

So I sang to myself quietly:
I am feeding myself
with the humble presence
of all around me;
I am feeding myself
with your soul, my mother earth;
make me cool and humble.
Bless me.

"I Told You I Like Indians"

You meet Indians everywhere.

Once I walked into this place—
Flagler Beach, Florida,
you'd never expect it—
a bar; some old people ran it.

The usual question, of course,
"You're an Indian, aren't you?"
"Yes, ma'am." I'm Indian alright.
Wild, ignorant, savage!
And she wants me to dance.
Well, okay, been drinking beer
all the way from Hollywood.
We dance something.

You're Indian aren't you?
Yeah, jeesus christ almighty,
I'm one of them.

I like Indians!

"There's an Indian around here."
What? And in walks a big Sioux.
Crissake man, how's relocation, brother?
He shakes my hand. Glad to see you.
I thought I was somewhere else.
We play the pingpong machine, drink beer,
once in a while dance with the old lady
who likes Indians.

I like Indians!

I *told* you
You meet Indians everywhere.

"What's Your Indian Name?"

It has to do with full moments
of mountains, deserts, suns, gods,
song, completeness.

It has to do with heroes, stories, legends
full of heroes and traveling.

It has to do with rebirth and growing
and being strong and seeing.

You see it's like this (the movement):
go to the water
and gather the straight willow stems
bring them home
work carefully at forming them
tie on the feathers
paint them with the earth
feed them and talk with them
pray.

You see, son, the eagle is a whole person
the way it lives; it means it has to do
with paying attention to where it is,
not the center of the earth especially
but part of it, one part among all parts,
and that's only the beginning.

From Sand Creek

"Rising in This Heart Which Is Our America"

That dream shall have a name after all,
and it will not be vengeful
but wealthy with love, and compassion and knowledge,
and it will rise in this heart,
which is our America.
It will rise in this heart,
which is our America.

Other Works

"Night Horses"

Quickly, before my breath
knows what I am doing, they roll
thunder away from me. Seeing
is a sudden strain; they are beyond.
My ken is only a drifting light
of cloud. It's fright I sense,

quickly, frantic and urgent
for my mind to settle in decision.

I merely went into the backyard
to get this morning's laundry.
And now the rolling fear at my feet,
in my stomach comes out of the dark.

But they are horse after all. Yes,
I see them soon clearly, this side
of shadows beyond. Their shapes
emerge into the forms I love, I know,
the nudge of their breaths enclosing
the air we breathe. They are dark
within the greater dark of night
at the other end of the clothesline.
Yet, for the moment, I could not know
why I was throttled by sudden motion
of fear, the entering quickly force.
I refused to accept the dark there.

Now the horses linger gently at the edge
of the assured moment; they wait for me.
Our knowledge of fear is vast; it is
our knowledge of the great dark of the spirit.

"Every Word, Everything"

Coming from the movie, Fatal Attraction
I was trying to recreate scenes,
thinking about them,
thinking of what they meant,
thinking like a man who loves film:
realism, super-realism, whatnot crap.

And then at the Tri-Met bus stop in Portland,
a man says, "Help me, help me,
help me, help me,"
over and over again.

* * *

He is dirty, sick-eyed, piss on his pants.
Two teenage girls run away
when he nears them
"Help me, help me, help me, help me."

I'm trying to remember who started
the flirtation, Glenn Close or what's his name.
Does it matter? Is it important?
Who wrote the script? Does it matter?

I try to think, but the movie makes no sense.
Help me, help me, help me, I feel huge.
Like a huge, empty, clumsy balloon, I feel
like imploring with my hands the Oregon sky,
I feel helpless, disconnected, unmanageable.

As the man lurches away, I don't recall
a single scene in Fatal Attraction,
but I remember every word, everything
that man said.

"Help me, help me, help me, help me."

N O T E S

1. "Washyuma Motor Hotel," *Going For The Rain* (New York: Harper & Row, 1976), p. 61.

2. For more information on Acoma oral tradition, see H. L. James, *Acoma: People of the White Rock* (West Chester, Pa.: Schiffer Publishing, 1988), with an introduction by Frank Waters.

3. Don Byrd, *Contemporary Poets* (Chicago: St. James Press, 1991), p. 727.

4. Ibid.

5. For a more complete look at the history of the Chicano civil rights movement, see Stan Steiner's *La Raza* (New York: Harper & Row, 1969), and Matt Meler's "King Tiger: Reyes Lopez Tijerina" in *Journal of the West*, vol. 27, no. 2 (April 1988), pp. 60–69.

6. "Sand Creek," *From Sand Creek*, (New York: Thunder's Mouth Press, 1981) p. 94.

7. Harold Jaffe, quoted in *Contemporary Authors* (Detroit, Mich.: Gale Research), vol. 134, 1992, p. 381.

8. Leslie Marmon Silko, in University of Arizona Press catalog (fall 1994).

9. Terry Tempest Williams, in University of Arizona Press catalog (fall 1994).

10. Harold Jaffe, quoted in *Contemporary Authors.*

ALBERTO RIOS

▲ ✣ ▼ ✣ ▼ ✣ ▲

Mexican-American and British, poet Alberto Rios grew up on the southwestern borderlands, a place often referred to as a third country where the cultures of the United States and Mexico meet, clash, and intertwine. Rios's poems and stories are a *mezcla* of English fairy tales and Hispanic *cuentos*; written in English but flavored by the sensibilities of his first language, Spanish. His work centers on life in the blue-collar barrios of Nogales, which straddles the Mexican border with Arizona.

Rios's writing might be called an urban version of the more rural southwestern magical realism of Rudolfo Anaya and Linda Hogan. And yet, it is rooted in the desert lore of his Mexican ancestors and in his mother's tales of snowdrifts towering over her head as a child in Lancashire. The task Rios sets for his writing is not to unify this duality, but to respect and appreciate it. His work helps readers negotiate the complex identities that are today's Southwest.

> *The West is a big place, but not my West. The West for me is where I lived—it is a house. And it is how I lived, and who I lived with. It's some people, and some streets, a border fence with Mexico in the distance, and an arroyo across the highway, a dry landscape, Coronado Elementary School, the Nogales Apaches High School fight song. My West is like that, a place to live. When I was old enough to think about the West, it was gone. It had moved into the realm of capital letters.*

> —ALBERTO RIOS

Arizona poet Alberto Rios has spent his life straddling the borders of the West. His father is Mexican, his mother British. He was born in Nogales, Arizona, in 1952, just two miles from the tall chain-link fence separating Mexico from the United States. He has relatives in three countries and on both sides of the Atlantic.

Like most of us, Rios grew up listening to stories, but few of us had the mix he did: Mexican *cuentos* [stories, tall tales] told in Spanish by his father's family (on both sides of the border), alongside English fairy tales, related in British English from his Lancashire mother (whose accent remains so pronounced, after forty years in the United States, that she is known in Nogales as "the English nurse"). When he writes, Rios says, he thinks in Spanish, but the words appear on the page in English.

Over the years, Rios has reaped many honors, including the prestigious Walt Whitman Award from the Academy of American Poets for an early collection of poetry, *Whispering to Fool the Wind* (1982). *The Iguana Killer* (1984), a collection of semi-autobiographical short fiction, received the Western States Book Award, and a volume of poems, *Teodoro Luna's Two Kisses* (1990), has recently been reissued by W. W. Norton in paperback. His eight books of stories and poems have been featured in over twenty anthologies.

The work of Alberto Rios is characterized by its balance of realism and fantasy, humor and tragedy—reflections of his childhood along the Mexico–United States border.

Cultural duality has always been a part of Rios's life. "I grew up around my father's [Mexican] family," he recalls, "but I look like my mother—which means I got to see two worlds from the beginning, and could even physically experience the difference growing up where I did: I could put, every day of my life, one foot in Mexico and one foot in the United States, at the same time."

Rios grew up speaking Spanish, until he entered public school in Nogales, Arizona. As they started first grade, Spanish-speaking children were told they would not be allowed to speak Spanish at school, even on the playground. Those who did would be physically punished if caught. This policy, aimed at achieving the same acculturation expected of Native Americans, was carried out across the Southwest.

Rios was caught. Being publicly spanked for speaking his father's language left a scar Rios carries today. The experience reverberated emotionally and resulted, for him and his classmates, in profound changes in their worldviews. By the time he was in junior high school—still no Spanish allowed—he could no longer speak it. "We knew one got swatted for something bad—our parents had taught us that. So if we got swatted for speaking Spanish, Spanish then must be bad. . . . If speaking Spanish was bad, we then must be bad kids. And our parents still spoke Spanish, so they had to be bad people. This was easy enough for children to grasp; so, though of course we loved them, we learned to be ashamed.

"Not until my last years of high school and college did I relearn Spanish. . . . The physical pain of being swatted, of thinking about being swatted—this doesn't go away so easily."

Rios still understood Spanish and engaged in the code switching practiced by children whose parents speak a language different from the one they must speak in school: when parents address their children in their native tongue, they answer in English. This weaving together of two languages lends an elusive rhythmic quality to Rios's poems. In reviewing Rios's *Five Indiscretions* (1985), one critic from the *New York Times Book Review* noted that "through his overlay of Spanish syntax on English he produces odd metaphors. . . . It is delightfully worth keeping the book open."[1]

Rios created his own communication strategies to cope with the multilingual world which surrounded him. As a child, he went several times a week to his paternal grandmother's house for lunch. He had ceased to speak Spanish, but she spoke no English; so they created a special, private means of communication: "What we had to do was invent a better language," Rios says, "something that wasn't an embarrassment for either of us. It had to be something that wasn't English or Spanish. So we made a language that exists between a grandmother and a grandson. She would cook and I would eat." Years later, in *Whispering to Fool the Wind*, Rios would write a poignant poem recalling the intricate, wordless conversations in her kitchen.

Rios's recollections of his childhood include the desert, mountains, canyons, and the rest of the natural world of the Southwest as well as the working-class barrios of Nogales. When he was five, his parents moved to a small neighborhood outside of town, into what was tactfully referred to as a "war bride neighborhood." Rios explains, "I was surrounded by people who were all in mixed marriages. The people across the street were Mexican-Japanese, my parents were Mexican-English, the couple next door was Mexican-Swedish, et cetera."

In his short story "The Secret Lion," adapted for television by the Public Broadcasting Service from Rios's collection *The Iguana Killer*, Rios writes about two young boys living on the outskirts of Nogales, exploring the surrounding desert. "My friend Sergio and I, we solved junior high school. We would come home from school on the bus, put our books away, change shoes, and go across the highway to the arroyo. It was the one place we were not supposed to go, so we did. It was our river, our personal Mississippi, our friend from long back."

Rios graduated from Nogales High School in 1970 and immediately entered the University of Arizona in Tucson. His parents were strong advocates of education; there was never any question that he would go to college even though his parents had no money for tuition. Rios paid his own way, and an early experience there changed his life forever.

As a young student, Rios had no idea of what exactly he wanted to study. For his first two years he was a political science major because, he claims, that's what his adviser was. Then, in his junior year, the University of Arizona computerized its registration system, and for the first time students could register for classes without direct approval from an adviser.

At that point, Rios says, he did what he thought all the students were doing:

I was thumbing through the entire university catalog, front to back, looking for the easiest courses I could find. This was my idea of playing school. School had always come at me, and I knew that what you did was to hit it back at itself. You took the easy courses because then you got good grades. It wasn't a mystery. I remember finding classes in the English department called Introduction to Poetry Writing and Introduction to Fiction Writing. And even more glaring, I read 'no final exam.' Aha! I thought, these are the classes for me, and I signed up for them.

And in fact, they absolutely were the easiest classes I'd ever taken—for the first month. Then at the end of the first month the teacher in the poetry class said, "All right, now go out and write one." And suddenly my mechanisms for school were attacked. There was nowhere I could go to get the answer, no book I could go to to copy it from. For the first time I was being asked to give something from the inside. That was an amazing revelation. It was an epiphany for me. At that point I became a creative-writing major.

Still, Rios worried that he would be unable to make a living as a writer; so he went back to school, earned a second degree in psychology, and then entered law school. His parents, he recalls, were ecstatic at this turn of events, but Rios wasn't. He did not enjoy what he was doing. After much soul-searching, he worked up the courage to call his parents and tell them he was dropping out of law school. "I felt bad for probably seven or eight minutes," he says, "and then I realized that I hadn't quit law school, I had quit writing, and it was time to go back."

He received his M.F.A. in creative writing from the University of Arizona in 1979, and in the same year published his first collection of poetry, the chapbook *Elk Heads on the Wall*, followed two years later by *Sleeping on Fists* (1981) and then the award-winning *Whispering to Fool the Wind* (1982). In 1982, Rios also began teaching at Arizona State University in Tempe, near Phoenix, where he remains to date.

Rios's work has long been inspired by Latin America. Critics have compared his writing to that of Gabriel García Márquez and Pablo Neruda for its mixture of fantastic and dreamlike elements with stark realism.[2] Rios himself acknowledges their impact on his work, saying that when he was first introduced to Latin American writing he found it foreign to his schooling but "familiar and friendly" to his upbringing. Although his father's family was not literary, they were "great storytellers. . . . They appropriated a great literary history that went back for centuries, telling stories that Cervantes would have told, but they attributed them to some cousin they knew, so these great, majestic, literary backgrounds became family to me. A lot of the stories, themes, and characters of great literature I grew up thinking were sort of mine—like just another family dinner."

In terms of his literary antecedents, Rios cites Whitman, Twain, Kafka, and Cortázar. Yet it was never specific writers, Rios claims, who influenced him the most, but a patchwork of "lines, juxtapositions of words, and ideas. I draw from the English and Spanish, and what I've tried to do is use them as binoculars, two lenses to see one thing more clearly. And that thing is the language that I write. It is mostly in English, but with the formality of Spanish. I'm writing in Spanish, though virtually every word is in English. That comes from a sense of rhythm and syntax, from hearing stories in Spanish, yet telling them in a language which will reach my audience. The stories are translatable into Spanish, but they'll carry an English sensibility equally into Spanish."

Rios has taken these divergent influences and added to them a rough-hewn naturalism which stares unblinkingly at the poverty and the beauty of life in what many call the "third country" of the borderland. His style is an unusual contrast of colloquial material and a formal poetics, which tends to short, regular, rhythmic lines. Perhaps because of his two-sided view of the world, Rios creates unusual metaphors, particularly apparent in *The Lime Orchard Woman* (1989): "A wood-nail / Trying to find a home in metal." Often these images combine the ordinary and the mythical, as in "The Sword Eusebio Montero Swallowed" from that collection. One critic for *Publishers Weekly* wrote of the poems in *The Lime Orchard Woman*, "Here the cerebral and the earthy are vividly combined, and the resulting tension between reality and fantasy yields fresh and often powerful imagery. Rios illustrates through startling juxtapositions. As the poems are neither linear nor logical, this technique is at once frustrating and provocative. . . . The raw power of the imagery lends the verses an almost surrealistic quality, enhanced by the richness of language and the originality of vision."[3]

The idea of the Mexican-American border as a third country, thirty miles wide and two thousand miles long, where Anglo, Hispanic, and Native American traditions combine—and sometimes clash—is one that surfaces often in Rios's writing. He sees the borderland not as a margin but as a heartland, a center positioned between extremes. "One thing that is important to me is duality, seeing a thing from two sides . . . to get at the middle by understanding that the only way to live it is to be on its extremities. We can find a middle ground if we can reach to both sides."[4]

For Rios, the West is not a melting pot where different cultures blend to the point of becoming indistinguishable, but rather a place where they meet, clash, and rub off on one another. This makes the West as a whole particularly hard for outsiders to grasp. Though many Anglo authors evaluate the West from the perspective of a "civilized" East Coast existence, Rios's West is very different: "The irony in all this, of course, is that I must seem some kind of opposite of myself. As a westerner, I'm an urban dweller, not a cowboy. I have been a cowboy, but I'm not now. I have cable, and I've been to England. Something about that changes the rules."

In the 1980s Rios began exploring his English roots; there are, after all, very few British-Mexican poets, and he has sought to know this past. After visiting England—bringing along his Mexican family and in-laws—he wrote a limited-edition collection of poems, *The Warrington Poems* (1989), where he describes the common ground in universal human experience which joined his parents.

Today Rios is receiving the attention rarely attained by poets of any color: in 1992, he won a Guggenheim Fellowship and signed on with a major New York publisher, W. W. Norton. His poems have been set to music by the Israeli songwriter David Broza. He has been appointed a regents professor at Arizona State University. His collection of short fiction, *Pig Cookies*, was released by Chronicle Books in San Francisco in spring 1995. Rios is at times gratified and at other times surprised by the attention. "Good writing, if it *is* good writing, will take care of itself. It doesn't matter where I'm sitting or where I'm doing it from; if I'm doing good writing I've got nothing to be afraid of."

▲ ✦ ▼ ✦ ▼ ✦ ▲

Rios is a short, muscular man with swept-back hair and twinkly blue eyes that seem more Irish than half-English. Rios and his wife, Maria Guadalupe Barrón (herself an educator and playwright), have traveled widely in Latin America. His conversation and appearance seem closer to those of a European-trained intellectual in Montevideo or Buenos Aires than of one who grew up in the raw, sewer-strewn barrios at the southernmost edge of our country.

Rios was interviewed at KJZZ-FM, Tempe, near his campus office at Arizona State University. His manners are cooperative and his spirit is quick-witted, even ebullient. Yet he, like John Nichols, chokes at having his work characterized as "southwestern" or at attributing his literary influences to specific works: "It's not just books that influence writers of this generation," he points out, "but film, television, and, of course, radio."

Growing up only miles from the Mexican-American border, he had access to two countries' media and developed complementary identities, as someone of British and Mexican descent. The tension between these two ways of looking at things, and the languages and cultures they either compromise or enhance (depending upon perspective), persists in his poetry.

Only when we spoke of his visits to Lancashire, where his mother was born, did his voice drop into sentimentality unlaced from the persona of the urbane, well-traveled raconteur.

It was not chic to grow up half-English in his Mexican world; adults often forget the pain of being different. In Rios's case, he was marked with the wrong blood, a cutting experience for a ten-year-old. Perhaps only in the relative tranquillity of middle age could he reclaim that bowl of porridge which awaits prodigal sons. Rios has managed to be less riven than Joy Harjo and Linda Hogan at being caught between cultures. Perhaps this is because he grew up with his Mexican identity close at hand: tangible in the tortillas he ate and the language he spoke on the street.

ALBERTO RIOS:

The oral tradition I most identify with is the oral history I was told as a child, my mother's British, Anglo traditions, and my father's history in Mexico. . . .

Growing up I heard about my father's family, because they were right in front of me—I heard about them and I knew who they were and what they looked like. My mother's family was in the realm of books, the realm of stories of princes and kingdoms and castles. England lends itself to that sensibility, and her telling me about snow that was taller than she was was certainly made up. Because of that, [her life for me] was relegated to the realm of fairy tales and books.

I didn't grow up in Mexico, I grew up right there on the border. I had a great deal of family in Mexico, so we did a lot of travel when I was young. I grew up with my father's family, speaking primarily Spanish as a young boy, except to my mother, who kept trying to learn Spanish.

When I was about five years old, we moved outside of Nogales. My parents were building this house and my mother got to choose what color to paint the walls. When she came to the kitchen she was talking to the workmen who were all Mexican and who spoke only Spanish. They asked her what color she would like the walls of the kitchen to be, and she wanted them to be yellow, so trying her best, she said, 'Lemon.' Which sounds like *limón*. The trouble is, we came back the next day, and the walls were bright, bright green, which is the color of a Mexican *limón*, a lime.[5] Not at all her version of a lemon. My mother left those walls painted that color for the next eight years. She said it was our lesson to ourselves, and I think in many ways it was a very good classroom.

I think Spanish has much more of a sense of formalism than English. And I relate Spanish now to all my older relatives— my grandmother, my great-grandmother, my great-aunts, those generations that were far more formal. They were always telling us to do things, and I remember getting those instructions to straighten up or say hello to somebody, so I have a more formal sense of what Spanish was growing up, that it was a corrective language, but also a more loving language. There was a lot more *cariño*. What's a good word for that? Ah, let me call it a sort of cuddling language. In Spanish everyone was known by their diminutive name, which was always a nicer version of the more formal sounding name—for me Alberto, which is a stern name. The diminutive is Albertito, and that shortens to Bertito, which is what my grandmother and great-grandmother and my great-aunts all call me, and my friends later called me Tito.

For me southwestern writing is more family-based rather than place-based. But I think people here live in a landscape that is clear, distinct from other landscapes, and absolutely an integral part of the work that I do. But there are some icons in the Southwest that point out a lack of understanding. I think particularly of the patio tiles that show a Mexican peasant leaning against a cactus. I always think that's a wonderful icon and clearly that would be from somebody that's writing *about* the Southwest, not writing from the inside. Anybody here knows better than to lean against a cactus. I think that's a good example of somebody imposing a view, as opposed to somebody simply sharing a view.

An Arizona writer is different from a New Mexico writer and very different from a Texas writer. I think we share various things, but there's a limit to what is shared and I think Arizona has developed a sensibility unto itself that is probably unknown to the larger literary world. Arizona is not close to the literary publishing houses, and so the kind of literature that gets shared here is probably kept here as well. It has to do with landscape, it has to do with the honest use of landscape without affectation. When you use a tortilla [in a literary context], for example, you must find a way to make it normal and not decoration.

Several years ago, I worked on what was then called the Papago Reservation near Sells, Arizona. I took the third-graders on a field trip, and as we were walking back to the school, they proposed playing a game. Sure, I agreed. What shall we play? Cowboys and Indians! they said. And then began to run. They shouted at me to run as well, because, they said, "The Indians are going to get you! The Indians are going to get you!" When we returned to the school, and calmed down, I asked them if they were Indians. "No," they said, "we are Papago."

And of course. They knew what Indians were, and they weren't exactly that. They had seen the movies with half-naked people yelling war whoops and shooting arrows. This isn't what they were. The people in their families wore boots, cowboy shirts, jeans. They drove pickup trucks, and they were good guys.

Good writing is political. I think that is one of the first true, important things we've got to understand as human beings. Clarity and communication is an overtly political act. When I say that my first language was Spanish, that's inaccurate. My first language was listening. And in that sense, clear writing, that is to say, the giving over of something clearly so that somebody who is listening can hear, is the first and most political act of all. I think I find the political in small places, I find it where it is honestly. I don't manufacture it, and I don't use it for decoration.

Business is a part of writing, but writing is going to take care of itself. What I had to come to terms with is the marketing angle; ultimately the way to keep on writing is to find some acceptance of the writing that you do . . . [and] publishing houses in the East command a different attention than those in the West. That's something the West is coming to terms with, not always successfully. . . .

We are always chagrined at attempts to market books in the West by writers who are from the West—because it's done through a middle person from the East. And it never works.

[East Coast publishers] view Hispanic writers as curiosities and, perhaps, as slow pieces without a lot of faith that the writing will persevere; that it is indivisible and has substance, that it will have meaning one century from now. . . . I do feel this recognition of difference: we have new directions, and that these directions [in Hispanic writing] won't be ignored and can't be ignored.

Ploughshares

For Christmas my son wanted and got a wooden map of the United States, the kind with the states sawn into puzzle pieces. He assembled the puzzle readily, and got all the states correctly placed, after only three or four times, and then he was ready for something more. *Dad, I'm going to rearrange the country,* he said, and then he did. When he was done, it was clear that people from Wisconsin would have to drink cheese coladas in what used to be Florida, and Maine residents were going to start ferrying across the Mississippi if they wanted to get to Virginia for peanuts and RC's. What was curious however, was that he didn't touch any of the western states—only all those scrunched up eastern ones. That's what he said—*Scrunched up. They need a little room.*

None of us seems quite able to get ahold of the West. Perhaps it's too big to consider, so it just gets left alone. We think ourselves incapable of defining it—which therefore makes it a scary place, ripe for conquest, for domination, for purchase. Those odd things we do, to that which we don't understand. . . .

I'm reminded of a small example about a central cultural difference between English speakers and Spanish speakers. In English, one says, *I dropped the glass,* should such a thing happen. It is an "I"-centered instance, rugged individualism in its smallest moment. In Spanish, one says, *"se me cayó el vaso,"* which means, "the glass, it fell from me." This is a different world view, a way of accommodating the world, of living with it, instead of changing it. Which is the better view is not the point, but I do think that our notions of the West as representing rugged individualism, may in fact, be faulty. There's a messy middle, something in between. I think that's the language of this place. It's a rugged pluralism.

The Lime Orchard Woman

"I Drive While Kissing You"

Riding car top down
On an Arizona road
Sunsets are a dime a dozen.
Hard times die here
Where the boys are men
And the women ride horses
Where they want.
Riding car top down
A car goes faster.
Everybody weighs less
And the stars
Pack a spark like a pin.
Everybody who used to be
Old now isn't,
And cows by the road
Make us laugh.
The road lights up
And the people let us through.
The road goes up
And won't come down.
I've taken a ride
Through the night
And the night is you.
Riding car top down
All steel and song,
I am the man
And the boy you knew.

"Listening for Tonight"

Today I have stayed with
The noises of the house,
Not music, not the radio as always.
Music like this, this kind of radio:
The kettle beginning, its tongue over teeth
Sound, the furniture truck too slowly

Going by as a June beetle might
The way they almost do not fly when they fly.
Then the creaks from the knees of the house
And the cats, who pay attention, every time.
Small dust blown against the window outside,
That noise I imagine I hear of crashing
In a surf of cellular things.
Shoes have left indentations in the carpet.
This secret catalogue of events:
People who will make noise later in the day,
Preparations of dinner tonight,
The kitchen cupboard opened,
The rocking chair making its name,
Noise of the breath of the woman
Who will sit there in it,
Who will rest at the end of one day's working.
Then the pencil, which will scratch
To destruction the minute structures
A page like this keeps invisible.
Noise that will be;
The rhythm hum of the circular fan;
The man who will drum
His fingertips, drips in the water of his shaving.
The noise this evening is making, and tomorrow,
The pointillist dream of it we can conjure:
This, I have heard the future
By listening.

Whispering to Fool the Wind

"Nani"

Sitting at her table, she serves
the sopa de arroz to me
instinctively, and I watch her,
the absolute mamá, and eat words
I might have had to say more
out of embarrassment. . . .
Nani never serves

herself, she only watches me
with her skin, her hair. I ask for more.

I watch the mamá warming more
tortillas for me. I watch her
fingers in the flame for me.
Near her mouth, I see a wrinkle speak
of a man whose body serves
the ants like she serves me, then more words
from more wrinkles about children, words
about this and that, flowing more
easily from these other mouths. Each serves
as a tremendous string around her,
holding her together. They speak
nani was this and that to me
and I wonder just how much of me
will die with her, what were the words
I could have been, or was. Her insides speak
through a hundred wrinkles, now, more
than she can bear, steel around her,
shouting then, What is this thing she serves?

She asks me if I want more.
I own no words to stop her.
Even before I speak, she serves.

Teodoro Luna's Two Kisses

"Anselmo's Moment with God"

Anselmo in a fit of pique
Over a spatula he could not find
As the eggs were burning
And as he did not yet have the services
Of the housekeeper Mrs. M.
He would have in later years,
Renounced his love of God
And of the world, right there.

* * *

He threw the drawer of utensils to the ground
And let the eggs burn dry
Until they gave texture to
And became part of the black iron pan itself.
Everyday for the rest of his life
He remembered that moment—
Himself but not the event:
His spatula became through the years
The Hand of God.

Of God's smell
He could not be certain:
Only that the burning of candles
Had for him a certain urgency.

Hispanics in the U.S.:
An Anthology of Creative Literature

"The Death of Rosa"

In 1851, a man was carved
from stone. Joaquín Murrieta's wife was raped
and thrown away by men who beat Joaquín,
but he escaped. They posted a reward
for all men named Joaquín; it was a name
not used by white men whom he killed now, paid
a little back; he knew a price the spit
of which not even rock could disregard.

In '53, his Rosa saw them shoot
a ghost. The man, Joaquín Murrieta, rides
the galloping Sierra Madres through
the Californias, where he never died
and where he meets with La Llorona, who
screams screams that comb his hair,
          that soothe his nights.

Five Indiscretions

"Taking Away the Name of a Nephew"

One of the disappeared looks like this:
One shirt, reasonable shoes, no laces, no face
Recognizable even to the mother of this thing.
Lump. Dropped egg, bag of old potatoes
Too old and without moisture, a hundred eyes
Sprouted out and gone wild into forest
Food for the maggot flies and small monsters.
Bag. Pulled by the tiestring
The laces around his ankles have become.
A crisp bag of seventeen birthdays
Six parties with piñatas and the particular
Memory of a thick hugging
His Tía Susí gave him with the strong arms
Her breasts were, how they had held him
Around his just-tall-enough throat and had reached
To touch each other behind the neck.

His memory of Susí was better than how the soldier held him.
She hoped this out of all things.
That she had made him warm.
In that body the three soldiers were fooled, tricked
A good hundred strings of wool put over their eyes:
They did not take away the boy.
They took away his set of hands and his spine
Which in weeks would look like the railroad tracks
Along the side of any young mountain.
One of the disappeared looks like this
The newspaper said. She had seen
The photograph which looked like all
Newspaper photographs,
Had thought, it does not say, *looked* like this,
But *looks* like this, still; had thought
What is being said here is that he did not die.

* * *

It was not death that took him

She thinks about things like this, this way. . . .

The Iguana Killer: Twelve Stories of the Heart

"The Secret Lion"

When we were young we moved away from town, me and my family. Sergio's was already out there. Out in the wilds. Or at least the new place seemed like the wilds since everything looks bigger the smaller a man is. I was five, I guess, and we had moved three miles north of Nogales where we had lived, three miles north of the Mexican border. We looked across the highway in one direction and there was the arroyo; hills stood up in the other direction. Mountains, for a small man.

When the first summer came the very first place we went to was of course the one place we weren't supposed to go, the arroyo. We went down in there and found water running, summer rain water mostly, and we went swimming. But every third or fourth or fifth day, the sewage treatment plant that was, we found out, upstream, would release whatever it was that it released, and we would never know exactly what day that was, and a person really couldn't tell right off by looking at the water, not every time, not so a person could get out in time. So, we went swimming that summer and some days we had a lot of fun. Some days we didn't. We found a thousand ways to explain what happened on those other days, constructing elaborate stories about the neighborhood dogs, and hadn't she, my mother, miscalculated her step before, too? But she knew something was up because we'd come running into the house those days, wanting to take a shower, even—if this can be imagined— in the middle of the day.

NOTES

1. Carol Muske, *New York Times Book Review*, Feb. 9, 1986, p. 28.
2. Ibid.
3. *Publishers Weekly*, Jan. 6, 1989, p. 96.
4. This construct is outlined in Tom Miller's *On the Border* (Tucson: University of Arizona, 1989).
5. In Mexico and Guatemala, *limón* means "lime" and *lima,* "lemon."

STAN STEINER

▲ ✛ ▼ ✛ ▼ ✛ ▲

The mythic West, the historic West, the new West—all were sources of inspiration for Stan Steiner. Like Abbey, Nichols, and Kingsolver, Steiner was originally an Easterner who fled West, seeking the font of the American soul.

An extraordinary storyteller in his own right, he spent his life chronicling the stories of groups largely silenced: Native Americans, Chicanos, Puerto Ricans, women, ranchers, farm workers, immigrants.

It was his job, Steiner believed, to record faithfully the voices of hyphenated Americans, and the road they were building into the twenty-first century for America and the American Southwest.

*I was on a panel once with a bunch of history professors.
. . . They were talking about myths of the American West,
myths of the cowboy, myths of the Indian. I told one of these
distinguished professors afterward that I once asked a
rancher what he thought about the mythic West and he said,
"If someone else ever comes up to me again and calls me a
myth, I'll kick him in the ass."*

—STAN STEINER

Historian, editor, and humorist, Stan Steiner spent a lifetime loving and writing about the American Southwest. In his thirty books, he sought not to destroy the many myths surrounding the land and its people, but rather to strip away the facade, the Hollywood and East Coast fantasies, to reveal the human beings beneath the myths. And real human beings, to Steiner, were somehow more real in the American West than anywhere else. The West, he believed, is a place where people are defined by the line at which Frederick Jackson Turner's frontier thesis becomes suddenly personal—a relation among individuals, rather than an abstract theory in a historian's textbook. For Steiner, here was the dwelling place of the American soul in all its fabulous, strife-torn diversity.

Like many of those extolling the West, he was originally from the East. Steiner was born January 1, 1925, in a long-vanished, rural section of Brooklyn, New York—in those years a small farming community. His childhood passed there and in rural New Jersey before Steiner's parents, Austrian immigrants, moved to Manhattan. The shock of the city soon drove him west, to discover America.

He volunteered for the army during World War II but was rejected because of his poor eyesight. When the war ended in 1945, Steiner and a buddy, catching the restlessness that gripped the country in the postwar years, bought rucksacks at a local secondhand store and set out for the West via "the rule of the thumb," as Woody Guthrie called it. For several years Steiner roamed throughout New Mexico, Arizona, Colorado, Wyoming, and Montana, traveling mostly by hitchhiking or by hopping freight trains. He recalls, "I'm one of the last writers I know . . . that has ridden the rails, the boxcars. The railroad bulls [security guards] and the police in those days, most of 'em had great sympathy for a kid on the road. They'd feed you. They would chase you off the train, but they would feed you. [laughs] I remember once we got into Des Moines, Iowa, in the middle of the night and we were so tired we couldn't make it to an alleyway and we fell asleep on the sidewalk in the middle of Main Street.

"Sure enough, around five in the morning some policeman appeared and tapped me on the soles of my shoes with his billy and said, 'Get in the patrol car.' My buddy and I got in and they drove us out to the farthest diner on the highway.

They gave us a nickel apiece for a cup of coffee, talked to us in a fatherly way, and said, 'Don't come back.' "

But the lure of the mythic West and the intense need to discover, explore, and redefine it gripped Steiner long before his first adventuresome rambles. At age twelve he read *Huckleberry Finn*, decided it was wonderful but out-of-date, and set about creating a modern rewrite of the Twain classic. In his own way, Steiner would eventually live a twentieth-century version of that timeless tale of discovery, recording in his books the voices of people as singular and fascinating as any fictional character Samuel Clemens invented.

This early love for the wonder of language and the written word stayed with Steiner even through his years as a high school football player when, he laughingly recalls, it wasn't "cool" to be caught reading anything other than a playbook. But on his way home from school one day, he happened upon a sale at a local used bookstore advertising books at seventeen cents a pound. Unable to pass up such a bargain, he purchased the several pounds of Shelley and Keats that inspired him to begin writing poetry.

Steiner attended the University of Wisconsin for several months, but soon dropped out, disillusioned with academic life. Back in New York, he worked as a dock organizer by day and wrote for various labor newspapers and periodicals at night. Here he found his kind of people—regular working Joes whose unrecognized contributions formed the backbone of the nation. He married Marjorie Fried in 1947 and had a son, Paul, in 1951. Motivated by both his love for children and for cooking, Steiner willingly became a househusband, working on his writing in between caring for his child and home. Eleven years later, Steiner and Marjorie were divorced, and in 1966 he married a university professor and renowned psychologist, Vera John, who would remain his lifelong companion. Along with her two children, Sandor and Suki, she joined Steiner on New York's east side.

By 1966, he had been working for several years on a book inspired by the various tribal peoples he had met, mostly by accident he claimed, during his wanderings in the West: Navajos (who fed him enormous amounts of mutton stew and wine); Pueblos, whose stately ceremonial dances fascinated him; and friends in the scattered tribes of Oklahoma and the northern plains. Less than a week after his wedding to Vera John, Steiner sold the manuscript for what was to become perhaps his most acclaimed work, *The New Indians* (1968).

He had become enthralled by the way these young Native Americans were breaking down the stereotypes imposed on them by Anglo society, while driving their own ancient traditions in new and startling directions. He created a book that was a compilation of their voices; not interviews, he insisted, but testimonials from people who had heretofore, willingly or unwillingly, been silent. It was a book, in fact, he had not actually wished to write, feeling that Indians themselves should be the authors.

Yet at the urging of a radical young Sioux named Vine Deloria, Jr. (who would become one of his closest friends and a highly acclaimed scholar and activist), Steiner finally agreed to act, as he called it, as "a human tape recorder." The book was an astounding success, and many claim it paved the way for the later success of such works as *Black Elk Speaks* and *Bury My Heart at Wounded Knee*.[1] In an appendix to *The New Indians* Steiner wrote:

> When the university experts and ordinary readers ask, as they do, how do you know these things to be true that you have written? I can only say, I do not. I know these people. . . . These things they told me and I tell you may be true. Or they may be dreams, which also may be true. But how did you study the Indians, what methods did you use? the questioners persist. I say, I did not study them. I used no methods. But you must have some technique of gaining the confidence of your "informants," they say with doubting brows. I say, I had no "informants." Just some friends, some enemies. The friends were truthful, I believe; the enemies may have lied to make a fool of me. What I have written is not a study, but a book of people full of the truths and lies people tell.[2]

For Steiner, "people" always meant more than just whites, and more than just men—it was those unsung others of every shade of black, white, and brown whom he felt made up the real American West, and he delighted in uncovering their stories. He wrote books not only about Native Americans, but also Mexican-Indians (*The Mexican Indians: Minority Rights Groups*, 1979), Puerto Ricans (*The Islands: The Worlds of the Puerto Ricans*, 1974), Chinese (*Fusang: The Chinese Who Built America*, 1979), Anglo ranchers (*The Ranchers: A Book of Generations*, 1980), and Chicanos (*La Raza: The Mexican Americans*, 1969). Several chapters of his final book, *The Waning of the West* (1989), concern the birth of the feminist movement in the West and issues of gender definitions and sexuality on the frontier.

Steiner's works have been overwhelmingly well received by critics and historians. The *New York Times Book Review* wrote of *The New Indians*, "The subject is timely and complex; here it is given both unity and perspective."[3] Of his 1976 book chronicling the cultural and ecological ravages of Anglo developers, *The Vanishing White Man*, *Publishers Weekly* said, "Partly a paean to the beauty of the American West, the narrative also interweaves a penetrating psycho-history of the white's relationship with the Indian. Powerful, eloquent, heartrending."[4] And critic F. W. Turner noted in *The Nation*, "One's admiration for Stan Steiner's work does not come easily. Rather it is like one's stubborn assent to Dreiser, whose sheer integrity and blood experience eventually must triumph. . . ."[5]

In his later years, Steiner grew ever more fascinated with the Southwest as the site of the clashing and coming-together of an amazing multitude of races, languages, and cultures. "You have the combination, not of three cultures, but of two dozen cultures in [New Mexico]," he insisted. "The cohesion and the conflict between those cultures in the past and in the present is exceedingly dramatic." His 1972 anthology, widely used in high school and college classrooms, *Aztlan: An Anthology of Mexican-American Literature*, was edited with Luis Valdez, a founder of Teatro Campesino.

When Vera John-Steiner was offered a professorship at the University of New Mexico in 1970, Stan and his family moved to the Southwest for good, settling in an old, tree-shaded adobe in Santa Fe, purchased with a down payment made from selling the manuscript for his acclaimed classic *La Raza*.

About this, one of his most widely read works, *Publishers*

Weekly noted that, "In Steiner, the case of today's Mexican Americans and the issues involved in their current struggle . . . has found a brilliant polemicist. Steiner vividly, without editorializing, tells the whole story."[6]

La Raza was assembled in the riot-torn years of the late sixties and spans the barrios of East Los Angeles, the agribusiness fields of Imperial Valley, and the remote Hispanic villages of northern New Mexico. Steiner spoke with the ranchers, housewives, radicals, mystics, and ex-cons who fill its pages.

"I wanted to do something about the Brown Berets," he recalls. "Most of these guys were ex-cons or ex–drug addicts who had really had a hard road. And suspicious, very suspicious of anyone who wanted to write about them. I said I wanted to sit down with four of these guys, leaders, and write it in their own words. We had a case of beer and some ham sandwiches and we sat in the basement of the drug rehabilitation center [in Los Angeles].

"It took me two years to get to that point because they would call me up and say, 'Stan, come down, I think we're going to talk to you.' So I would come to L.A. and be met by a guy who would say, 'Drive to the corner of such-and-such, park your car, and get into the blue car across the street'; then we would go to another corner and another car and then finally he said, 'Go down the alley, through the basement window, out on the porch, across the field and someone will talk to you.' So I did that and when I got there there were three huge police dogs ready to chew me up. I did that three times [over the course] of two years. The fourth call came finally, and we went through the same procedure but this time they talked.

"I came home and I wrote the chapter and I sent it back to L.A. and waited. Finally, a guy named Fred knocked on the door here. I could see he was carrying the chapter and I said, 'Want to come in?' He said, 'No, I just have a message from the *hombres* for you.' I said, 'What's the message?' He said, 'Either you change it or we'll kill you.' So I changed it. That was harsh criticism."

Not all the chapters were as harrowing to write as the one on the Brown Berets, however. Most people were eager to speak. Like the voices of Native Americans in *The New Indians*, these were the voices of people who had been silent for too long. Many sensed that in Steiner they had found someone who believed they should be heard.

As a stylist, Steiner's prose was airy and accessible, with a deceptive transparency. A master of collecting stories and history, he relished oral performance, rendering what he was told with a light but dexterous hand. As compelling as Studs Terkel, he, too, had a distinctive, gritty style. Whatever one told him, it read like the Bible by the time Steiner was through.

In *La Raza* Steiner began developing his own frontier theory that grabbed Turner's thesis and gave it a hard, postcolonial twist. He recorded the Southwest from the point of view of the colonized, the insurgent, the hard-hit, and the down-on-their-luck. Steiner loved the Southwest, old and new, and gloried in the romance of life on its borders. Yet he never allowed the myths to blind him to the harsh realities of the region's history. Poverty, alcoholism, drug abuse, broken treaties, police brutality, racism, cultural genocide—if his subjects wanted to speak about the hard facts of life in their West, Steiner would record them.

In *La Raza* he wrote, "Life in the barrios is like living in 'a colony' to Esteban Torres, director of the East Los Angeles Labor Community Action Committee. He believes the second class citizenship in city services [such as water and postal delivery] is due to the lack of the communities' control of their civil life. . . . Torres says: Our money flows out rather than in, and this leaves the barrio impoverished. 'East Los Angeles is a colony.' . . . 'We have a colonial mentality?' says [another] barrio leader. 'Of course! You treat us like colonials.' "[7]

And later, in a chapter entitled "The Conquered Country," a former president of the Mexican-American Political Association in Denver tells Steiner, " 'We are a conquered people. . . . The behavior of the police toward our people will not let them forget that.' " Steiner continues, "One young man tells me: 'The cops are just nothing but Anglo *Pachucos*. Man, we learn everything we know about street fights from them. They teach us from when we were little kids. It's like basic training, except they use live ammo.' "[8]

Stan Steiner believed the West was the most important part of America, the place where the diversity of cultures and people were defining what it meant to be American. His dry wit and boundless energy made him a sought-after lecturer at over a dozen universities, from Berkeley to the Sorbonne. He was on the editorial board of the Western Historians Association, several journals for Hispanics, the National Indian Youth Council, and the Mark Twain Society. He edited anthologies of Native American, Mexican-American, and Puerto Rican literatures, as well as several encyclopedias. His essays appear in over fifty university textbooks; he wrote and consulted on a dozen scripts for movies and documentaries in the United States, Sweden, Italy, Germany, and the Netherlands; and he appeared himself on "The Today Show" and other talk shows in a score of major cities in the United States and Europe.

He was a tireless promoter of other writers, particularly southwestern authors with limited access to the distant publishing houses of the East. Writers from the region seem exotic and foreign to New York publishers, he realized, and as a result, many talented authors and great books were ignored. One of his later achievements was founding the Santa Fe Writers' Co-op, a group of authors who cooperatively distributed their work. (Five other members are included in this volume: Anaya, Chavez, Hillerman, Nichols, and Tapahonso.) He told *Contemporary Authors*, "The crisis in publishing is not a crisis of writers and their books; rather it is a crisis of conscience on the part of the publishers. And they are incapable, so it seems, of solving the crisis. That is why I think the writers and readers have to step in and do what the publishers don't seem able to do: to broaden the book market; to discover new readers; to encourage a greater, not a smaller, breadth for books and for writers."

When asked what, exactly, was his career, he replied, "None that I know of. . . . Writing is not a career; it is a religion."[9]

Steiner found his place of worship in the American West, and his last book, *The Waning of the West* (1990), was his declaration of love to that place: essays on everything from space-age "cosmic cowboys" like astronaut Chuck Yeager to the practical difficulties faced by the pioneers in having sex in covered wagons.

Probably most importantly, Steiner introduced the Southwest to a generation of writers and educators. At a memorial service in 1988 at the Santa Fe Public Library, John Nichols said, "*The New Indians* and *La Raza* were among the first books to articulate the Southwest for me when I arrived in New Mexico." Anthropologist Alfonso Ortiz, having taught Steiner's books at Princeton, reflected, "Steiner, alone among modern writers about Indians, understood that one is most free when one can count on support of a group or tribe."[10]

By the end of his career, Steiner could bask in the honors which had come his way: the Ainsfeld Wolf Award for *La Raza*, a Golden Spur from the Western Writers of America, and a National Endowment for the Arts grant. In the mid-1980s, he developed Parkinson's disease and his productivity slowed.

Stan Steiner died of a heart attack on January 12, 1987. He was seated at his battered manual typewriter in his home in Santa Fe, working on the manuscript for *The Waning of the West*, struggling with a chapter on the modern westerner. The last sentence he typed read, "Who was this new man?" Some would say it was Steiner himself.

▲ ✧ ▼ ✧ ▼ ✧ ▲

Stan Steiner's interview for this book was one of the last he gave.[11] The radio series (and this volume) had its genesis in the quiet book-lined study where he spoke, the former home of anthropologist Clyde Kluckhohn.

In his study, which looked out over the piñon-juniper forest of Santa Fe, books stuffed into every cranny absorbed his words. Though Steiner spoke with the passion that had carried him through some thirty volumes, underneath his words was a faint wheeze. It told of too many hard years at the writer's life: waking up before dawn to edit an underground labor newspaper, which had to be mimeographed in a private home; too many years of cigarettes and alcohol; too many years of sitting in his tiny study, writing while the outside world passed by.

Short, broad-chested, with thick gray-white hair hanging down over his forehead, Steiner was a rugged man. His face had the sharp angles of someone used to forswearing dinner when his cash was low, or staying up all night talking with his "sources," which he always insisted were not sources but friends.

He liked rugged things, like the manual Royal typewriter be-

*cause he could throw it across the room when it betrayed him:
"What computer would allow me to do that and then pick it up
in the morning and start all over again," he asked with a smile.
Though there were few omens of his sudden death from a heart
attack, except his increasing unwillingness to venture far from his
study, this interview became a testament. The volumes that had
bounded his writing life looked down on us, like sentinels from
the peoples whose histories he wrote: the Puerto Ricans, the Chinese, the Native Americans of many tribes, the Hispanics and
Chicanos, the Venezuelans, and of course the ranchers—all
watched in quiet sympathy as we talked.*

STAN STEINER:

When I did *La Raza*, I would tell everyone, Cesar Chavez,
Rich Taylor, everyone, "I'm your *hermano*. I may be your older
brother or your younger brother, but I'm your *hermano*. If you
can't understand that and be part of it, if you can't let an Anglo
be a Chicano, I can't write about you. I have to become who
you are. It doesn't mean I believe what you believe, or speak
the way you speak or come from the same culture. . . ."

I keep telling people, don't interview anybody, talk to them
like an *hermano*, like a member of the family, and then you can
perhaps get some glimmer of their soul and if you can write
that down you've gone way beyond an interview.

When I was younger, I used to set appointments, schedule
a plan, go from state to state. I stopped doing that a few years
ago. I just see what happens. I figure, if the interview doesn't
come off, then God didn't want it to, and who am I to defy
God?

If I'm writing about American Indian people, or Hispanos or
Chicanos, I ask them first—before the project starts—do they
trust me to write it? Do they want me to write it? If they don't,
I won't write it.

What I called the generation of new Indians came on the
scene in the sixties and seventies, and most were veterans of
Korea and Vietnam. They were a new Indian . . . and they had
their feet in both worlds. I knew a lot of them were very fine

writers and I kept asking them to write a book about what their generation felt.

They said, "You write it." I have the feeling I was like an Indian scout hired by Custer except history had reversed itself and here the white guy was the scout for the Indians. . . . A dear friend of mine, Vine Deloria, was insisting I write this book called *The New Indians*, and I was insisting he write this book called *The New Indians*. Then he sent a letter to 250 tribal chairmen saying "Stan Steiner will visit you soon and write what is in your heart." I blew up. I told him, I can't even write what's in my own heart, much less 250 tribal chairmen. But I was stuck. I had to write the book.

I spent about a year or two writing *The Ranchers* but I spent thirty, forty years thinking about it and talking to these ranchers and finally I got to the point where I said [to myself], "For God's sake, stop bellyaching and scrounging around. Put it down on a tape and let the world hear it." That was not a decision, that was thirty, forty years of culmination of knowing these people, knowing what they want, what they didn't want, how they talked. If you do that it takes a lot of time. It's not like sitting in your study in Beverly Hills turning out manuscripts from newspaper clippings and telephone conversations.

You're talking to an old westerner, old-time rancher, and you ask him something, he's bound to say, "I reckon I don't know much about that." Then you know you have a good interview 'cause he's gonna talk for eight hours about what he don't reckon he knows much about. The only thing that is better is if the man or woman says, "Don't have what you would rightly call education." Then you know he's mad as hell and he's gonna talk for three days.

I had a very sweet reaction from an old Hispano farmer up in northern New Mexico who I wrote about and sent my chapter to. I drove into the valley and he came down in his pickup truck and said, "Stan, you got me just right. I give you an acre of land." That's the best literary criticism I ever got. Of course he never gave me an acre of land.

I think it was Abe Rosenthal in the *New York Times* who said, "The country stops west of the Hudson." We, of course, live a little west of the Hudson. We have a hard time, living out here and trying to communicate with the publishing world. Publishing exists in one city—New York—and there's no other industry in the country that exists in one city. So western writers are really foreigners. One of the editors of the *New York Times* said about two years ago that people who live outside of New York are more remote than European peasants; [laughs] they think of us as European peasants!

So the Santa Fe Writers' Co-op was really formed so we could get our voices heard. That was the rational reason. But I think the underlying reason it's gone on is that it has built a small community of writers, it's given them some self-respect, and it's even given some people courage to write books they would never dare write before.

When we [the Santa Fe Writers' Co-op] were trying to figure out how can we reach the most people in the state of New Mexico, it came right to everybody: the state fair. More people attend the state fair than live in the state. . . . The writers actually built a booth and put it next to the Cow Pavilion. Everybody thought we were crazy, but that's a western marketing technique . . . and a lot of cowboys bought books.

Of course we had some disasters. We had a book a day that we raffled. We had the author of the book sitting there to autograph it for whoever won. One writer [David Dunaway] had the bright idea to get one of the rodeo queens to come and pick the winning raffle for the book. Well, she let her horse pick it and the horse stuck his nozzle into the barrel and ate the goddamn tickets!

Since the publishing industry isn't here and we have no ready access to readers, most people here don't write for New Mexico, they write for back East.

It's not easy, but the publishing industry . . . is going to have to discover the rest of America. And it's going to have to discover a new kind of book.

EXCERPTS

The New Indians

A few years ago, in the tribal newspaper of the Navajos, there appeared this classified advertisement:

SWAP, SELL, OR TRADE
Well trained roping horse. Rodeo experience.
Weight 1150 lbs. 14 hands high. Excellent
condition. Will sacrifice. Owner in college.

He put his cowboy boots, his worn jeans, his one tie, his high school diploma, his rock-n-roll records in his broken suitcase. He tied his suitcase with a rope—perhaps the lasso he had used in bull-dogging calves in the Indian rodeos.

He walked in bare feet, one last time, down the dirt road to the blacktop road and on to the crossroad of the super-highway. Then he put on the new shoes he had bought. He looked back at the open country, he turned his back on his indecision, and he walked down the superhighway toward Albuquerque and the University of New Mexico.

The cowboy who had sold his horse was one of thousands of an entire generation beginning a journey be-tween two worlds. Until then he may have been just another "invisible Indian," his thoughts, like himself, kept within the confines of his reservation. Now he was on the open road, where the white man could really see him. He had become visible.

He was the new Indian.

The Ranchers

. . . One night we were in this bar [in western Montana] where I hadn't been in ten years. And [Bill] started telling stories; he loved to talk. He started bellyaching about all the things changing in the valley, how the valley was no longer ours, how everything was mechanical. And he starts talking about "Tokyo quarter horses."

Well, I didn't know what a "Tokyo quarter horse" was. He says: "It's a Honda!"

And we all rode on horseback before and now we ride Hondas. . . . So it's still the same energies, the same life, the same ethos. Things are not really destroyed; they are not really gone. In a different way they become the same sort of things. . . .

People in the valley where I grew up, it seems to me they are still living there and they're still comfortable living there. Most of them go on doing whatever they did. Go to town. Go to the store.

But so what? It doesn't matter. People still make love and have children and tell stories in styrofoam houses. . . .

So a lot of us who grew up in the West I think have given up. Really in a cynical and bad sort of way. To us it may seem that our world has completely changed and it is never going to be as it was when I was a child. Never. . . .

And things will not be like they were. Of course. They can't possibly be like they were, because they never were in the first place.

So to me the thing is not to give in, to accept a false idea of ourselves. But to make things the way we want them to be. To me the West is not dead. It doesn't have to be dead. . . . Even though it's not there anymore—it is. The valley I grew up in was full of horses. . . . And in my head the horses are still there. . . . And in this world I feel like a very, very old man. That's because the past is still alive in all of us.

La Raza: The Mexican Americans

It is a long, hot summer afternoon. Four young men from the poorest barrios of East Los Angeles lounge about beneath the lazy palm trees. In the suburban house of shabby elegance, mocked by once-gracious lawns and broken garden urns, the young men of the streets eat cheese sandwiches and drink beer and philosophize about bygone Aztec kingdoms and utopias of brown power and poetry they have liked and the police who have beaten them up. Summer days inspire dreams. And these "young toughs," as the police call them, are romantic and wistful.

Who are these young dreamers? They are the Chicanos of La Junta.

All summer the Los Angeles Police Department has feared trouble in the barrio from these youths. "The *placas* [police] have treated us like *pendejos* [idiots, literally, pubic hairs]," the Chicanos say, "because they do not understand us." These young men are rebels, but are philosophical about their rebellion.

José: "If you have a rebellion you have to have something to rebel against. So you may become racist. Stone racist. Is 'brown power' racist? No, 'brown power' is cultural. So it doesn't have to become racist."

Hector: "I wonder. Why do militants create a lot of alienation in their communities?"

José: "Man, we're not rebelling. We're building something. We're trying to create less alienation and more community unity. A man without knowledge of his people is like a tree without a root. What we're trying to do is get people this cultural consciousness. Brown power is to know your culture."

In Search of the Jaguar: Growth and Paradox in Venezuela

On the night that I came to this country someone had crept into the darkened zoo in the city of Mérida, high in the Andes. The man, whom the newspapers called the "lover of animals," had opened the door of the cage of the jaguars. And two of the caged animals had escaped into the night. In the city, the morning after, there was no panic. The marketplace was crowded and the traffic did not diminish and the children played a new game called "jaguar."

The man who had opened the cages of the jaguars had left a note. It said: "These animals are not being treated with dignity. So I have freed them."

And in the city it was said: "The jaguars have gone home to the mountains. No one can live in someone else's cage."

One man said to me: "That man, he did not free the jaguars. He has freed himself. It is not the Venezuelan way to live in a cage."

The Waning of the West

"Love in a Covered Wagon"

On the trail men suffered hardships and endured pains they never had experienced back East as schoolteachers, clerks or small-town farmers. It both hardened and weakened them. And, as their wives sadly noted in endless diary entries, the deprivations and humiliations of the journey seemed to be more traumatic for the men than for the women.

As if to protect themselves, men adopted a new image of manhood; it was tough, vigorous and taciturn. They were influenced, in many ways, by the behavior of the Indian men whom they met, and imitated. Romance, to the pioneer man, might have seemed a sign of vulnerability. . . .

As a result, there arose two very different, if not opposed, ways of looking at love in the West. One was as romantic as the other was laid-back, bold as the other was timid, as openly passionate as the other was quietly embarrassed, and as feminine as the other was masculine. Both were as uniquely Western as the frontier. . . .

In the decades after the Civil War the settlement of the West was replaced by its conquest. The pioneers' attempts at friendship with the native people were doomed by "wars of annihilation" and the inevitable playing out of the expansionist impulses that united under the banner of "Manifest Destiny." In the minds of many Easterners, they were destined to dominate the native land and native women; the U.S. Army adopted the figure of the "kneeling squaw" as its target in rifle practice. . . .

Even so, the later immigrants to the West brought these ideas with them, and sought to impose their Victorian beliefs about femininity on the proud and independent women of the frontier. In the eyes of these men, the women of the

West had to be fitted into the masculine stays and mental corsets of the women of the East. The reality of life on the prairies and in the mountains, however, did not easily bend itself to fit these male myths. . . .

By the end of the century, romance *in* the West had become inseparable from romance *of* the West. Many of the ideas and beliefs about love on the frontier came from the pens of Eastern writers seeking to glorify love in a covered wagon and romance on the frontier in order to satisfy their own need for the passion they had expurgated from their lives; it was a paradox of puritanism.

N O T E S

1. Brandt Morgan, *The Reporter*, Jan. 28, 1987.

2. *The New Indians* (New York: Harper & Row, 1968), p. 291.

3. N. Scott Momaday, *New York Times Book Review*, March 17, 1968, p. 22.

4. *Publishers Weekly*, June 21, 1976, p. 83.

5. F. W. Turner, *The Nation*, quoted in *Contemporary Authors* (Detroit, Mich.: Gale Research Inc., 1992), vol. 39, p. 403.

6. *Publishers Weekly*, Nov. 3, 1969, p. 44.

7. *La Raza* (New York: Harper & Row, 1969), p. 156.

8. Ibid., pp. 163–64.

9. In *Contemporary Authors*.

10. Ibid.

11. This interview, conducted just a month before Stan Steiner's death, is printed in a more complete version posthumously in *The Waning of the West* (New York: St. Martin's Press, 1990).

LUCI TAPAHONSO

▲ ❖ ▼ ❖ ▼ ❖ ▲

Ethereal yet immensely powerful, the works of Navajo poet Luci Tapahonso seem as native to the Southwest as the yellow sandstone and fragrant sage of her home in Shiprock, New Mexico. Like Joy Harjo and Simon Ortiz, Tapahonso draws from the oral traditions in which she was raised—in her case, the flowing rhythms of the Beauty Way and other Navajo chants. These rhythms and traditional songs are incorporated organically into her work.

Her poetry is rooted in the remote mesa country of the Navajo reservation; but she does not ignore the problems of modern urban Indians—alcoholism, poverty, racism. Her poems unite these harsh realities with the harmony of vision so important to her Navajo worldview.

> The cashier looks up smiling
> first smile in 20 minutes of Navajo customers
> "Oh—that's okay. Are you Navajo?
>   I swear, you don't have an accent at all!"
> She's friendly too quick and I am uneasy.
> I say to the people behind me
> "Ha' 'at'ii sha'ni?
>   Why is she saying that to me?"
> We laugh a little under our breaths
> and with that
> I am another Navajo
> she doesn't greet or thank
>
> —LUCI TAPAHONSO[1]

Luci Tapahonso has become one of the most widely read Native American poets writing today. Her books are immensely popular among Navajos and equally well received by non-Indian audiences. In constant demand as a reader, she appears in such diverse venues as elementary school auditoriums on the Navajo reservation, National Public Radio's "All Things Considered," and the Gorky Institute of World Literature in Moscow.

Her seven books of poetry and short fiction have made Luci Tapahonso a leading voice among southwestern writers. Her poems explore the starkly beautiful and often pain-ridden life on the Navajo reservations. Racism and unemployment are vividly yet compassionately portrayed in her work. Tapahonso's shy humor masks her underlying hope to create a body of literature in which young Indians can finally find a source of strength.

Perhaps more than any other Native American poet writing today, Tapahonso has combined the musical roots of Native poetry and its traditional forms (chants, songs, and prayers) with an unvarnished presentation of the lives of modern Indians, on and off the reservations. The songlike qualities of her poems grow from musical traditions of the Navajo and her unique, singsong speaking voice.

Tapahonso was born November 8, 1953, and raised in the small, dusty town of Ganado on the Navajo reservation near Shiprock, New Mexico—a high, arid plateau of rough, reddish-yellow sandstone, scrub piñon pines, and sage-covered flats backed by immense expanses of sky. The countryside is dominated by the imposing bulk of Shiprock, a fluted, wind-carved formation which resembles the prow of an enormous ship thrusting up hundreds of feet from the desert floor, visible for many miles in any direction. The rock, considered a holy place by the Navajo, is the spiritual center of the reservation.

When introducing herself, in proper etiquette of the Diné (the Navajo name for their tribe), Tapahonso identifies her clan membership within the Navajo Nation. "My mother's clan is Too dik'oozhi (Saltwater Clan), which is what I am, and my father's is To dichi'ii'nii (Bitterwater Clan)." When Navajo people introduce themselves, especially to other Navajos, identifying one's clan establishes possible kinship relations which exist in a complexity staggering to outsiders.

Tapahonso's grounding in her Navajo culture gives shape and structure not only to her poetry, but to her life, and she is sharply aware of her responsibilities both as a mother within her tribe, and as its most prominent poet. She fully expects to live her final years on the reservation, in the home of her mother, which according to tradition will become the home of her daughters and their daughters, and their daughters' daughters.

"In a way, we [Navajo people] take a lot of things for granted," she reflects. "There's poetry and rhythm inherent in the way that we talk; songs, prayers, the way people tell stories, the fact that we know from our heart exactly what our great-grandmother was like, even though maybe she died forty years before we were born. We know so much about our relatives we could go anyplace and know that we're surrounded by people that care about us and recognize us as one of them. We take these things for granted, not realizing that people in the larger society don't have those sorts of gifts."

Tapahonso's calm certainty regarding the continuation of her family and of Navajo tradition is rooted in what she describes as a typically Navajo childhood on a farm north of Shiprock. She is the middle child of eleven (Tapahonso has seven sisters and three brothers), and relatives were as much a part of her life as her parents and siblings. "My extended family consists of various uncles and half brothers and half sisters and cousins and aunts," she recalls. "Probably there weren't less than twenty or twenty-five people at our house at one time when I was growing up."

All this community enriched her sense of belonging to the world of drive-up restaurants and to that of traditional ceremonies such as the Blessing Way: "I grew up with people who were pretty aware of both worlds: for events we would sing Navajo songs and we just sort of knew them, like everybody knows 'Mary Had a Little Lamb.'"

This double life which is the reality for many Native Americans today, and the struggle to balance both sides in some kind of harmony, informs much of Tapahonso's work. The stress of trying to live in both worlds at once has been a shattering experience for many Indians.

She traces much of her strength and stability to her childhood. The family farm was a large one and by age four the children helped to harvest corn, alfalfa, watermelons, and fruit from their small orchard, and cared for the horses, sheep, chickens, and turkeys. "We always had lots of chickens. That was my responsibility, so I pretty much grew up with chickens." She laughs, "As an adult, I don't want any chickens!"

The farm was also starkly isolated in the rough, ocher-colored high-desert plains. "We didn't have electricity in our home until I was almost in high school," Tapahonso recalls, "so I wasn't exposed to a lot of things. Just in my adult life I began to learn about 'Leave It to Beaver' and 'I Love Lucy.'

"The kinds of memories I have of my childhood are really sensual kinds of memories; sounds of birds, or roosters and chickens outside the window, scratching in the dirt, my parents talking early in the morning about what they're going to do that day, or their plans for the next week, talking about the children, or my mother singing while she cooks breakfast. One of my best memories is of my mother making bread, and that slapping sound of the bread as she's forming dough. They have a joke at home; they say if you're Navajo, you're supposed to be able to make bread by flipping the dough back and forth between your hands, making it nice and smooth without rolling it out. If you have to use a rolling pin, you're not really a Navajo!"

Although her father completed only the fifth grade, Tapahonso describes him as extremely well read and a tireless proponent of education. He worked much of his life as a livestock inspector for the Navajo Nation. As a young man he was a foreman in the uranium mines in northwestern New Mexico. Her mother worked part-time in the dormitories of Indian boarding schools, her love of children making her a favorite among students. Tapahonso's parents made sure their children understood the importance of education, and taught them to recite their ABCs in English before they started school. Severely punished as students for speaking Navajo, they had their children memorize in English their address and census numbers to ensure that Luci and her siblings would not suffer the same humiliation. They also made sure the children were well versed in Navajo traditions, to help them survive their excursions into the white world.

For Tapahonso, these encounters began at a public grade school. During her first year, a teacher recognized her natural talent for music. Her parents decided to make the financial sacrifice of sending young Luci to a private school where she would receive more personal attention. Thus she attended the Navajo Methodist Mission School in Farmington, New Mexico, a boarding school thirty long miles from her home at Shiprock. Children were allowed to visit their families only at Christmas or for emergencies, rules typical in such institutions, which were often dedicated in those days not only to educating Indian children, but attempting to sever them from their reservations and families in order to more fully integrate them into white society.

It was a difficult time for Tapahonso, who still remembers her first harsh lessons in the religion of white people. "I didn't really know much about Christian religion, so I was very horrified and scared for many years about the world ending, because that was what I grasped [of Christianity]—people dying. To have a bad thought and to die because of it—and *burn*, even worse! It took me a long time to realize there was more to Christian religion than that."

Tapahonso survived boarding school, however, and graduated from Shiprock High School in 1971. Her creativity, first identified as musical talent, manifested itself even more fully in writing. She recalls hearing and reading phrases that she liked because they sounded good, then repeating them secretly to herself until she had memorized them. As she edited the school newspaper and later acted as a stringer for various local newspapers, she also began writing poetry. In 1974, she took part in a training program for investigative reporting at the National Indian Youth Council, which led her to study journalism at the University of New Mexico in 1976.

She wearied of the limitations of daily journalism, and on a whim enrolled in a creative-writing class taught by the prominent Native American author Leslie Marmon Silko, part of the Indian renaissance taking place at the University of New Mexico during the 1970s whose members included Simon Ortiz, Joy Harjo, Paula Gunn Allen, and N. Scott Momaday. This class changed Tapahonso's life. Silko waxed enthusiastic about her creative abilities, both as a poet and as a writer of fiction, and helped get her first short story, "The Snake Man," published in 1978. Tapahonso changed her major to creative writing, receiving her B.A. from the University of New Mexico in 1980 and her master's degree in 1983.

In Albuquerque, exposure to Indian writers such as Silko and Acoma poet Simon Ortiz as well as to the Red Power Movement (documented in Stan Steiner's *The New Indians*) changed forever the way Tapahonso thought about writing. Like most schoolchildren in the 1960s and 1970s, Tapahonso's initial experiences with literature did not include any Native American writers; and she herself had not considered becoming a "real" poet until she began studying with Silko. "When I was growing up, I read Robert Frost and Shakespeare, and I memorized them, but I didn't really know anything about their birch trees or early English," she says. "The writing wasn't mine and it didn't do anything for me. When I go to schools now, the children relate to my poetry, and they like it because they didn't know about poetry that has to do with fry bread or mutton stew or Kool-Aid."

Success came early for Tapahonso. She published her first book of poetry, *One More Shiprock Night*, in 1981. Acoma Pueblo artist Earl Ortiz, who became Tapahonso's first husband, illustrated this volume. Her second collection, *Seasonal Woman* (1982), was illustrated by internationally renowned Native American artist R. C. Gorman. Critic Floyce Alexander wrote, "Luci Tapahonso's *Seasonal Woman* establishes the presence of a new and potentially important voice among younger American poets. . . . Like so much of the powerful poetry now being written by young Native American writers, Tapahonso's work tells the truth."[2]

Tapahonso's truth is a piquant mixture of Navajo and Anglo worlds, or more specifically of a new Navajo world, one that has interacted with twentieth-century white America and come away changed, sometimes for worse, sometimes for better. Tapahonso attributes the success of her work to its dynamic mix of Indian and Anglo influences. She explains, "Parts of contemporary Navajo culture, cowboys and rodeos, being in love with somebody, sometimes knowing that it's not going to work out, and still continuing it—these are very common and accepted by Navajo people, because that's the way our lives are. My poetry is accepted because of those kind of things."

In 1980, Tapahonso began teaching at the elementary school in San Felipe Pueblo, New Mexico; but by 1983 she had accepted a position as an instructor at the Southwestern Indian Polytechnic Institute in Albuquerque, then in 1985 began teaching poetry, literature, and women's studies at the University of New Mexico. In 1987, she published her third collection of poems, entitled *A Breeze Swept Through*, again garnering critical and popular praise.

Stylistically, her poetry is characterized by short line length, the incorporation of dialogue in both Navajo and English, and a reliance on the meter of traditional chants and songs. Her images are a vibrant mix of a spiritually alive landscape and a people caught between an ancient worldview and the buzzing, high-technology angst of twentieth-century America. Her characters, often poised on the shaky borderland between Native and Anglo worlds, speak the same lilting, Navajo-accented English as Tapahonso herself.

Her writing evokes an almost childlike simplicity with its lyric, singsong movement of verses, yet the poems have an immediate, sometimes brutal strength. John Nichols, author of *The Milagro Beanfield War*, says of Tapahonso, "I don't know how to explain it other than [to say] the poetry itself is so disarmingly simple—compassionate and very powerful. I love it when she reads her work. She is so gentle, almost ethereal, and very, very powerful at the same time."[3]

Part of the impact of Tapahonso's writing comes from its intimate physical connection to the high desert and mesa country of Shiprock. The careful reader finds the land, whether the obvious subject in a poem or not, as a solid, living force behind her work: the immensity of space, where neighbors live twenty miles apart and the nearest town is a hundred miles distant; the drama of light and shadow, as the sun filters down past red rock buttes ten stories high; and the almost overwhelming expanse of night sky whose stars glitter undimmed by city lights.

To Tapahonso, anyone writing in the Southwest will be influenced by the force of this powerfully symbolic landscape: "To me, a southwestern writer would be one that's concerned with the land. To all people indigenous to the Southwest, the land is crucial to the way one feels; it shapes one's philosophy about life, work ethic—it shapes just about everything." *A Breeze Swept Through* is particularly rooted in Tapahonso's—and many Navajos'—powerful sense of place, a homeland where, she says, she can stand on the farm where she grew up and point to the distant mesas, eagles circling above, where her mother and father came from. Here there is little separation between rock and home, animal and human, religion and daily life.

This reverence informs her writing, whether set in the concrete cityscape of Albuquerque or among the Gothic cathedrals of Paris. The sense of the spiritual is something she cultivates in her own life and in her two daughters, Lori and Misty Dawn. It is part of their heritage as Navajos, and its continued animation is vital to succeeding generations.

"It's easy to separate church and politics [in the Anglo world] although I think if you looked at it in a finer sort of way, you'd see that maybe the connections aren't that separate. But with Navajo people, the way that one believes and certainly the way that one behaves, the way that one talks, has much to do with what you know about creation stories, and about your own sense of history."

Part of that history, Tapahonso notes in her soft voice, involves its legacy of environmental and occupational disease—particularly in families such as hers, who worked and lived near the infamous uranium mines operating there in the 1940s and 1950s. Few safety measures were taken to protect workers in those days. Tapahonso recalls that miners were not even advised to wear masks to filter the toxic dust. Local families often used the large stones quarried and discarded by the mines to construct the walls of their houses, unaware of their radioactive content. "My brother died from cancer and my sister from leukemia," Tapahonso says quietly. "And all that was unnecessary, because the federal government didn't take precautions—perhaps didn't think the people were important enough to take precautions."

Navajo traditions of spirituality live in a curious balance in Tapahonso's poetry alongside mines, pickup trucks, motel rooms, and the taste of Hills Brothers coffee. A compulsion to record this diverse iconography, so central to a nonromanticized view of the Navajo, left her little choice as to a career. "I write because I have no choice. When I realized that I really liked writing poetry, I knew I would do it regardless of anything else. If I don't write, I feel like I'm neglecting a part of myself and neglecting a part of other people, for sure. It's sort of like the feeling you get when you know that you should have fed your kids at noon and it's now two o'clock and you still haven't fed them! It doesn't matter that I'm being published. If I had not been published, I would still be doing the same thing."

That Tapahonso could feel that she is neglecting not only herself but other people as well when she is not writing reflects the responsibility she feels as a poet: "I write what's important to me as an individual, as a mother, as a daughter, as a Navajo person." She views herself, she says unabashedly, as a good writer with an important message and the means to relate it properly. She bristles slightly when people label her "the Navajo woman poet," objecting to the subtle implication that she is somehow the only Navajo woman writing poetry. "There are a lot of Navajo people who are writing, but the exposure and the opportunity to be published isn't there for them," she says. "The sacrifice that I've had to make is to leave [the reservation]."

Tapahonso currently lives in Lawrence, Kansas, where she teaches at the University of Kansas and where her husband, Bob Brown, directs the renowned Haskell Indian Institute. Yet she still considers the reservation her real home. The songs of Navajo tradition find their way into everything she writes, intertwined now with the grasslands, cottonwoods, and river bottoms of eastern Kansas. The songlike quality of that poetry springs from a life full of singing. "For Navajos there are songs for everything," she explains. "There are songs for putting children to sleep, songs for when you're cooking, songs for riding horses, traveling songs for when you're going a long distance, songs for planting, songs for weddings, songs to protect your home and songs if you're building a home, and there are songs that are really sacred, in prayers and in ceremonies."

Translating the rhythms of Navajo songs into English is a difficult feat, however, and one that Tapahonso struggles with continually. She composes mentally in both languages. Increasingly, her poems incorporate Navajo words and phrases or even alternate verses of English and Navajo. Often, the poems are stated in English, but follow the traditional Navajo song structure of four repeating stanzas.

In recent works, Tapahonso expresses herself in prose poems and stories. In 1993, she published her most recent work, *Sáanii Dahataal: The Women Are Singing*, a collection of poems and short stories. Critic David Biespiel wrote in the *New York Times* that this book succeeds when "seen against the Navajo belief that the world is first conceived in thought and then comes to form through speech and song. . . . She is at her best when describing the human voice, revealing an intimacy with the sound of speech. . . . Ms. Tapahonso speaks the observed and spiritual world into existence."[4]

As in her earlier works, she draws inspiration from her tribe's treasury of folklore and creation tales but grounds them in the present: "In a lot of the [Navajo] stories, there's a sense that this has happened before, that this is very old, that there's so much behind this story in terms of how many times it's been told and where it occurred. It's very visual because a lot of the stories refer to actual places that you can see and that you can go to, in contrast to 'Little Red Riding Hood' or the Bible stories."

This connection of place and consciousness is particularly clear in the short story entitled "Just Past Shiprock," from *Sáanii Dahataal: The Women Are Singing*. The narrator tells of a childhood trip in the back of the family pickup to visit relatives at a distant hogan (a traditional Navajo round house constructed of earth and logs). The bed of the truck is packed with young children. When their play becomes rambunctious, the oldest girl gently brings the children in line by telling a story, passing along an important lesson about memory and respect alongside a piece of tradition whose origin dates to people who passed that way on horseback over a century before.

The girl points to a nearby mesa and tells the children that a long time ago a family traveled through with a baby girl who became sicker and sicker. The family finally realized their tiny daughter was going to die and stopped their horses at the bottom of the mesa.

> They knew it was no use going on. They just stopped and held the baby. By then, she was hardly breathing, and then finally she just stopped breathing. They just cried and walked around with her.
>
> In those days, people were buried differently. The mother and father wrapped her in a pelt of sheepskin and looked for a place to bury her. They prayed, sang a song, then put the baby inside. They stacked rocks over this place so that the animals wouldn't bother her. Of course, they were crying as they rode home.
>
> Later on, whenever they passed by those rocks, they would say, "Our baby daughter is right there," or "She would have been an older sister now." They wiped their tears, remembering her. A lot of people knew that the baby was buried there—that she was their baby and that they still missed her. They knew that and thought of the baby as they passed through here.
>
> So that's why when we come through here, remember those rocks and the baby who was buried there. She was just a newborn. Think about her and be quiet. Those rocks might look like any others, but they're special.[5]

For Tapahonso and many Navajo, the land is not simply something one walks on or something that's "down there." The Diné, in their stories, evolved from the land, and the land becomes them. In Navajo, the word for land means "our mother." That maternal relationship is carried in people and in the landscape itself, which defines one's well-being, one's emotions, and the songs one sings.

Tapahonso published *Bah's Baby Brother Is Born*, a children's book on Fetal Alcohol Syndrome, in 1995, as well as *Dineh ABC: A Navajo Alphabet* (1995) from Macmillan. *Blue Horses Rush In* (1995), a collection of poems and stories, was published by the University of Arizona Press along with an anthology Tapahonso edited entitled *Hayoolkal: An Anthology of Navajo Writers* (1995).

▲ ✧ ▼ ✧ ▼ ✧ ▲

Luci Tapahonso was interviewed in the living room of her sub-urban house on the mesa at the edge of Albuquerque just as she was selling it in preparation for her move to the University of Kansas. Throughout our talk, her teenage daughter, taller than her mother by a head, darted in and out, stopping occasionally to eavesdrop on what the world wanted of her mother.

Tapahonso dresses conservatively or in farmer's jeans: the rough-and-tumble kind, no designer label. Like many Navajo, Tapahonso has a squarish face and a broad, rounded brow. The first thing one notices about her is her silky black hair down to her waist, and the second is her voice: equally silky but subtle, maternal. It is a voice that never seems to hurry and speaks so gently that later, in the studio at KUNM-FM, we had to check twice before setting our recording levels.

It is also a voice never far from a song. Even if transcribed ethnomusicologically, the lilting rise and fall, the tonal shadings of her language, cannot be captured with precision. With few other authors does one feel as little ego or pretension. Like Simon Ortiz, Tapahonso finds herself representing her tribe's culture to the world. This unalterable connection has given her a sense that her life counts; and though incidents have given birth to memorable poetry, her individual experience matters little compared to transmitting her people's traditions.

Her feelings for the land of the Navajo are almost palpable. Like the young Wordsworth hugging a tree (in the introduction to the "Intimations of Immortality" ode), Tapahonso embraces a whole landscape: the pink-and-red sandstone with its table mesas, the olive gray of the mineral-rich plains.

This is a hard land, but there is little that is hard in Tapahonso's manner. Her recollections of boarding school carry the agony imposed by a system that allowed visits to her family only on holidays. This, the Board of Indian Education thought long ago, was the perfect way to detribalize Indians. That painful isolation is relieved by a charming smile as she reflects on the cliques at school and the many different ways of being Navajo. Then she laughs as she remembers listening to the radio buried in her pillow after lights out, marveling at the distant world that crackled in her ears.

LUCI TAPAHONSO:

My father worked at various jobs; early on he worked in a uranium mine. He was a foreman in what were called "dog mines" in the northwestern part of New Mexico. They were really unregulated. A lot of my relatives live out in that area around Red Rock and Cove, where these mines were located. Luckily, my father took precautions, even though at that time it wasn't part of the standard procedures to wear a mask or something over your face when you were working in the mines. Today the cancer rate in that area is really high—people even built their homes with the rocks they brought out of those mines. But this was in the 1940s and there were no paying jobs and people couldn't subsist anymore on the traditional life-styles that we had before. In terms of economics it was necessary, but in terms of human spirit, our lives, and the future of our children, it was a really terrible risk to have taken.

Education was really important for my family. My parents' experiences were sometimes very negative. During the time [they went to school] they weren't allowed to speak Navajo, and they were punished severely for not speaking English, but they came to school able to speak only Navajo. Therefore they didn't speak at all, because they didn't know English. So when we were growing up, they made sure that when we started school we knew our ABCs, our census numbers, our parents' census numbers, our address, all sorts of information memorized before we went so that their experience wouldn't be repeated.

When I was at boarding school, we couldn't have radios, and we were only allowed to watch cartoons on Saturday morning and "Lassie" on Sunday afternoon. I did sneak a radio in once and I fell asleep listening to it. The dorm mother took it from me, and that's the last I saw of it! I remember that when I came home at Christmastime one year everybody was talking about the Beatles, "Oh the Beatles this" and "The Beatles that" and "Oh their hair." This was when the Beatles were very big, and I didn't even know who the Beatles were! They said to me, "Don't you know who the Beatles are?" And I said, "Yeah." They said, "Who?" And I didn't say anything for a while, then

I said, "Everybody knows who the Beatles are!" They thought it was so funny that I didn't know who they were. Everybody in the country knew, I suppose, except people at Navajo Mission school!

Later on, when I was in public high school, there were actually two parts at school—divisions. One was people that listened to rock and roll. They were called "The Cats" and they dressed in go-go boots and those sort of things. Then there were the ones that more often the Indian people went with called "The Stomps." They listened to country music and went to rodeos and western dances and wore boots and big belt buckles.

I think my childhood was very happy . . . filled with a lot of songs and stories, and a lot of attention from both of my parents.

When we went out in the fields and we would hoe or irrigate, even though it was hard work and the sun was real hot, what made it good was that my mother would always tell us things. We would always say to her, "Tell us that story . . ." about a particular thing, or "When you went to school, what kind of things did you have to do?" We had the kind of chores that allowed time to talk and to visit as well as to get work done.

It was different for me [on the reservation] because things weren't convenient. [Today] the kids run down and rent VCRs and watch movies. It seems like things are very easy. And it's nice, in a sense, because it was very hard in the wintertime, especially in the wintertime, to be having to haul water or go out and get wood, which we still do, and bring in coal when it's really cold outside, pipes freeze and all kinds of stuff. It was hard in that sense, so I'm glad that it's easier for them. But I also think that the kind of childhood we had really made you appreciate material things. As materialistic and frivolous as a microwave might be, to me it's just a marvel because it sure beats going and building a fire and waiting for it to warm up!

My children don't refer to their cousins as their cousins, which would be putting them at a distance. They really think of each other in the extended family as brothers and sisters, which is the way it's supposed to be. They have a real sense of their identity as Navajo people and their place in America as Indian people.

Sometimes when I translate things from Navajo the passage sounds so dry in English, but it has an actual image that goes with it in Navajo. Navajo is very different [from English] in that the language encompasses so much more. Visually, it's very rich, and just one word can have connotations that are emotional as well as physical and social. To me, English is very male, and not flexible. You have to say so much to say one thing.

[For Navajos] the skill of being an orator is very much valued, being able to get up and talk in front of people and not stutter, being able to think on your feet and say things in a way so that, at home, people will say, "They speak in the right way, they speak in a beautiful way." There's so much emphasis on the way people talk that when you listen to these people, whether it's in the setting [of an event] or just sitting at the kitchen table, there's always a certain rhythm, certain language markers that exist within the language. To me, language is having a sense of how that works, as well as having a message, saying something important.

I really like James Wright, and when my daughter was about five, she went through a phase where she wanted me to read just James Wright when she fell asleep. So I would read her his poetry. She liked the rhythm and the way that the words sound, and it was very much the same thing for me, except I liked also the things he dealt with—very painful and difficult things sometimes, but dealt with in a very elegant way. I think that is really important in poetry. One has to address and reflect the kind of society that we live in regardless of how hard that might be or how distasteful. That's part of why we write.

Some of the poems that I work on are combined with songs. Those are poems that, as I'm thinking them or writing them, a song naturally comes with it, becomes a part of it. But in written material, the song can't really be there, so the song will only exist if I read the poem and sing it.

[Sometimes] people think that if you're not tall and if you don't wear a headdress and buckskin and beads, then you can't be Indian. Or that if you talk English well, or you're dressed like a "regular" American you can't be Indian. I was on the East Coast and I came into a classroom before the person who was to introduce me was there. This young woman came in and said, "Are *you* the speaker?" I said, "Yes." And she said, "Oh, I thought you were Indian." I said, "I am." And she said, "But you dress like us, and you talk English!" [laughs] She was really disappointed!

America has ignored us for so long that it's real difficult for general America to finally acknowledge the existence of Indian people. Ideally, according to history books, we've all been banished or become part of the American "melting pot," which is not the case. A lot of people are very ignorant about Indian people. Just recently have things begun to be corrected, but it's part of that memory vacuum in this country which has existed for a long time.

Politically the kind of things that are important to me are social issues such as racism, economics, the insistence of keeping our Navajo culture intact. I think those are really important. But also understanding and accepting the way we live today, being able to confront those issues and say, "Well, that's the way things are now." A large part of healing and moving forward is being able to address things and accept them and then progress from there.

EXCERPTS

A Breeze Swept Through

"A Song in Four Parts"

I
that handsome man with grey-blue eyes
would drive 100 miles to have lunch with me
he would, smiling like that.

he distracts me,
nowadays i struggle to complete
projects
(i used to be so diligent!)

* * *

be serious, i tell myself, focus on
work
my mind rebels and flies across
town
to where he sits at his desk
smiling and talking into the phone

(Sings in Navajo)

II
i should not have spoken to you today
perhaps a smile or a simple "hi" would have sufficed
not that nonsensical rambling I lapsed into

i saw that look of pain and confusion in your eyes
i do that quite well by now
by now, i have had
some instances of practice,
nervous training—putting people
on edge
occurs quite naturally by now.
i won't speak to you when i am this way.

(Sings in Navajo)

III
i almost danced even closer against you
as we danced around that far corner

just in time, i didn't
instead, i looked out at faces alongside the dance floor

away from your eyes
i didn't want to see what you might have
thought

had I moved   oh so slowly
into the empty curve of your arm.

(Sings in Navajo)

IV
i have been there
oh yes   these nights
                    the breathing land
                    draws us in
                    the full moon reaches out
                    precisely for you
                    precisely for me
                    these shiny highways become trails for
                    where
                    we would go if i wanted, i want
                    we would pass curving hills
                    pass horses grazing in the moonlight
                    i would leave with you now if you
                    asked.
it is on these nights
i am not sure of my own life   my life becomes a magnet
                                for what i can't understand.

(Sings in Navajo)

Seasonal Woman

"There Have Been Nights"

There have been nights
        I sang '49 songs
        volcano cliffs, south mountain
        red rocks park, summit, stone house
        those times stomping the ground
        I saw my voice rising out of me
        drifting mingling with bonfire smoke
        such a powerful feeling like that

there have been nights
        I sat alone on the living room couch
        with willie nelson/don williams crooning
        it's not supposed to be this way
            in semi-darkness

ring phone ring ring ring
I need a voice to talk to now
tell me that story again about your horses
weren't their names bill and charley?
    tell me stories about anything
    anything on nights like this

there have been nights/ or nightdreams
    I can't be too sure now
    he held me   talking quietly
    around midnight   voice and breath
    surrounding me in the warm dark
    and I felt breathless from
        drifting in senses
        swimming in his motion

there have been nights
there have been nights like that
    so I hardly remember the days that followed.

"Listen"

> Once in high school a friend
> told me: Don't marry a man who
> can't sing. There's something
> wrong if a man can't sing in Indian.

I tell my daughters:
When your daddy or your grandpa is singing—
be still and listen. It's important to listen,
let the song come inside you. Even if it's a
silly song or a hunting song—it's important to
listen and see how he is when he sings.
It helps you grow strong, feel good about yourself.

Listen to your father
see how he looks into your face as he sings
notice the rises and falls of his voice
            the vibrations inside
as he holds you

and just before you fall asleep, daughters
when he kisses your forehead lightly
                    careful not to wake you

if you could see his face
                    the half-smile as he covers you
                    sometimes he has to untangle the both
                    of you
                    bending over your bed and chuckling
                    softly
                    over the way you girls sleep—
                        all scrunched together
                        legs and arms all over.

he takes a deep breath
                    as he turns out the light
                    smiling a little

                    his own prayer after the songs.

"Pay Up or Else"

Vincent Watchman was shot
in the head February 12
because he owed 97¢ at
                    a Thrift-Way gas station.

While he lay dead,
the anglo gas boy said
                    I only meant to shoot out
                    his car tires and scare him.
He fired 2 poor shots—one in the head,
                    one in the rear window and
                    the police cited him for
                    shooting a firearm within city limits.

Meanwhile, Thrift-Way officials in Farmington
expressed shock
                    It's not company policy, after all,
                    to shoot Navajo customers who run

overflows in the self-serve pumps.
This man will definitely be fired.

There is no way that such an action
can be justified, the official said

while we realized our lives weren't worth a dollar
and a 24-year-old Ganado man never used
the $3 worth of gas he paid for.

"Raisin Eyes"

I saw my friend Ella
with a tall cowboy at the store
the other day in Shiprock.

Later, I asked her
Who's that guy, anyway?
Oh, Luci, she said (I knew what was coming.)
it's terrible. He lives with me
and my money and my car
But just for awhile.
He's in AIRCA and rodeos a lot
and I still work.

This rodeo business is getting to me
you know and I'm going to leave him
Because I think all this I'm doing now
will pay off better somewhere else
but I just stay with him and it's hard
because
he just smiles that way you know
and then I end up paying entry fees
and putting shiny Tony Lamas on lay-away again.
It's not hard.

But he doesn't know when
I'll leave him and I'll drive across the flat desert
from Red Rock in blue morning light
straight to Shiprock so easily.

And anyway
my car is already so used to humming
a mourning song with Gary Stewart
complaining again of aching and breaking
down and out love affairs.

Damn.
These Navajo cowboys with raisin eyes
and pointed boots are just bad news,
but it's so hard to remember that
all the time.

She said with a little laugh.

NOTES

1. "Hard to Take," *Seasonal Woman* (Santa Fe: Tooth of Time Press, 1982), pp. 17–18.

2. Floyce Alexander, quoted by Joseph Bruchac in *MELUS*, vol. 11, Winter 1984, pp. 85–91.

3. John Nichols, interview with David K. Dunaway, April 19, 1988.

4. David Biespiel, *New York Times Book Review*, Oct. 31, 1993, p. 40.

5. *Sáanii Dahataal: The Women Are Singing* (Tucson: University of Arizona Press, 1993), pp. 5–6.

FRANK WATERS

▲ ❖ ▼ ❖ ▼ ❖ ▲

Mystic, ethnologist, and author, Frank Waters ranks as western literature's renaissance man. Waters's life spans virtually the whole of the twentieth century, from the administration of Teddy Roosevelt to that of Bill Clinton. Like the work of scholar-novelist Rudy Anaya, Waters's work in fiction and ethnology is vision-centered. His *Book of the Hopi* traces the roots of today's southwestern Indians in the ruins of the vanished Anasazi.

A native of Colorado, Waters draws a spiritual connection from mountains, whether those of his Rocky Mountain boyhood, the snowcapped Sangre de Cristos of his summer home in Taos, New Mexico, or the rugged, dusty ranges surrounding his winter home in Tucson, Arizona. He also has a powerful bond with the Native tribes he has written about for fifty years, despite the discouragement of publishers who told him repeatedly throughout the 1930s and 1940s that Americans did not want to read about Indians.

The great difference between the Indian conception of the environment—that is, the land and the world of nature—and the English-American-Anglo view—is that land, the earth, to us is just inanimate Nature to be exploited at will for our benefit. The Indian viewpoint is that the earth is a living entity and must be respected and protected. So what we're learning is what the Indian has always known; how to respect the earth instead of ruining it—because we know that by ruining

the earth, destroying Nature, we're destroying ourselves.
We're too a part of Nature.

—FRANK WATERS

The work of nonagenarian Frank Waters, who is today re-ferred to as the dean of western writing, has spanned historical eras and multiple careers. A noted novelist, historian, and eth-nologist, Waters has written over·twenty books in the last six decades—almost three-quarters in print today. Read primarily on college campuses in the United States and Europe, he is sometimes called America's best-known unknown writer when compared with other major American authors of this century. As critic Alexander Blackburn wrote, "Waters may one day be seen as . . . having revealed [the West's] complex civilization as William Faulkner revealed that of the South."[1]

Frank Waters was born in Colorado Springs, at the foot of Pikes Peak, on July 25, 1902. Automobiles were largely un-known, airplanes were yet to be invented, and blocks of ice were still delivered to homes in Colorado Springs by horse-drawn wagons. From this beginning, Waters would one day write about the ultimate harbinger of the modern age—the development of the first atomic bomb in Los Alamos, New Mexico, only two hundred miles south of his boyhood home, in *The Woman at Otowi Crossing* (1966). In this and a dozen other novels Waters explores a uniquely southwestern dichot-omy: traditional Native American mysticism coexisting with twentieth-century technology. The characters of Waters's imagination inhabit a world charged with the Southwest's vi-brant cross-fertilizations, with its sometimes violent clashes of Hispanic, Indian, and white cultures.

Waters's unusual historical span allows him a far-reaching vision. He was among the first Anglo novelists to seek an ac-curate spiritual understanding of Native worldviews. Critics have noted that his ideas are early predecessors to today's environmental and New Age movements. Yet what has always made Waters's books different from the Smithsonian Institu-tion's ethnographies is the way he engages Indian cultures per-sonally, respectfully. His work has set a broad stage on which the literature of the Southwest has unfolded over the last half century.

From early childhood, Waters moved between different worlds. Colorado Springs had originally been settled by wealthy British expatriates and was known as "Little London." When gold was discovered in nearby Cripple Creek, the town became a tourist resort and retirement village for the wealthy. Waters's father, Jonathan, was a prominent builder who constructed many of the new schools, businesses, and mansions which quickly filled the town. Jonathan Waters was also part Cheyenne.

When the displaced Ute tribes were allowed to return to Colorado from the West Coast, they erected their smoke gray conical lodges each summer on the mesa just west of Colorado Springs. Although the Indians were shunned by most "respectable" townspeople, Waters's father visited the Utes whenever he could, taking his son in their buckboard wagon, and once spending a summer with the boy on a Navajo trading post.

"I have known Indians since I was a little boy," Waters reflects, "and I feel at home with them. It seems wherever I went [in the Southwest, Mexico, Guatemala] I was with Indians." Just as Tony Hillerman found early community with the Potawatomi of Oklahoma, whose school he attended, many of Waters's later writings took up Indian-Anglo crossings.

As a youth, Waters also imbibed a quasi-mystical connection to the desert earth, the rhythm of the seasons, the ebb and flow of nature. The drama of the outdoors was as real to him as the Zane Grey novels to which he was addicted—ironically, as it turns out, for he would spend much of his life challenging the stereotypes Grey portrayed.

The symbolic representation of the natural world in myths is at the center of Waters's work. Besides Native American mysticism, his work eventually drew upon Hinduism and Buddhism, the nature mysticism of the American Romantic writers and philosophers, and the oral tradition of the Hispanic West.

Waters's life was characterized by a series of spiritual epiphanies. His first vision occurred on a summer afternoon when he was ten years old. There, in the shadow of the Rockies, the boy was sitting one day on the talus dump of tailings from his grandfather's gold mine. Pikes Peak loomed above him as he played with handfuls of sand: "I noticed in my hand all the infinitesimally little particles of sand. And it suddenly seemed to me that all these particles of matter were bound together with a strange affinity, as if fitted together by a pattern. It was a revelation. I got the feeling then that the whole world was fitted together like that."

This vision guided Waters's life, helping him move not only between cultures, but also within them, drawing connections between disparate worlds where others had seen only separation. Waters's wide-ranging career reflects this fluidity—he has been a wildcatter, an engineer, a screenwriter, a public-relations writer, an army propaganda expert, and a lecturer in addition to producing essays, biographies, novels, and works of ethnography. None of his books was a major commercial success, a fact which he credits with forcing him to become a better writer. "Having to hunt for a job was the best thing that happened to me because I was thrown in with new people and new experiences—and that, of course, is the kind of material that a writer uses—life."

When he graduated from high school, Waters attended Colorado College in Colorado Springs for three years, studying engineering, before deciding that he was not cut out for what he considered dry, mathematical work. In 1925, he dropped out of college and caught a train to Salt Creek, Wyoming, where he worked in the oil fields as a roustabout. He earned what was then good money: fifty cents an hour for laying ten-inch pipe across the vast western prairie, ten hours a day. The oil company subtracted from their workers' daily wages fifty cents for every meal and another fifty cents for the privilege of sleeping in the company bunkhouse. On weekends, the work crews traveled to a squatter camp, which according to Waters looked like a Hollywood set for a wild West movie, to drink bootleg beer.

While in the oil fields, Waters befriended an elderly man whose daughter lived in California. The daughter asked her father to come and live with her in Los Angeles. The old man invested his life's savings in a Star roadster which he soon discovered he was unable to drive. He promised Waters a free ride to California if he would drive him there in his new car. Waters agreed, leaving the oil fields for good. "I went, and finally found a job in Los Angeles with the telephone company,"

Waters laughs, "and of course life catches up to you—the job was as an engineer."

He was sent by the phone company to work on the California-Mexico border, in Imperial Valley. It was his first time living in the desert, and he was instantly fascinated. Here in the eerie quiet, broken only by wind and an occasional truck, he wrote his first novel, *The Lizard Woman* (published as *Fever Pitch* by Liveright in 1930). Although today Waters considers the book "inept," it caught the eye of the first publisher to read it, the pioneering Horace Liveright. Liveright declared that the book would be a financial failure, but he felt Waters had great potential and he would option Waters's next three books if he would promise to learn how to spell. Waters did, and he credits Liveright with launching his writing career.

Finally, in 1935, Waters quit the phone company to write full-time, although he continued working periodically at an astonishing variety of jobs, from newspaper editor to information officer at the atomic testing grounds in Los Alamos, to help support himself. He had already written another novel, *The Wild Earth's Nobility* (1935), the first in his Colorado mining trilogy, followed by *Below Grass Roots* (1937) and *Dust within the Rock* (1940).[2]

While writing these books, Waters lived off and on in Mora, a small Hispanic village in northern New Mexico, just south of the Colorado border. This is the place where canyon meets pine in New Mexico, a landscape of brown earth, cactus, and cottonwoods hugging the banks of streams tumbling down between red sandstone cliffs. This unity of physical features, of rivers and valleys that cross state boundaries, is a metaphorical characteristic of the Southwest. The Ute tribes of Utah live isolated from Anglo settlement by a range capped by the mountain they call "Sleeping Lady"; north of Taos, where *People of the Valley* is set, the San Luis valley eventually joined Anglo and Hispanic communities. Mora had remained genuinely isolated since the nineteenth century, a close-knit, self-sufficient village of Hispanic farmers. In the late 1930s, Waters was one of only three Anglos in Mora, all residents of the historic turn-of-the-century Butler Hotel. From its porch he traced, with the irony of a Swift or a Voltaire, the arrival of the great train of Progress. Yet *People of the Valley* (1941) really con-

cerns not simply the arrival of the modern era but its antici-
pation: "There was no traffic, no business—just people living
on the land there in that beautiful little valley. The story is
what confronted them when the government wanted to come
in and build a dam—and take over their land."

Fifty miles south of the San Luis Valley rises Taos, New Mexico, where the Taos Indians constructed their pueblo, perhaps
the most elaborate such structure still standing, in the shade
of what the Spaniards called the Sangre de Cristo (Blood of
Christ) Mountains. Waters settled on the slopes of these dramatically high, snowy peaks. This is the high country which
joins the deserts and mesas of central New Mexico with the
southernmost extension of the Rocky Mountains—a mountain-
scape that reminded Waters of his boyhood. High above, in
the crevasses of the peaks, lie the pine-fringed, crystal blue
lakes sacred to the Taos. This became the backdrop for Waters's most famous book, *The Man Who Killed the Deer* (1942).

While still a newcomer in Taos, one afternoon Waters wandered into the local courthouse in time to witness the trial of
a young man from Taos Pueblo, charged with killing a deer out
of season in the national forest above the pueblo. The man
was unrepentant; his people knew no seasons on feeding their
families. Before he could be sentenced, an old white trader
stepped forward, without explanation, and paid the young
man's fine.

The little drama and the cultural contradictions it contained
haunted Waters. Several days later, as he stood before his
bathroom mirror, he stared absently down into his shaving
bowl. In it he saw reflected three figures—an Indian, a white,
and a Hispanic—discussing the trial of the man who killed the
deer. In that instant, he says, he knew exactly what he wanted
to write.

The book is more than one man's story. It concerns the
continuing fight of the people of Taos Pueblo, inflamed by the
trial, to regain possession of their most holy site, the sacred
Pine Lake in the middle of the national forest (where the dis-
puted deer was killed). The conflict is complicated by the reactions of Hispanic farmers and Anglo businessmen to Indian
claims of land ownership. Through it all, the pueblo struggles
to accommodate Anglo-educated Indians like Martiniano, the

man who kills the deer, and the outside world he represents, within the mythic and religious realities of Pueblo life. The actual legality of the killing of the deer is, as the Pueblo elders describe it, merely a pebble thrown in a lake. The pebble quickly disappears. What is important is not the small truth of the stone, but the ever-expanding ripples it creates.

The Man Who Killed the Deer was such a pebble. Its reputation grew, with translation after translation. Though the book was critically well received, it was esoteric: "In those days no one wrote about Indians," Waters recalls. "National prejudice was still strong, and nobody would *read* about Indians. So I wrote book after book about Indians, and each one of them was a complete flop the minute it came off the press. Why I persisted I just don't know, except that I simply couldn't help it."

Beginning in 1942, Waters spent two years in the army preparing training films, writing for the Office of Inter-American Affairs in Washington, D.C., then working as an information officer at the Los Alamos National Laboratory in New Mexico. In the late 1940s, he spent a short time as a screenwriter in Hollywood—a job he quickly came to detest because of the titanic egos he encountered. The film, *River Lady*, was finally produced in 1949 by Universal-International Studios, but Waters had no regrets about leaving Hollywood. If he had been too successful, he insists, he would now be "just sitting around all day, repeating myself constantly. I would've had nothing to write about and I would've gone to pot."

Waters returned to New Mexico and over the next decade wrote novels as well as essays and other nonfiction, among them *The Yogi of Cockroach Court* (1947), *Diamond Head* (1948), and *The Earp Brothers of Tombstone: The Story of Mrs. Virgil Earp* (1960). In 1960, when he was fifty-eight, he received what he considered the chance of a lifetime. A man from the Bay Foundation in New York, which was contributing money to the Western Apache to aid them in improving their cattle-breeding programs, met a Hopi Indian named Oswald Fredericks White Bear. The administrator felt his foundation might assist the Hopi tribe as well, if someone could tell their story. The administrator wrote to Waters, asking if he would speak with

White Bear. Waters lived for the next three years on the remote Hopi reservation at Pumpkin Seed Point, Arizona.

One of the first to befriend him was a traditional Hopi religious leader who told Waters that if he were honest and sincere in what he planned to write, he would receive four specific dreams that would let the elders know his "heart was right." To Waters's surprise, less than a week after this encounter he had the first dream; he was subsequently initiated into the Hopi world. The Hopi are notoriously wary of outsiders—both whites and Indians of other tribes—but Waters gained their confidence. Thirty traditionalist Hopi elders contributed to this classic ethnological study of Hopi religion, mythology, legend, and ritual—*Book of the Hopi* (1963).

Waters has always been keenly aware of the fine line between writing about Native Americans and exploiting their cultures by revealing matters they wish secret. As he had done with *The Man Who Killed the Deer*, Waters sent *Book of the Hopi* to the tribal council before publication, asking if confidences had been violated. Both books passed this test.

In 1965, two years after the publication of *Book of the Hopi*, Waters wandered into a small bookstore in Flagstaff, Arizona, not known then as a leading book town. He noticed an exceptionally tall stack of *Book of the Hopi*. Curious, he asked the clerk, "Who in the world buys these books?", to which she replied, "Well, the Hopis buy them."

After working with the Hopi, Waters received a Rockefeller grant to research the life and religion of pre-Columbian Indians in Mexico and Guatemala. This resulted in his nonfiction book *Mexico Mystique: The Coming Sixth World of Consciousness* (1975).

Throughout the next two decades, into his nineties, Waters has continued to write. In 1966 he had published *The Woman at Otowi Crossing*, based on the life of a remarkable woman, Edith Warner, who ran a tearoom at the train station below Los Alamos, where the first atomic bombs were developed. A number of legends grew up around her, passed on by the Native American and Hispanic communities who still remember her. He published yet another novel, *Flight from Fiesta*, in 1986, which takes place in Santa Fe.

Critics have generally been kind to Waters, despite the fact that he holds no university degrees in the subjects he studies. The editor of *Western American Literature*, Thomas Lyon, has written that Waters (and his range of subjects) is representative of southwestern regionalism.[3]

Waters became interested in anthropology early in his writing career. In 1950, he published *Masked Gods*, a retelling of Native American ritual from a Jungian perspective, today recognized as a classic overview of Navajo and Pueblo worldviews. Harvard anthropologist Clyde Kluckhohn wrote of *Masked Gods*, "Mr. Waters has synthesized in an altogether new way an amazing amount of material. . . . I found myself questioning familiar assumptions and, more importantly still, realizing for the first time some of the hidden premises in my habitual thinking about the cultures of the Southwest. This is a heady wine. It is not, however, old wine in a new bottle. It is a new vintage from a rare soil. The roots are deep in the writer's personal life."[4]

Today Frank Waters divides his time between Taos and Tucson, Arizona; the clean mountain air of the desert in winter relieves his weak lungs. He follows with interest the environmental movement, seeing parallels with a Native American mythos he documented decades earlier. As with Johnny Appleseed, the results of his travels and long research have been fruitful, not in the first generations to read them, in the 1930s and 1940s, but in subsequent ones in many countries. With time has come tranquillity despite the physical frailties of a body approaching its century mark. He refuses to speak about current projects before they are finished, but Waters continues to write, to read, to wonder, and to explore with a mind that remains undimmed. His conversation shows signs of a lifetime synthesizing myths and languages.

The man who admits an early addiction to Zane Grey finds literary predecessors in the memoirs of the friars and conquistadores and in the journals of pioneer settlers winding their way down the Santa Fe Trail, each phrase scrawled between bumps of a wagon wheel. This is, after all, a college dropout with seven honorary doctorates, whose books are standard texts in many university classes, and whose novels have been translated into a dozen languages.

▲ ❖ ▼ ❖ ▼ ❖ ▲

At first glance, at age ninety-three, Frank Waters resembles the craggy slopes of the mountain near which he was born, Pikes Peak. Though Waters always claimed to love the desert the way a sailor loves the sea, there is something of the Rockies in every conversation with the man widely called "the dean of western writers." Our interview, in the studios of KUAT-FM in Tucson (the city where he winters) shifted between sharply etched recollections of growing up eighty years ago in Colorado Springs and his childlike wonder at the workings of the universe. It is a cliché to speak of the way the elderly recapitulate childhood, yet it is a fact that their recollections return to early childhood; they wonder as they wander in time.

Waters's long, rangy body more closely resembles that of a Mexican vaquero *than a former writer for Hollywood and Los Alamos National Laboratory. Though his movements are slow and tentative, his mind is quick. He is always ready to pluck an index card off his desk to write down a helpful citation.*

In the studio his voice, like his lungs, is weak, but he reads with the deliberate care of the professional. After he began a passage, it was as if we had entered a tunnel, and he and the listener had somehow wandered off together—into an aviary or a horse pen, or perhaps into the zócalo (town square) of a small village on a summer's evening as the old men gathered to tell their tales.

FRANK WATERS:

Looking back over all my books, it seems that every one establishes a definite, separate sense of place. My first early books, the Colorado Mining Trilogy, were on the Pikes Peak region of Colorado, and the desert country. Then Taos and the Taos Pueblo, Santa Fe, and then two books on Arizona, and a book on Mexico. Each reflects a sense of place.

Places have a certain spirit, a sense of rhythm, the same as people. And out in the West places are distinctive and widely separated.

I lived on Bijou Street [in Colorado Springs]. The Santa Fe Railroad track ran on a high embankment a short distance away, and later I became a newsboy at the train station. When I would hear those trains "in the block" as they said, and the sound of the steam whistles, that was sweet music indeed.

We had some very fancy wagons, like the Pan-Dandy Bread wagon that would stop in the street right opposite our house. It was drawn by a beautiful team of mares. On winter mornings I'd hitch my sled to the back of that wagon and get a free ride to school. Then the tradesmen would come—the scissors- and knife-sharpening man with his portable grinding wheel; the iceman; the rags, bottles, and sacks man. These were the people that kept this little world going.

Wherever I've been, there have been mountains very close. The desert mountains have influenced me. I have a love of the desert that I developed when I went down to Lower California. For me, the desert has the same attraction that to other people, the ocean, the sea, has. When I'm out in the midst of the desert, I have that feeling that a sailor must have on the sea.

I think the shift in consciousness [we need] is an enlargement, an expansion of our perspective. A child's consciousness is merely an awareness of his immediate family and the little world he lives in. And then, as he develops more and wider experiences of people and places, his consciousness expands. Unfortunately, most men and women stop growing at that point.

Your imagination is always reaching out to become aware of things beyond the sensory limits. I think that is the point we've reached now, with our microscopes and our telescopes and our trips to the moon—they are revealing an immense world that our consciousness is trying to embrace. . . . With psychology, meditation practices of the East, we're trying to find a correspondence between the world outside and the world inside.

You can lead a horse to water, but you can't make him drink. You can preach to a man, you can give him the best books to read, and nothing sinks in. But suddenly one day, he's going to get thirsty. You don't know how this comes, but all these things are unconsciously working, and suddenly they come into focus.

* * *

The Woman at Otowi Crossing is modeled on a woman named Edith Warner. I changed her name and her life—this is not a biography. But it is the story of the myth about her that has grown up and is believed by her Spanish and Indian neighbors. She ran a little tearoom at the bottom of Los Alamos Mesa, which then was called "The Hill" and is where the atomic bomb was created. It just seemed such a remarkable instance. An Indian pueblo right at the bottom of "The Hill" carrying on their ages-old ceremonial life, and then these atomic scientists carrying on a different life up above. I thought the difference between the two was just too remarkable to ignore.

[In the book] the woman is called Helen Chalmers. She kept a secret journal. She has a series of paranormal experiences. Jack, a friend and former lover, takes a dim view of these experiences, which explains the tenor of her journal excerpt which I'm going to read. She has dedicated the journal to him.

EXCERPTS

The Woman at Otowi Crossing

There is no such thing as time as we know it. The entire contents of all space and time coexist in every infinite and eternal moment. It is an illusion that we experience them in a chronological sequence of "time." . . . I didn't learn this gradually during all my lonely years running this obscure tea room at a remote river crossing. I was trying to escape a miserable past, suffering the makeshifts of the day, dreading the future. Then suddenly it all spun before me like a wheel turning full circle. Everything I had known and would ever know congealed into one rounded, complete whole. And it's been that way more or less ever since.

Perhaps none of us really ever learn anything by degrees. We just keep on absorbing things subconsciously, without realizing what they mean. Till suddenly, for no apparent reason, it all comes into focus with a blinding flash. Civilizations like people must evolve the same way. Not continuously. But by steps. Sudden unfoldments and blossomings, like the

Renaissance and the Atomic Age, followed by another dormant period of darkness and ignorance. . . .

What determines when we are ready for these mysterious upsurges and Emergences? . . . All I know is that it started late that afternoon when we were waiting for the last run on the Chile Line. We heard her whistle as she came around the bend. I was thinking then in terms of time. That this was the last lonely screech from my darling little narrow gauge and a life going from me forever—and with it my livelihood from a lunch room here. I didn't know that it was whistling in a new life, a whole new era. But these, I found, were illusions, too. There are no beginnings, no ends, nothing new. Everything has always been within us, just waiting to be recognized.

People of the Valley

For months a somber gray had overhung the valley, blotting the beauty and obscuring the blue. Fall it was and still raining—an incessantly dripping mist, a sparse quick splatter, the lash of a heavy storm.

The earth was soggy. Adobe walls kept crumbling. Anemic, water-logged corn straddled puddles. Beasts and birds of the field dragged hoof and claw as if too discouraged to shake off the clinging mud. When the sky appeared to be clearing, the river bloated with more debris; there had been another heavy rise [rain] up one of the tributary cañons.

"Mother of God!" a man would exclaim, tramping in from the fields. "I have not seen it so wet in thirty years." . . .

Mid-November it is, and the Saint's Day of the village. The late morning stillness of the deserted fields is broken by a faint wailing chant. A thousand crows, polished like ebony, flap up cawing from the tawny stubble. A lone mallard shoots like an arrow from the marsh. A shaggy stallion wheels from his mares, flings up his head and stares over the fence.

The chanting wails louder. It comes from twenty men in a column of twos crossing the fields from El Alto de los

Herreras. Their boots are muddy, their denim trousers ragged, but they wear neckties and wrinkled Sunday coats. All are bareheaded. Their eyes are raised to a banner of red silk lettered with faded gold. It flaps between two poles which the men in front are carrying.

As the column crosses the creek by the old mill and enters the village, the wail rises higher and falls lower. A red rooster flees squawking. A wagon draws aside to let the men pass. Clutching their rebozos to be sure their heads are covered, a few hurrying women fall in behind the column.

All cross the little plaza behind the general store. Beyond the rows of empty wagons and tethered horses the bell of the church is ringing. The tall poles dip, and the red banner slides through the adobe arch of the courtyard wall. The chanting ceases. The bell stops ringing. And in the silence, down the dark nave between cottonwoods, the people pass into the church.

The Man Who Killed the Deer

[Martiniano] went to the trading post. The adobe-brick walls of Byers' new room had been laid and settled. The big pines for vigas cut last fall had seasoned all winter. Now Byers needed help in carpentering and carving. Martiniano was glad to accept the employment he offered; it would give him money and work for the several weeks remaining until he had to prepare his land for spring planting.

Both men worked silently and slowly, without shirking, but with time out for cigarettes and coffee, and for frequent trips to town after more materials.

"This strange white trader!" thought Martiniano. "No wonder the old men trust him. No wonder I like him. He understands. He knows much, thinks well and says little. That is the mark of a good man." But there was nothing to say to him.

Byers, rattling around, was as conscious of the one who worked beside him. But in the one there were two. There was a jim-dandy carpenter and craftsman who knew tools and how to use them, a young fellow who had been to school, spoke English and Spanish, was intelligent and matter-of-fact. There was another, dark-faced and somber, with long hair braids down his back, who squatted patiently, hour after hour, beside the long roof support he was carving. He worked with a mindless preoccupation. His toes dug into the ground, his thigh muscles corded. A gentle tremor flowed up the red-brown torso revealed by his gaping shirt. . . . Meanwhile he sang softly of gathering clouds and of the tall rain walking through the corn. . . . It was all one flowing whole, passing from toes to finger-tips, into and up the wood—a simple design springing evenly and effortlessly from nerve and muscle and bone.

Masked Gods

The only Indians left as integral groups today exist within the immemorial boundaries of their ancient homeland. The village Pueblos and semi-nomadic Navajos, fringed by the mountain Utes and desert Apaches—these today are the last homogenous remnants of what we call the Vanishing American. And they all live within the one last wilderness of what they may well call Vanishing America.

We today call it the Four Corners, because here in this upland wilderness exists the only point where four states touch: Utah, Colorado, New Mexico, and Arizona. Yet its geographical boundaries and the legendary significance of its name stem back to a prehistoric tradition that immemorially antedates the discovery of the continent by Europeans.

[Navajos,] "Dinneh"—"The People." This came to be their name in their own tongue, just as Apaches to the south called themselves "Inde" or "Tinde"—"The People." Here was the vast open land over which they roamed to raid and besiege the pueblos, and here was The People arising from it. It was as simple, as subtle, as arrogantly strong as that.

The Pueblos, high and safe on their rocky mesas in the center of this grassy sea, called themselves "Hopituh"— "The People of Peace."

This was the only real difference between them. For the

nomads, ostensibly still a people of constant and turbulent change, had made the transition to the Rock. The land itself was their Rock. To it they were rooted as securely as the Cliff Dwellers to their cliffs. . . .

Then suddenly, about seven hundred years ago, something happened. We believe it was a great drought beginning in 1276. Year after year for twenty-three years the rainfall lessened. The springs failed. The crops dried up. The game dwindled. One by one the great pueblos were abandoned, their populations wandering away on long hegiras seeking new homesites near water.

What we have left, washed up on today's beach, are hewn stones, fragments of pottery, ears of corn, and desiccated bodies perfectly preserved in the dry air, ruins of whole pueblos. All empty kachina masks of a vanished civilization.

But no post mortem is necessary; this ancient civilization still exists if we know where to look for it. From the sun temples of Mesa Verde its light flickered to the pyramid sun temples of Aztec Mexico, and was reflected from those of Inca Peru. In the modern Pueblo and Navajo ceremonials of today we find embodied the same ancient rituals. It is all one vast continuity spanning both time and space—an American Way still rooted in the soil and the soul of a continent.

NOTES

1. Alexander Blackburn, *A Sunrise Brighter Still: The Visionary Novels of Frank Waters* (Athens, Ohio: Swallow/Ohio University Press, 1991), p. 4.

2. The trilogy was later combined and reissued as *Pike's Peak: A Family Saga* (Athens, Ohio: Swallow/University of Ohio Press, 1971).

3. Thomas Lyon, *Writer's Forum*, Fall 1985, pp. 180–194.

4. Clyde Kluckhohn, foreword to *Masked Gods* (Albuquerque: University of New Mexico Press, 1950), pp. 7–8.

SELECTED BIBLIOGRAPHY

▲ ❖ ▼ ❖ ▼ ❖ ▲

EDWARD ABBEY

Primary Bibliography

The Brave Cowboy. New York: Dodd, Mead, 1956.
Fire on the Mountain. New York: Dial Press, 1962.
Desert Solitaire: A Season in the Wilderness. New York: McGraw-Hill, 1968.
Black Sun. New York: Simon and Schuster, 1971.
The Monkey Wrench Gang. Philadelphia: Lippincott, 1975.
The Journey Home: Some Words in Defense of the American West. New York: Dutton, 1977.
Abbey's Road: Take the Other. New York: Dutton, 1979.
Good News. New York: Dutton, 1980.
Slumgullion Stew: An Ed Abbey Reader. New York: Dutton, 1984.
Beyond the Wall: Essays from the Outside. New York: Henry Holt, 1984.
Confessions of a Barbarian. Dual edition, Santa Barbara: Capra Books, 1986.
One Life at a Time, Please. New York: Henry Holt, 1988.
Fool's Progress. New York: Henry Holt, 1988.

Secondary Bibliography

Library Journal, Jan. 1, 1968; July 1977.
New York Times Book Review, Jan. 28, 1968; July 31, 1977; August 5, 1979.
Washington Post Book World, March 24, 1968; June 25, 1979.

The New Yorker, July 17, 1971.

Christian Science Monitor, July 27, 1977.

New York Times, June 19, 1979.

Washington Post Book Review, May 30, 1982.

Publishers Weekly, Oct. 5, 1984.

Berry, Wendell. "A Few Words in Favor of Edward Abbey." *Resist Much, Obey Little: Some Notes on Edward Abbey*. Eds. Hepworth, James; McNamee, Gregory. Salt Lake City: Dream Garden, 1985.

Bryant, Paul T. "Edward Abbey and Environmental Quixoticism." *Western American Literature*, May 1989, v. 24(1): 37–43.

Davis, Carl L. *Thoughts on a Vulture: Edward Abbey, 1927–1989*. RE Arts & Letters: A Liberal Arts Forum, Fall 1989, v. 15(2): 15–23.

Dougherty, Jay. " 'Once more, and once again': Edward Abbey's Cyclical View of Past and Present in *Good News*." *Critique: Studies in Contemporary Fiction*, Summer 1988, v. 29(4): 223–32.

Eastlake, William. "A Note on Ed Abbey." *Resist Much, Obey Little: Some Notes on Edward Abbey*. pp. 20–22.

Herndon, Jerry A. " 'Moderate Extremism': Edward Abbey and 'The Moon-Eyed Horse'." *Western American Literature*, Aug. 1981, v. 16(2): 97–103.

Jimerson, Kay. "New America Studies in the American West." *This Is About Vision: Interviews with Southwestern Writers*. Eds. Balassi, William; Crawford, John F.; Eysturoy, Annie O. Albuquerque: Univ. of New Mexico Press, 1990. pp. 53–60.

McClintock, James I. "Edward Abbey's 'Antidotes to Despair.' " *Critique: Studies in Contemporary Fiction*, Fall 1989, v. 31(1): 41–54.

Murray, John A. "The Hill beyond the City: Elements of the Jeremiad in Edward Abbey's 'Down the River with Henry Thoreau.' " *Western American Literature*, Feb. 1988, v. 22(4): 301–6.

Ronald, Ann. *The New West of Edward Abbey*. Albuquerque: Univ. of New Mexico Press, 1982. p. 255.

————. *A Literary History of the American West*. Fort Worth: Texas Christian Univ. Press, 1987. pp. 604–11.

Scheese, Don. "Desert Solitaire: Counter-Friction to the Machine in the Garden." *North Dakota Quarterly*, Spring 1991, v. 59(2): 211–27.

RUDOLFO ANAYA

For a more complete bibliography of works by and about Rudolfo Anaya *see* Cesar Gonzalez-T.'s *Rudolfo Anaya: Focus On Criticism*, La Jolla, CA: Lalo Press, 1990; and Maria Teresa Huerta Marquez's *A Selected Bibliography* in *Contemporary Author's Autobiography Series*, vol. 4.

Primary Bibliography

Bless Me, Ultima. Berkeley: Tonatiuh-Quinto Sol Intl., 1972.
Heart of Aztlan. Berkeley: Editorial Justa, 1976.
Bilingualism: Promise for Tomorrow. Screenplay, Bilingual Educational Services, 1976.
Tortuga. Berkeley: Editorial Justa, 1979.
Cuentos: Tales from the Hispanic Southwest. Translated by Rudolfo Anaya, Santa Fe: Museum of New Mexico Press, 1980.
The Silence of the Llano. Berkeley: Tonatiuh-Quinto Sol Intl., 1982.
A Chicano in China. Albuquerque: Univ. of New Mexico Press, 1986.
Alburquerque. Albuquerque: Univ. of New Mexico Press, 1992; paperback edition, New York: Warner Books.
The Anaya Reader. New York: Warner Books, 1995.
Zia Summer. New York: Warner Books, 1995.

Editor of:

Cuentos Chicanos: A Short Story Anthology, with Antonio Marquez. Albuquerque: Univ. of New Mexico Press, 1980.
A Ceremony of Brotherhood, 1680–1980, with Simon J. Ortiz. Albuquerque: Academia, 1981.
Aztlan: Essays on the Chicano Homeland, with Francisco Lomelf. Albuquerque: Academia/El Norte, 1989.

Secondary Bibliography

Anaya, Rudolfo. "La Llorona, El Kookooee, and Sexuality." *The Bilingual Review/La Revista Bilingüe*, Jan.–Apr. 1992, v. 12(1): 50–55.

Anaya, Rudolfo A.; Lomeli, Francisco A.; eds. "Myth, Identity and Struggle in Three Chicano Novels: Aztlan . . . Anaya, Mendez and Acosta." *Aztlan: Essays on the Chicano Homeland.* Albuquerque: Academia/El Norte, 1989. v. 248: 219–29.

Anaya, Rudolfo A. "The Silence of the Llano: Notes from the Author." *MELUS: The Journal of the Society for the Study of the Multi-Ethnic Literature of the United States*, Winter 1984, v. 11(4): 47–57.

———. "The Myth of Quetzalcoatl in a Contemporary Setting: Mythical Dimensions/Political Reality." *Western American Literature*, Nov. 1988, v. 23(3): 195–200.

Anderson, Robert K. "Marez y Luna and the Masculine-Feminine Dialectic." *Crítica Hispánica.* 1984, v. 6(2): 97–105.

Crawford, John. "Rudolfo Anaya." *This Is about Vision: Interviews with Southwestern Writers.* Eds. Balassi, William; Crawford, John F.; Eysturoy, Annie O. New America Studies in the American West. Albuquerque: Univ. of New Mexico Press, 1990. pp. 83–93.

Daghistany, Ann. "The Shaman, Light and Dark." *Literature and Anthropology.* Studies in Comparative Literature 20. Eds. Dennis, Philip; Aycock, Wendell. Lubbock: Texas Tech Univ. Press, 1989. pp. 193–208.

Dasenbrock, Reed Way. "Intelligibility and Meaningfulness in Multicultural Literature in English." *PMLA: Publications of the Modern Language Association of America*, Jan. 1987, v. 102(1): 10–19.

Elias, Edward. "Tortuga: A Novel of Archetypal Structure." *The Bilingual Review/La Revista Bilingüe*, Jan.–Apr. 1982, v. 9(1): 82–87.

Lamadrid, Enrique. "The Dynamics of Myth in the Creative Vision of Rudolfo Anaya." *Paso por Aquí: Critical Essays on the New Mexican Literary Tradition, 1542–1988.* Ed. Gonzales-Berry, Erlinda. Albuquerque: Univ. of New Mexico Press, 1989. pp. 243–54.

Schiavone, Sister James David. "Distinct Voices in the Chicano

Short Story: Anaya's Outreach, Portillo Trambley's Outcry, Rosaura Sanchez's Outrage." *The Americas Review: A Review of Hispanic Literature and Art of the USA*, Summer 1988, v. 16(2): 68–81.

Vassallo, Paul, ed. *The Magic of Words: Rudolfo A. Anaya and His Writings*. Albuquerque: Univ. of New Mexico Press, 1982.

DENISE CHAVEZ

Primary Bibliography

Nacimiento. Drama, first produced in Albuquerque, 1979.

Plaza. Drama, first produced at the Joseph Papp Festival Latino in New York, and the Scotland Arts Festival in Edinburgh, 1984.

The Last of the Menu Girls. Houston: Arte Publico Press, 1986.

Face of an Angel. New York: Farrar, Straus and Giroux, 1994.

Secondary Bibliography

Castillo, Debra A. "The Daily Shape of Horses: Denise Chavez and Maxine Hong Kingston." *Dispositio: Revista Americana de Estudios Semióticos y Culturales/American Journal of Semiotic and Cultural Studies*, 1991, v. 16(41): 29–43.

Chavez, Denise. "The Blessing of a Desert Land." *New York Times Magazine*, May 16, 1993.

———. "Heat and Rain: Testimonio." *Breaking Boundaries: Latina Writing and Critical Readings*. Eds. Horno-Delgado, Asuncion; Ortega, Eliana; Scott, Nina M.; Sternbach, Nancy Saporta; Miller, Elaine N. Amherst: Univ. of Massachusetts Press, 1989. pp. 27–32.

Eysturoy, Annie O. "New America Studies in the American West; Denise Chavez." *This Is about Vision: Interviews with Southwestern Writers*. Eds. Balassi, William; Crawford, John F., Eysturoy, Annie O. Albuquerque: Univ. of New Mexico Press, 1990. pp. 157–169.

Gray, Lynn. "Interview with Denise Chavez." *Short Story Review*, Fall 1988; v. 5(4): 2–4.

Green, Stacy. "Bilingual Play Accents Individuality." *New Mexico Daily Lobo*, Nov. 24, 1982.

Heard, Martha E. "The Theatre of Denise Chavez: Interior Landscapes with 'sabor nuevomexicano'." *The Americas Review: A Review of Hispanic Literature and Art of the USA*, Summer 1988, v. 16(2): 83–91.

Quintana, Alvina Eugenia. *Chicana Discourse: Negations and Mediations*. Dissertation Abstracts International (ISSN Pt. A, 0419–4209; Pt. B, 0419–4217; Pt. C, 1042–7279), Mar. 1990, v. 50(9): 2916A.

Rosaldo, Renato. "Post-Contemporary Interventions; Fables of the Fallen Guy." *Criticism in the Borderlands: Studies in Chicano Literature, Culture, and Ideology*. Eds. Calderon, Hector; Saldivar, Jose David; Hinojosa, Rolando. Durham: Duke Univ. Press, 1991. pp. 84–93.

Sagel, Jim. "Writer Wanders Through Familiar Rooms." *Journal North*, August 4, 1982.

JOY HARJO

Primary Bibliography

The Last Song. Puerto Del Sol Press, 1975.

What Moon Drove Me to This? I. Reed Books, 1980.

She Had Some Horses. New York: Thunder's Mouth Press, 1983.

Secrets from the Center of the World. Collaboration with Stephen Strom, Tucson: Univ. of Arizona Press, 1989.

In Mad Love and War. Middletown, CT: Wesleyan Univ. Press, 1990.

Fishing. Miniature Fine Press, Oxhead Press, 1992.

The Woman Who Fell from the Sky. New York: W. W. Norton, 1994.

A Love Supreme. New York: W. W. Norton, forthcoming.

The Good Luck Cat. New York: Harcourt Brace, forthcoming.

Secondary Bibliography

Ruppert, James. "Paula Gunn Allen and Joy Harjo: Closing the Distance Between Personal and Mythic Space." *American Indian Quarterly*, 1983, v. 7 (1): 27–41.

Bruchac, Joseph. "Interview with Joy Harjo." *North Dakota Quarterly*, Spring 1985.

Harjo, Joy. "The Creative Process." *Wicazo Sa Review*, Spring 1985, vol. 1, no. 1.

Johnson, J. "Revolving Worlds: The Evolving Worlds of Joy Harjo." *World Literature Today*, Summer 1992.

Lang, Nancy Helene. *Through Landscape toward Story/through Story toward Landscape: A Study of Four Native American Women Poets*. Diss., Indiana University of Pennsylvania, 1991.

Scarry, John. "Representing Real Worlds: The Evolving Poetry of Joy Harjo." *World Literature Today*, 1992.

Smith, Patricia Clark and Paula Gunn Allen. "Earthly Relations, Carnal Knowledge: Southwestern American Indian Women Writers and Landscape." *The Desert Is No Lady: Southwestern Landscapes in Women's Writing and Art*. New Haven: Yale Univ. Press, 1987.

TONY HILLERMAN

Primary Bibliography

The Blessing Way. New York: Harper & Row, 1970.

The Fly on the Wall. New York: Harper & Row, 1971.

Dance Hall of the Dead. New York: Harper & Row, 1973.

The Great Taos Bank Robbery and Other Affairs of Indian Country. Albuquerque: Univ. of New Mexico Press, 1973.

The Listening Woman. New York: Harper & Row, 1977.

The People of Darkness. New York: Harper & Row, 1980.

The Dark Wind. New York: Harper & Row, 1982.

The Ghostway. New York: Harper & Row, 1985.

Skinwalkers. New York: Harper & Row, 1986.

A Thief of Time. New York: Harper & Row, 1988.

Talking God. New York: Harper & Row, 1989.

Coyote Waits. New York: HarperCollins, 1990.

Sacred Clowns. New York: HarperCollins, 1992.

Secondary Bibliography

Bakerman, Jane S. "Cutting Both Ways: Race, Prejudice, and Motive in Tony Hillerman's Detective Fiction." *MELUS: The Journal of the Society for the Study of the Multi-Ethnic Literature of the United States*, Fall 1984, v. 11(3): 17–25.

Bakerman, Jane S. "Tony Hillerman's Joe Leaphorn and Jim Chee." *Cops and Constables: American and British Fictional Policemen.* Eds. Bargainnier, Earl F.; Dove, George N. Bowling Green, OH: Popular, 1986. pp. 98–112.

———. "Joe Leaphorn and the Navaho Way: Tony Hillerman's Indian Detective Fiction." *Clues: A Journal of Detection,* Spring–Summer 1981, v. 2(1): 9–16.

Bernell, Sue; Karni, Michaela. "New America Studies in the American West; Tony Hillerman." *This Is about Vision: Interviews with Southwestern Writers.* Eds. Balassi, William; Crawford, John F.; Eysturoy, Annie O. Albuquerque: Univ. of New Mexico Press, 1990. pp. 41–51.

Doerry, Karl W. "Literary Conquista: The Southwest as a Literary Emblem." *Journal of the Southwest,* Winter 1990, v. 32(4): 438–50.

Erisman, Fred. "Tony Hillerman's Jim Chee and the Shaman's Dilemma." *Lamar Journal of the Humanities,* 1992, v. 17(1): 5–16.

———. "Hillerman's Uses of the Southwest." *Roundup Quarterly,* Western Writers of America, Inc., Summer 1989, v. 1(4): 9–18.

———. *Tony Hillerman.* Western Writers Series, 1987. Boise: Boise State Univ., 1989. p. 51.

Hillerman, Tony. "Mystery, Country Boys, and the Big Reservation." Winks, Robin W., ed. *Colloquium on Crime: Eleven Renowned Mystery Writers Discuss Their Work.* New York: Scribner's, 1986. pp. 127–47.

———. "Making Mysteries with Navajo Materials." Eds. Dennis, Philip; Aycock, Wendell. *Literature and Anthropology.* Studies in Comparative Literature 20. Lubbock: Texas Tech Univ. Press, 1989. pp. 5–13.

Parfit, Michael. "Weaving Mysteries That Tell of Life among the Navajos." *Smithsonian,* Dec. 1990, v. 21(9): 92–105.

Parker, Betty; Parker, Riley. "Hillerman Country." *Armchair Detective: A Quarterly Journal Devoted to the Appreciation of Mystery, Detective, and Suspense Fiction,* Winter 1987, v. 20(1): 4–14.

Pierson, James C. "Mystery Literature and Ethnography: Fictional Detectives as Anthropologists." *Literature and Anthropology.* Eds. Dennis, Philip; Aycock, Wendell. Studies in

Comparative Literature 20. Lubbock: Texas Tech Univ. Press, 1989. pp. 15–30.

Quirk, Tom. "Justice on the Reservation." *Armchair Detective: A Quarterly Journal Devoted to the Appreciation of Mystery, Detective, and Suspense Fiction*, Fall 1985, v. 18(4): 364–70.

Schneider, Jack W. "Crime and Navajo Punishment: Tony Hillerman's Novels of Detection." *Southwest Review*, Spring 1982, v. 67(2): 151–60.

Strenski, Ellen; Evans, Robley. "Ritual and Murder in Tony Hillerman's Detective Novels." *Western American Literature*, Nov. 1981, v. 16(3): 205–16.

Ward, Alex. "Navajo Cops on the Case." *New York Times Magazine*, May 18, 1989, pp. 38–39.

LINDA HOGAN

Primary Bibliography

Calling Myself Home. New York: Greenfield Review Press, 1978.

Daughters, I Love You. Denver: Loretto Heights College Press, 1981.

Eclipse. Los Angeles: American Indian Studies Center, 1983.

Seeing Through the Sun. Amherst: University of Massachusetts Press, 1985.

The Stories We Hold Secret: Tales of Women's Spiritual Development. New York: Greenfield Review Press, 1986.

The Big Woman. Ithaca, N.Y.: Firebrand Books, 1987.

Savings: Poems. Minneapolis: Coffee House Press, 1988.

Mean Spirit: A Novel. New York: Atheneum, 1990.

Red Clay: Poems and Stories. New York: Greenfield Review Press, 1991.

Secondary Bibliography

Berner, Robert. "Linda Hogan." *World Literature Today*, Autumn 1989, v. 63.

Bruchac, Joseph. "To Take Care of Life: An Interview with Linda Hogan." Sun Tracks: An Amer. Indian Lit. Ser. 15. Ed. Bruchac, Joseph. *Survival This Way: Interviews with Amer-*

ican Indian Poets. Tucson: Univ. of Arizona Press, 1987. pp. 119–33.

Casey, John. "Review, *Mean Spirit.*" *American Book Review*, August 1991.

Cincotti, Joseph. *New York Times Book Review*, Feb. 24, 1991.

Lang, Nancy Helene. *Through Landscape toward Story/Through Story toward Landscape: A Study of Four Native American Women Poets* (Dissertation abstract number DA9123672; Degree granting institution: Indiana Univ., Pennsylvania), Dissertation Abstracts International (ISSN Pt. A, 0419–4209; Pt. B, 0419–4217; Pt. C, 1042–7279), Sept. 1991 v. 52(3): 918A.

Miller, Carol. "The Story Is Brimming Around: An Interview with Linda Hogan." *Studies in American Indian Literature: The Journal of the Association for the Study of American Indian Literature*, Winter 1990, v. 2(4): 1–9.

Scholer, Bo. " 'A heart made out of crickets': An Interview with Linda Hogan." *The Journal of Ethnic Studies*, Spring 1988, v. 16(1): 107–17.

Smith, Patricia Clark. "New America Studies in the American West: Linda Hogan." *This Is about Vision: Interviews with Southwestern Writers.* Eds. Balassi, William; Crawford, John F.; Eysturoy, Annie O. Albuquerque: Univ. of New Mexico Press, 1990. pp. 141–55.

BARBARA KINGSOLVER

Primary Bibliography

The Bean Trees. New York: Harper & Row, 1988.
Homeland and Other Stories. New York: Harper & Row, 1989.
Animal Dreams. New York: HarperCollins, 1990.
Holding the Line. ILR Press, 1989.
Pigs in Heaven. New York: HarperCollins, 1993.

Secondary Bibliography

Antioch Review, Dec. 1990.
Bloomsbury Review, Nov./Dec. 1990, p. 3.
Booklist, March 1, 1988; Aug. 1990.
Books of the Southwest, May 1988; Aug. 1989.

Christian Science Monitor, April 22, 1988.
Contemporary Literary Criticism, 1990.
Courier Journal (Louisville, Ky.), April 24, 1988.
English Journal, Oct. 1990.
Kirkus Reviews, June 15, 1990.
Library Journal, Feb. 1, 1988; Aug. 1990; Nov. 1, 1989.
Los Angeles Times Book Review, Sept. 9, 1990.
The New Yorker, April 4, 1988; Dec. 10, 1990.
New York Times Book Review, April 10, 1988; Sept. 2, 1990; Jan. 7, 1990; May 6, 1990.
Publishers Weekly, Jan. 15, 1988; June 22, 1990.
Time, Sept. 24, 1990, p. 87.
Tribune Books, Aug. 26, 1990.
Washington Post Book World, Sept. 2, 1990.
Women's Review of Books, Jan. 1990; April 1990.

TERRY MCMILLAN

Primary Bibliography

Mama. New York: Houghton Mifflin, 1987.
Disappearing Acts. New York: Viking, 1989.
Breaking Ice: An Anthology of Contemporary African–American Fiction. New York: Viking, 1990.
Waiting To Exhale. New York: Viking, 1992.
A Day Late and a Dollar Short. New York: Viking, 1995.

Secondary Bibliography

Belles Lettres, Sept.–Oct. 1987, 3(1).
Booklist, Jan. 1, 1987.
Ebony, May 1993.
Library Journal, Jan. 1987.
New York Newsday, Sept. 10, 1989.
New York Times Book Review, Aug. 6, 1989.
New York Times Magazine, Aug. 9, 1992.
The New Yorker, March 16, 1987.
The Observer, May 10, 1987; Feb. 4, 1990.
People Weekly, Jan. 1993.
Publishers Weekly, Nov. 28, 1986; July 13, 1992.

The Village Voice, March 24, 1987.
Davis, Thulani. "Don't Worry, Be Buppie: Black Novelists Head for the Mainstream." *Village Voice Literary Supplement*, May 1990, v. 85, 26–29.

JOHN NICHOLS

Primary Bibliography

The Sterile Cuckoo. New York: David McKay, 1965.
The Wizard of Loneliness. New York: G. P. Putnam's Sons, 1966.
The Milagro Beanfield War. New York: Holt, Rinehart and Winston, 1974.
The Magic Journey. New York: Holt, Rinehart and Winston, 1978.
A Ghost in the Music. New York: Holt, Rinehart and Winston, 1979.
If Mountains Die. New York: Knopf, 1979.
The Nirvana Blues. New York: Holt, Rinehart and Winston, 1981.
The Last Beautiful Days of Autumn. New York: Holt, Rinehart and Winston, 1982.
On The Mesa. Santa Fe: Peregrine Smith, 1986.
American Blood. New York: Henry Holt and Company, 1987.
A Fragile Beauty. Santa Fe: Peregrine Smith, 1987.
An Elegy for September. New York: Henry Holt and Company, 1992.

Secondary Bibliography

Best Sellers, Jan. 15, 1965; Nov. 1979.
New York Times Book Review, Jan. 17, 1965; March 6, 1966; April 16, 1978; June 10, 1979; Oct. 28, 1979; June 5, 1988.
Book Week, Jan. 24, 1965; Feb. 20, 1966.
Saturday Review, Jan. 30, 1965; Feb. 26, 1966.
Christian Science Monitor, Feb. 4, 1965.
America, Feb. 26, 1966.
Atlantic, March 1965.
The Nation, June 20, 1987.
American West, April 1988.

Books, July 1990.

Library Journal, Aug. 1990.

Nichols, John. "The Writer as Revolutionary." *Old Southwest/ New Southwest: Essays on a Region and Its Literature*. Lensink, Judy Nolte (ed.). Tucson: Tucson Public Lib., 1987. pp. 101–11.

Bus, Heiner. "John Nichols' *The Milagro Beanfield War* (1974): The View from Within and/or the View from Without?" *Missions in Conflict: Essays on U.S.–Mexican Relations and Chicano Culture*. Eds. Bardeleben, Renate von; Briesemeister, Dietrich; Bruce-Novoa, Juan. Tubingen: Narr, 1986. pp. 215–25.

Myers, Thomas. "Dispatches from Ghost Country: The Vietnam Veteran in Recent American Fiction." *Genre*, Winter 1988, v. 21(4): 409–28.

Thompson, Phyllis. "New America Studies in the American West: John Nichols." *This Is about Vision: Interviews with Southwestern Writers*. Eds. Balassi, William; Crawford, John F.; Eysturoy, Annie O. Albuquerque: Univ. of New Mexico Press, 1990. pp. 119–27.

Ward, Dorothy Patricia. *Literature of Conscience: The Novels of John Nichols*. Dissertation Abstracts International (ISSN Pt. A, 0419–4209; Pt. B, 0419–4217; Pt. C, 1042–7279), Nov. 1990, v. 51(5): 1615A–1616A.

Wiggs, Terry. "Magical Realism and John Nichols' Milagro." *Conference of College Teachers of English Studies*, Sept. 1988, v. 53: 15–21.

Wild, Peter. *John Nichols*. Western Writers Series, 75. Boise: Boise State Univ., 1986. p. 52.

SIMON ORTIZ

Primary Bibliography

Naked in the Wind. Quetzal-Vihio Press, 1971.

Going for the Rain. New York: Harper & Row, 1976.

Good Journey. New York: Turtle Bay Books, 1977.

The People Shall Continue. Chicago: Children's Press, 1977.

Fight Back: For the Sake of the People, for the Sake of the Land. Albuquerque: Institute for Native American Development, Univ. of New Mexico, 1980.

From Sand Creek: Rising in This Heart Which Is Our America. New York: Thunder's Mouth Press, 1981.

Fightin': New and Collected Stories. New York: Thunder's Mouth Press, 1983.

Woven Stone: Poetry and Prose. Tucson: Univ. of Arizona Press, 1991.

After and Before the Lightning. Tucson: Univ. of Arizona Press, 1994.

Secondary Bibliography

Bruchac, Joseph. "The Story Never Ends: An Interview with Simon Ortiz." Ed. Bruchac, Joseph. *Survival This Way: Interviews with American Indian Poets.* Sun Tracks: An Amer. Indian Lit. Ser., 15. Tucson: Univ. of Arizona Press, 1987. pp. 211–29.

Evers, Lawrence J. "The Killing of a New Mexican State Trooper: Ways of Telling a Historical Event." *The Wicazo Sa Review: A Journal of Indian Studies*, Spring 1985, v. 1(1): 17–25.

Gleason, Judith. "Reclaiming the Valley of the Shadows Parnassus." *Poetry in Review*, Fall–Winter 1984, v. 12(1): 21–71.

Hoilman, Dennis. "The Ethnic Imagination: A Case History." *Canadian Journal of Native Studies*, 1985, v. 5(2): 167–75.

Lincoln, Kenneth. "Dolphin 9: Common Walls: The Poetry of Simon Ortiz." *Coyote Was Here: Essays on Contemporary Native American Literary and Political Mobilization.* Ed. Scholer, Bo. Aarhus, Denmark: Seklos, Dept. of Eng., Univ. of Aarhus, 1984. pp. 79–94.

Manley, Kathleen; Rea, Paul W. "An Interview with Simon Ortiz." *Journal of the Southwest*, Autumn 1989, v. 31(3): 362–77.

Oandasan, William. "Simon Ortiz: The Poet and His Landscape." *Studies in American Indian Literature: The Journal of the Association for the Study of American Indian Literature*, 1987, v. 11: 26–37.

Ortiz, Simon J. " 'That's the Place Indians Talk About.' " *The*

Wicazo Sa Review: A Journal of Indian Studies, Spring 1985, v. 1(1): 45–49.

———. "Dolphin 9: Always the Stories: A Brief History and Thoughts on My Writing." *Coyote Was Here: Essays on Contemporary Native American Literary and Political Mobilization.* Ed. Scholer, Bo. Aarhus, Denmark: Seklos, Dept. of Eng., Univ. of Aarhus, 1984. pp. 57–69.

Ruoff, LaVonne Brown. "Simon Ortiz: A.S.A.I.L. Bibliography 7." *Studies in Amer. Indian Lit.*, Summer–Fall 1984, v. 8(3–4): 57–58.

Silko, Leslie Marmon. "Language and Literature from a Pueblo Indian Perspective." Eds. Fiedler, Leslie A.; Baker, Houston A., Jr. *English Literature: Opening Up the Canon.* Sel. Papers from the Eng. Inst. 4. Baltimore: Johns Hopkins Univ. Press, 1981. pp. 54–72.

Smith, Patricia Clark. "Coyote Ortiz: Canis latrans latrans in the Poetry of Simon Ortiz." Ed. Allen, Paula Gunn. *Studies in American Indian Literature: Critical Essays and Course Designs.* New York: Mod. Lang. Assn. of America, 1983. pp. 192–210.

Warner, Nicholas O. "Images of Drinking in 'Woman Singing,' Ceremony, and House Made of Dawn." *MELUS: The Journal of the Society for the Study of the Multi-Ethnic Literature of the United States*, Winter 1984, v. 11(4): 15–30.

Wiget, Andrew. *Simon Ortiz.* Western Writers Series 74. Boise: Boise State Univ., 1986. p. 53.

ALBERTO RIOS

Primary Bibliography

Elk Heads on the Wall. Mango Press, 1979.

Sleeping on Fists. Dooryard Press, 1981.

Whispering to Fool the Wind. New York: Sheep Meadow Press, 1982.

The Iguana Killer: Twelve Stories of the Heart. New York: Blue Moon Books, 1982.

Five Indiscretions. New York: Sheep Meadow Press, 1985.

The Lime Orchard Woman. New York: Sheep Meadow Press, 1989.

Teodoro Luna's Two Kisses. New York: W. W. Norton, 1990.

The Warrington Poems. Pyracantha Press, 1991.

Secondary Bibliography

Village Voice Literary Supplement, Oct. 1982.

New York Times Book Review, Feb. 9, 1986.

Library Journal, May 1, 1985; Feb. 15, 1989; Sept. 15, 1990.

American Book Review, May 1987.

Publishers Weekly, Jan. 6, 1989.

Booklist, Nov. 1, 1990.

Cardenas, Lupe; Alarcon, Justo. "Entrevista con Alberto Rios." *Confluencia. Revista Hispánica de Cultura y Literatura,* Fall 1990, v. 6(1): 119–28.

Rios, Alberto. "Becoming and Breaking: Poet and Poem." *Ironwood,* Fall 1984, v. 12(2 [24]): 148–52.

————. "Chicano/Borderlands Literature and Poetry." *Contemporary Latin American Culture: Unity and Diversity.* Ed. Guntermann, C. Gail. Tempe: Center for Latina American Studies, Arizona State Univ., 1984. pp. 79–93.

Rosaldo, Renato. "Post-Contemporary Interventions; Fables of the Fallen Guy." *Criticism in the Borderlands: Studies in Chicano Literature, Culture, and Ideology.* Eds. Calderon, Hector; Saldivar, Jose David; Hinojosa, Rolando. Durham: Duke Univ. Press, 1991. pp. 84–93.

Saldivar, Jose David. "Towards a Chicano Poetics: The Making of the Chicano Subject, 1969–1982." *Confluencia: Revista Hispánica de Cultura y Literatura,* Spring 1986, v. 1(2): 10–17.

STAN STEINER

Primary Bibliography

The Last Horse. New York: Macmillan, 1961; Holt, Rinehart and Winston, 1973.

The New Indians. New York: Harper & Row, 1968.

George Washington: The Indian Influence. New York: G. P. Putnam's Sons, 1970.

La Raza: The Mexican Americans. New York: G. P. Putnam's Sons, 1970.

The Tiquas: The Lost Tribe of City Indians. New York: Crowell, Collier, Macmillan, 1972.

The Islands: The World of the Puerto Ricans. New York: Harper & Row, 1974.

The Vanishing White Man. New York: Harper & Row, 1976.

The Mexican Indians. London: The Minority Rights Group, 1978.

In Search of the Jaguar: The Paradox of Development in Venezuela. New York: New York Times Books, 1979.

Fusang: The Chinese Who Built America. New York: Harper & Row, 1979.

The Ranchers: A Book of Generations. New York: Knopf, 1980.

Spirit Woman. New York: Harper & Row, 1980.

Dark and Dashing Horsemen. New York: Harper & Row, 1981.

The Waning of the West. New York: St. Martin's Press, 1989.

Co-editor, *The Way: An Anthology of American Indian Literature*. New York: Knopf, 1972.

Co-editor, *Aztlan: An Anthology of Mexican American Literature*. New York: Knopf, 1972.

Co-editor, *Borinquen: An Anthology of Puerto Rican Literature*. New York: Knopf, 1973.

Co-editor, *Native American Writing*. PEN Quarterly, 1974.

Secondary Bibliography

America, Nov. 13, 1976.

Contemporary Authors, 1971, 1976, 1982, 1989.

Los Angeles Times, May 19, and Dec. 5, 1980.

The Nation, Oct. 2, 1976.

The New Republic, March 24, 1979.

New York Times, Jan. 15, 1987.

Publishers Weekly, June 21, 1976; June 23, 1989.

The Reporter, Jan. 28, 1987.

Deloria, Vine. "Stan Steiner Reviewed." *New York Times Book Review*, September 12, 1976.

Momaday, N. Scott. "Tribal Spirit." *New York Times Book Review*, March 17, 1968.

Steiner, Stan. "Militance among the Mexican Americans: Chicano Power." *The New Republic*, June 20, 1970. pp. 8–9.

Streisand, Anna. "Stan Steiner." *Literature By and About the American Indian*. Urbana, Ill.: National Council of Teachers of English, 1973.

Wiznitzer, Martine. "Stan Steiner and 'La Raza.'" *Partisans*, Nov. 1970, v. 6(3).

LUCI TAPAHONSO

Primary Bibliography

One More Shiprock Night. San Antonio: Tejas Art, 1981.

Seasonal Woman. Santa Fe: Tooth of Time, 1984.

A Breeze Swept Through. Los Angeles: West End, 1991.

Sáanii Dahataal: The Women Are Singing. Tucson: Univ. of Arizona Press, 1993.

Bah's Baby Brother Is Born. National Organization on Fetal Alcohol Syndrome, 1994.

Dineh ABC: A Navajo Alphabet. New York: Macmillan, 1995.

Blue Horses Rush In: Poems and Stories. Tucson: Univ. of Arizona Press, 1995.

Editor, *Hayoolkal: An Anthology of Navajo Writers*. Tucson: Univ. of Arizona Press, 1995.

Secondary Bibliography

Bruchac, Joseph. "A MELUS Interview: Luci Tapahonso." *MELUS*, Winter 1984, v. 11.

Bruchac, Joseph. "For What It Is: An Interview with Luci Tapahonso." Sun Tracks: An Amer. Indian Lit. Ser., 15. Ed. Bruchac, Joseph. *Survival This Way: Interviews with American Indian Poets*. Tucson: Univ. of Arizona Press, 1987. pp. 271–85.

Crawford, John; Eysturoy, Annie O. "New America Studies in the American West; Luci Tapahonso." *This Is about Vision:*

Interviews with Southwestern Writers. Eds. Balassi, William; Crawford, John F.; Eysturoy, Annie O. Albuquerque: Univ. of New Mexico Press, 1990. pp. 195–202.

"Luci Tapahonso." *The Maazo Magazine: A Magazine for the Navajo Nation,* Spring 1985.

Moulin, Sylvie. "Nobody Is an Orphan." *Studies in American Indian Literature: The Journal of the Association for the Study of American Indian Literature,* Fall 1991, v. 3(3): 14–18.

Smith, Patricia Clark; Allen, Paula Gunn. "Earthly Relations, Carnal Knowledge: Southwestern American Indian Women Writers and Landscape." *The Desert Is No Lady: Southwestern Landscapes in Women's Writing and Art.* Eds. Norwood, Vera; Monk, Janice. New Haven: Yale Univ. Press, 1987. pp. 174–96.

FRANK WATERS

Primary Bibliography

The Wild Earth's Nobility: A Novel of the Old West. New York: Liveright, 1935.

Below Grass Roots. New York: Liveright, 1937.

Dust Within the Rock. New York: Liveright, 1940.

People of the Valley. Swallow Press, 1941.

The Man Who Killed the Deer. Swallow Press, 1942.

The Yogi of Cockroach Court. Swallow Press, 1947.

Masked Gods: Navajo and Pueblo Ceremonialism. Albuquerque: Univ. of New Mexico Press, 1950; reprinted, New York: Ballantine, 1975.

Book of the Hopi. New York: Viking, 1963.

The Woman of Otowi Crossing. Swallow Press, 1966.

Pumpkin Seed Point. Swallow Press, 1969.

Pike's Peak: A Family Saga. Contains *The Wild Earth's Nobility, Below Grass Roots,* and *Dust Within the Rock.* Swallow Press, 1971.

Mexico Mystique: The Coming Sixth World of Consciousness. Swallow Press, 1975.

Flight from Fiesta. Rydal, 1986.

Secondary Bibliography

For a more complete list of works about Frank Waters, see the journal *Studies in Frank Waters*, The Frank Waters Society.

Adams, Charles. "Charles Adams on: *Pike's Peak*." *Writers' Forum*, Fall 1985, v. 11: 195–208.

———. "Frank Waters." *A Literary History of the American West*. Eds. Westbrook, Max; Maguire, James H. Fort Worth: Texas Christian Univ. Press, 1987. pp. 935–57.

———. "New America Studies in the American West: Frank Waters." *This Is about Vision: Interviews with Southwestern Writers*. Eds. Balassi, William; Crawford, John F.; Eysturoy, Annie O. Albuquerque: Univ. of New Mexico Press, 1990. pp. 15–25.

Blackburn, Alexander. "Alexander Blackburn on: *The Woman at Otowi Crossing*." *Writers' Forum*, Fall 1985, v. 11: 171–79.

———. "Frank Waters: The Colorado College Symposium." *Writers' Forum*, Fall 1985, v. 11: 164–221.

———. "Frank Waters's *The Lizard Woman* and the Emergence of the Dawn Man." *Western American Literature*, Aug. 1989, v. 24(2): 121–36.

———. "The New Age of Frank Waters." *Journal of the Southwest*, Winter 1988, v. 30(4): 535–44.

———. "Pastoral, Myth, and Humanity in *People of the Valley*." *South Dakota Review*, Spring 1990, v. 28(1): 5–18.

Geertz, Armin W. "Reflections on the Study of Hopi Mythology." *Religion in Native North America*. Ed. Vecsey, Christopher. Moscow: Univ. of Idaho Press, 1990. pp. 119–35.

———. "Thomas J. Lyon on: *The Man Who Killed the Deer*." *Writers' Forum*, Fall 1985, v. 11: 180–94.

McAllister, Mick. "Homeward Bound: Wilderness and Frontier in American Indian Literature." *The Frontier Experience and the American Dream: Essays on American Literature*. Eds. Mogen, David; Busby, Mark; Bryant, Paul. College Station: Texas A & M Univ. Press, 1989. pp. 149–58.

———. "The Emergence of Helen Chalmers." *Women and Western American Literature*. Eds. Stauffer, Helen Winter; Rosowski, Susan. Troy, N.Y.: Whitston, 1982. pp. 100–23.

———. "Meru, the Voice of the Mountain." *South Dakota Review*, Summer 1989, v. 27(2): 27–35.

Smith, Curtis C. "Frank Waters' Minorities: Romance and Realism." *MELUS: The Journal of the Society for the Study of the Multi-Ethnic Literature of the United States*, Winter 1984, v. 11(4): 73–83.

Sturdevant, Katherine Scott. "Frank Waters and His Work." *Sundays in Tutt Library with Frank Waters*. Ed. Sturdevant, Katherine Scott. Colorado Springs: Hulbert Center for Southwestern Studies, Colorado Coll., 1988. pp. 56–67.

Waters, Frank. "Roots and Literary Influences." *Old Southwest/ New Southwest: Essays on a Region and Its Literature*. Ed. Lensink, Judy Nolte. Tucson: Tucson Public Lib., 1987. pp. 7–15.

SELECTED BIBLIOGRAPHY OF
SOUTHWESTERN LITERATURE

▲ ✤ ▼ ✤ ▼ ✤ ▲

Allen, Paula Gunn. *The Woman Who Owned the Shadows*. San Francisco: Spinsters Ink, 1983.

———, ed. *Spider Woman's Granddaughters*. New York: Fawcett Columbine, 1989.

Anaya, Rudolfo. "The Myth of Quetzalcoatl in a Contemporary Setting: Mythical Dimensions/Political Reality." *Western American Literature*, Nov. 1988, v. 23(3).

Anderson, John Q.; Gaston, Edwin; Lee, James; eds. *Southwestern American Literature: A Bibliography*. Chicago: The Swallow Press, 1980.

Applegate, Frank. *Indian Stories from the Pueblos*. Philadelphia: Lippincott, 1929.

Armas, José. "Chance to Tell Mestizo Story Lost." *The Albuquerque Journal*, Oct. 11, 1992.

Austin, Mary. *Land of Journeys' Ending*. New York: Houghton Mifflin, 1908.

———. *Land of Little Rain*. New York: Houghton Mifflin, 1903.

———. *Lost Borders*. New York: Houghton Mifflin, 1909.

Balassi, William; Crawford, John F.; Eysturoy, Annie O., eds. *This Is about Vision: Interviews with Southwestern Writers*. Albuquerque: University of New Mexico Press, 1990.

Bandelier, Adolph. *The Delight Makers*. New York: Dodd, Mead, 1890.

Baumann, Richard. *Verbal Art as Performance*. Rowley, Mass.: Newbury House, 1977.

Berkhofer, Robert. *The White Man's Indian*. New York: Knopf, 1979.

Bernstein, Richard. "Unsettling the Old West." *New York Times Magazine*, March 18, 1992.

Blackburn, Alexander, ed. *Writers' Forum: Frank Waters*. Colorado Springs: University of Colorado, 1985.

Bowden, Betsy. *Chaucer Aloud: The Varieties of Textual Interpretation*. Philadelphia: University of Pennsylvania Press, 1987.

Bowden, Charles. "Useless Deserts & Other Goals." *Old Southwest/New Southwest: Essays on a Region and Its Literature*. Tucson: Tucson Public Lib., 1987.

Briggs, Charles. *Competence in Performance: The Creativity of Tradition in Mexicano Verbal Art*. Philadelphia: University of Pennsylvania Press, 1988.

Bruce-Novoa. *Retrospace: Collected Esays on Chicano Literature—Theory and History*. Houston: University of Houston, Arte Publico Press, 1990.

Brumble, H. David. *American Indian Autobiography*. Berkeley: University of California Press, 1988.

Campa, Arthur L. "Spanish Traditional Tales in the Southwest." *Perspectives in Mexican American Studies*, 1988, v. 1.

Candelaria, Cordelia. *Estudios Chicanos and the Politics of Community*. Boulder: National Association for Chicano Studies, 1988.

———, ed. *Multiethnic Literature of the United States: Critical Introductions and Classroom Resources*. Boulder: University of Colorado, 1989.

Carteret, John D. *The Old Stone Corral*. Cincinnati: published by author, 1888.

Cather, Willa. *Death Comes for the Archbishop*. New York: Knopf, 1927.

———. *The Professor's House*. New York: Knopf, 1925.

Chavez, John R. "The Image of the Southwest in the Chicano Novel, 1970–1979." *The Bilingual Review/La Revista Bilingüe*, Sept.–Dec. 1987–1988 v. 14(3).

Chronicles of American Indian Protest. The Council on Interracial Books for Children. Greenwich, Conn.: Fawcett, 1971.

Cooper, Guy H. "Coyote in Navajo Religion and Cosmology." *Canadian Journal of Native Studies*, 1987, v. 7(2).

Cronyn, George W., ed. *American Indian Poetry*. New York: Liveright, 1934.

Dary, David. *Cowboy Culture: A Saga of Five Centuries.* New York: Knopf, 1981.

Dasenbrock, Reed Way.. "Southwest of What?: Southwestern Literature as a Form of Frontier Literature." *Desert, Garden, Margin, Range: Literature on the American Frontier.* Ed. Heyne, Eric. New York: Twayne, 1992. p. 182.

———. "Forms of Biculturalism in Southwestern Literature: The Work of Rudolfo Anaya and Leslie Marmon Silko." *Genre,* Fall 1988, v. 21(3).

Dobie, J. Frank. *Buried Treasures of the Southwest.* New York: Literary Guild of America, 1931; 2nd edition, 1987.

———. *Coronado's Children.* New York: Grosset & Dunlap, 1930.

———. *Guide to Life and Literature of the Southwest.* Dallas: SMU Press, 1952.

———. *The Oral Tradition of the American West,* 2nd edition. New York: Literary Guild of America, 1990.

Doerry, Karl W. "Literary Conquista: The Southwest as a Literary Emblem." *Journal of the Southwest,* Winter 1990, v. 32(4).

Dorris, Michael. "Indians in Aspic."

"Don't Fence Them Out." *Newsweek,* July 13, 1992.

Dozier, Edward P. *The Pueblo Indians of North America.* Prospect Heights, Ill.: Waveland, 1970.

DuBuys, William. *Enchantment and Exploitation.* Albuquerque: University of New Mexico Press, 1985.

Dunaway, David King; Baum, Willa. *Oral History: An Interdisciplinary Anthology.* Tennessee, AASLH, 1984.

Ellis, Richard N. "Duke Indian Oral History Collection." *New Mexico Historical Review,* July 1973, v. 48(3).

Elsasser, Nan; MacKenzie, Kyle; Tixier Vigil, Yvonne, eds. *Las Mujeres: Conversations from a Hispanic Community.* New York: McGraw-Hill, 1980.

Erisman, Fred. "Hillerman's Uses of the Southwest." *Roundup Quarterly,* Western Writers of America, Inc., Summer 1989, v. 1(4).

Farah, Cynthia. *Literature and Landscape.* El Paso: University of Texas, El Paso, 1989.

Fergusson, Harvey. *Rio Grande.* New York: Tudor, 1933.

Finnegan, Ruth. *Oral Literature in Africa*. London: Clarendon Press, 1970.

Gaston, Edwin. *The Early Novel of the Southwest*. Albuquerque: University of New Mexico Press, 1961.

Gattuso, John, ed. *A Circle of Nations: Voices and Visions of American Indians*. Hillsboro, Ore.: Beyond Words Publishing, 1993.

————, ed. *Voices and Visions of American Indians*. Hillsboro, Ore.: Beyond Words Publishing, 1993.

Gibson, Arrell Morgan. "The Author as Image Maker for the Southwest." *Old Southwest/New Southwest: Essays on a Region and Its Literature*. Lensink, Judy Nolte, ed. Tucson: Tucson Public Lib., 1987.

Grey, Zane. *Light of the Western Stars*. New York: Black's Readers, 1914.

————. *The Rainbow Trail*. New York: Black's Readers, 1915.

————. *Riders of the Purple Sage*. New York: Black's Readers, 1912.

Hepworth, James; McNamee, Gregory. *Resist Much, Obey Little: Some Notes on Edward Abbey*. Salt Lake City, Utah: Dream Garden, 1985.

Herrera-Sobek, Maria. *The Mexican Corrido*. Bloomington: Indiana University Press, 1993.

Hymes, Dell, ed. *In Vain I Tried to Tell You: Essays in Native American Ethnopoetics*. Philadelphia: University of Pennsylvania Press, 1981.

Kramer, Jane. *The Last Cowboy*. New York: Harper & Row, 1978.

Krupat, Arnold. *A Study of Native American Autobiography*. Berkeley: University of California Press, 1985.

Krutch, Joseph Wood. *The Voice of the Desert*. New York: Sloane Assoc., 1955.

Kurath, Gertrude Prokosch. *Music and Dance of the Tewa Pueblos*. Santa Fe: Museum of New Mexico Press, 1973.

Lang, Nancy Helene. *Through Landscape toward Story/Through Story toward Landscape: A Study of Four Native American Women Poets*, Diss., Indiana University of Pennsylvania, 1991.

Lensink, Judy Nolte. *Old Southwest/New Southwest: Essays on a Region and Its Literature*. Tucson: Tucson Public Lib., 1987.

Limon, Jose E. *Mexican Ballads, Chicano Poems: History and Influence in Mexican–American Social Poetry*. Berkeley: University of California Press, 1992.

Loeffler, Jack. *Headed Upstream: Interviews with Iconoclasts*. Tucson: Harbinger House, 1989.

Lummis, Charles. *The Land of Poco Tiempo*. Albuquerque: University of New Mexico Press, 1929.

———. "Does the Land Speak? Frank Waters and the Southwest." *Sundays in Tutt Library with Frank Waters*. Eds. Sturdevant, Katherine Scott; Gordon, Joseph T. Colorado Springs: Hulbert Center for Southwestern Studies, Colorado Coll., 1988.

———. "Beyond the Frontier Mind." *Old Southwest/New Southwest: Essays on a Region and Its Literature*. Lensink, Judy Nolte, ed. Tucson: Tucson Public Lib., 1987.

Major, Mabel. *Southwest Heritage*. Albuquerque: University of New Mexico Press, 1972.

Major, Mabel; Pearce, T. M. *Southwest Heritage: A Literary History*. Albuquerque: University of New Mexico Press, 1972.

Miller, Tom. *On the Border*. Tucson: University of Arizona Press, 1989.

Momaday, N. Scott. "Landscape with Words in the Foreground." Lensink, Judy Nolte, ed. *Old Southwest/New Southwest: Essays on a Region and Its Literature*. Tucson: Tucson Public Lib., 1987.

———. *The Way to Rainy Mountain*. Albuquerque: University of New Mexico Press, 1969.

Monk, Janice; Norwood, Vera. "Angles of Vision: Enhancing Our Perspectives on the Southwest." *Old Southwest/New Southwest: Essays on a Region and Its Literature*. Tucson: Tucson Public Lib., 1987.

Nichols, John. "The Writer as Revolutionary." *Old Southwest/New Southwest: Essays on a Region and Its Literature*. Lensink, Judy Nolte, ed. Tucson: Tucson Public Lib., 1987.

Norwood, Vera. "Crazy-Quilt Lives: Frontier Sources for Southwestern Women's Literature." *The Desert Is No Lady: Southwestern Landscapes in Women's Writing and Art*. Eds. Norwood, Vera; Monk, Janice. New Haven: Yale University Press, 1987.

Norwood, Vera; Monk, Janice. *The Desert Is No Lady: Southwestern Landscapes in Women's Writing and Art*. New Haven: Yale University Press, 1987.

Philippi, Donald L. *Songs of Gods, Songs of Humans*. San Francisco: Northpoint Press, 1982.

Pike, Albert. *Prose, Sketches, and Poems, Written in the Western Country*. Boston: Light & Horton, 1834.

Pilkington, William T. "The Southwest." *A Literary History of the American West*. Eds. Westbrook, Max (pref.); Maguire, James H. (intro.). Fort Worth: Texas Christian University Press, 1987.

Powell, Lawrence Clark. *Heart of the Southwest*. University of Arizona Press, 1955.

————. "The Fountain and the Well: Sources of Southwestern Literature." Lensink, Judy Nolte, ed. *Old Southwest/New Southwest: Essays on a Region and Its Literature*. Tucson: Tucson Public Lib., 1987.

Rebolledo, Tey Diana. "Hispanic Women Writers of the Southwest: Tradition and Innovation." *Old Southwest/New Southwest: Essays on a Region and Its Literature*. Lensink, Judy Nolte, ed. Tucson: Tucson Public Library, 1987.

Robb, J. D. *Hispanic Folk Songs of New Mexico and the Southwest*. Norman: University of Oklahoma Press, 1973.

Rodenberger, Lou. "The Southern Border." *A Literary History of the American West*. Eds. Westbrook, Max; Maguire, James H. Fort Worth: Texas Christian University Press, 1987.

Rothfork, John. "The Failure of Southwest Regionalism." *South Dakota Review*, Winter 1981, v. 19(4): 85–97.

Rudnick, Lois. "Re-Naming the Land: Anglo-Expatriate Women in the Southwest." *The Desert Is No Lady: Southwestern Landscapes in Women's Writing and Art*. Eds. Norwood, Vera; Monk, Janice. New Haven: Yale University Press, 1987.

Ruoff, Lavonne Brown. "American Indian Literature: Introduction and Bibliography." *American Studies International*, Oct. 1986, v. 24(2).

Sanders, Scott P. "Southwestern Gothic: Alienation, Integration, and Rebirth in the Works of Richard Shelton, Rudolfo Anaya, and Leslie Silko." *Weber Studies: An Interdisciplinary Humanities Journal*, Fall 1987, v. 4(2).

Sando, Joe. "Modern New Mexico's Shared Roots: Shared Culture of Pueblos and Spaniards." *Pueblo Indian Historian*.

————. *Pueblo Nations, Eight Centuries of Pueblo Indian History*. Santa Fe: Clear Light Publishers, 1992.

Savage, William W. *Cowboy Life: Reconstructing an American Myth*. Norman: University of Oklahoma Press, 1975.

Shorris, Earl. *Latinos: A Biography of the People*. New York: Norton, 1989.

Smith, Patricia Clark; Allen, Paula Gunn. "Earthly Relations, Carnal Knowledge: Southwestern American Indian Women Writers and Landscape." *The Desert Is No Lady: Southwestern Landscapes in Women's Writing and Art*. Eds. Norwood, Vera; et al.

Sonnichson, C. L. *The Southwest in Life and Literature*. New York: Devin-Adair, 1962.

Text and Performance Quarterly (formerly *Literature in Performance*). Speech Communication Association, 1988.

The Santa Fe Magazine of the Arts. "Rethinking Representation: Native American Culture," Aug. 1993.

Tyler, Hamilton A. *Pueblo Gods and Myths*. Norman: University of Oklahoma Press, 1964.

Vansina, Jan. *Oral Tradition, Significance, and Social Context*. Chicago: Aldine Pub., 1977.

Ward, Dorothy Patricia. *Literature of Conscience: The Novels of John Nichols*. Boulder: University of Colorado, Nov. 1990.

Waters, Frank. "Roots and Literary Influences." *Old Southwest/ New Southwest: Essays on a Region and Its Literature*. Lensink, Judy Nolte, ed. Tucson: Tucson Public Lib., 1987.

Weigle, Marta. *Brothers of Light, Brothers of Blood*. Albuquerque: University of New Mexico Press, 1976.

West, John O. *Cowboy Folk Humor*. Little Rock: August House, 1990.

————. *Mexican-American Folklore*. Little Rock: August House, 1990.

White, Jon Manchip. *A World Elsewhere: Life in the American Southwest*. College Station: Texas A&M University Press, 1989.

Wissler, Clark. *Indians of the United States*. New York: Doubleday, 1966.

Zwinger, Ann. "Writers of the Purple Figwort." *Old Southwest/ New Southwest: Essays on a Region and Its Literature*. Lensink, Judy Nolte, ed. Tucson: Tucson Public Lib., 1987. pp. 143–54.

PERMISSIONS

▲ ❖ ▼ ❖ ▼ ❖ ▲

ON THE LITERARY SCENE

☐ **CONCEIVED WITH MALICE** *Literature as Revenge in the Lives and Works of Virginia and Leonard Woolf, D.H. Lawrence, Djuna Barnes, and Henry Miller.* **by Louise De Salvo.** Full of enticing literary gossip, the author vividly describes how these great literary figures each perceived an attack on the self—and struck back through their art, creating lasting monuments to their deepest hurts and darkest obsessions. "Delicious, intelligent, irresistible, one of the darker pleasures."—Carole Maso, author of *The American Woman in the Chinese Hat*   (273234—$13.95)

☐ **WRITING THE SOUTHWEST by David King Dunaway.** The common thread that links such writers as Edward Abbey, Tony Hillerman, Joy Harjo, Barbara Kingsolver, and Terry McMillan is an understanding of the interplay between humans and the earth. This compelling collection offers outstanding selections of contemporary southwestern literature along with a biographical profile, a bibliography, and an original interview with each of the 14 authors included.
(273943—$12.95)

☐ **A SENSE OF WONDER** *On Reading and Writing Books for Children.* **by Katherine Paterson** This book is a collection of more than three dozen critical essays on reading and writing for children that were originally published as two books, *Gates of Excellence* and *The Spying Heart.* Combined for the first time in one volume, these writings come from speeches Katherine Paterson has given all over the world, from her book reviews, and from articles she has authored on her craft.   (274761—$12.95)

☐ **THE SEED AND THE VISION** *On the Writing and Appreciation of Children's Books.* **by Eleanor Cameron.** The National Book award-winning author is back with another superb collection of essays about the transforming power of children's fiction and the sources of its inspiration. Involving, provocative, and informative, it illuminates the maturity and complexity of what we call "children's literature."   (271835—$14.95)

☐ **THE READING GROUP BOOK** *The Complete Guide to Starting and Sustaining A Reading Group, with Annotated Lists of 250 Titles for Provocative Discussion.* **by David Laskin and Holly Hughes.** This lively, down-to-earth book is a complete guide to reading groups—from getting one going to sparkling lively discussions to revitalizing a long-established group. This one-stop handbook covers the history of reading groups, how to attract those who love good books and good conversation, even what food to serve.
(272017—$9.95)

Prices slightly higher in Canada.